Blowing the Whistle

Blowing the Whistle

The Organizational and Legal Implications for Companies and Employees

Marcia P. Miceli
The Ohio State University

Janet P. Near
Indiana University

LEXINGTON BOOKS
An Imprint of Macmillan, Inc.
NEW YORK
Maxwell Macmillan Canada
TORONTO
Maxwell Macmillan International
NEW YORK   OXFORD   SINGAPORE   SYDNEY

This book is published as part of the Lexington Books Issues in Organization and Management series, Arthur P. Brief and Benjamin Schneider, consulting editors.

Library of Congress Cataloging-in-Publication Data

Miceli, Marcia P.
  Blowing the whistle : the organizational and legal implications for companies and employees / Marcia P. Miceli, Janet P. Near.
      p.   cm.—(Issues in organization and management series)
  Includes bibliographical references and index.
  ISBN 0-669-19599-5
  1. Whistle blowing. 2. Whistle blowing—Law and legislation —United States. I. Near, Janet P. II. Title. III. Series.
HD60.M54   1992
302.3'5—dc20   91-46201
                                                              CIP

Lexington Books
An Imprint of Macmillan, Inc.
866 Third Avenue, New York, N.Y. 10022

Maxwell Macmillan Canada, Inc.
1200 Eglinton Avenue East
Suite 200
Don Mills, Ontario M3C 3N1

Macmillan, Inc. is part of the Maxwell Communication Group of Companies.

Printed in the United States of America

printing number
1 2 3 4 5 6 7 8 9 10

To Ryan Farquer, Joey Near,
Chris Near, and Sean Farquer

Contents

Foreword

This is an important book. It is so for a number of reasons. First, the behavior addressed, whistle-blowing, has potentially profound consequences for those who engage in it, for the organizations that employ these whistle-blowers, for the customers or clients these organizations supposedly serve, and, perhaps, even for society-at-large. To some, whistle-blowers are heroes; to others villains; but, to virtually no one are they inconsequential.

Second, Miceli and Near's book is important because it represents the very best the social sciences have to offer in attempting to understand an applied problem. The authors, based upon their own insightful investigations and a meticulous review of the literature, advance a tightly woven and comprehensive theory of the whistle-blowing phenomenon that likely will serve as a guide to research for years to come.

Finally, the book is important because it goes beyond theorizing to suggest how whistle-blowing might be managed both from an organizational as well as a societal perspective. In sum, we are very pleased to welcome Miceli and Near's book to our series for its theoretical and practical insights to the problem of whistle-blowing.

Arthur P. Brief
Benjamin Schneider

Preface

It is a rare day that the news media do not carry at least one account of whistle-blowing—the disclosure by organizational members of illegal, immoral, or illegitimate organizational acts or omissions to parties who can take action to correct the wrongdoing. This suggests that whistle-blowing is fairly common and likely on the upswing, as the editor of the *Harvard Business Review* has pointed out (Ewing, 1983). While whistle-blowing may be threatening to some managers or co-workers, it often can improve long-term organizational effectiveness, because whistle-blowers may suggest solutions to organizational problems. More importantly, organization members, stockholders, and society, in general, can benefit from the cessation of organizational wrongdoing, such as fraud, unfair discrimination, or safety violations. In an era where taxpayers must spend billions to bail out financial institutions, where oil spills create environmental havoc and cost many person-hours and dollars to rectify, and sexual harassment issues arise in a context as unlikely as the nomination process for a member of the highest court in the land, many observers have asked, "why didn't someone do something earlier?"

This book examines the phenomenon of whistle-blowing. One of our purposes is to address the questions of why and how whistle-blowers decide to take action. A second purpose is to explore decisions concerning the form of opposition. For example, why do some whistle-blowers act in concert with fellow organization members, while others act alone? What are the predictors of anonymous whistle-blowing? A third purpose is to examine what happens after a report is made. Whistle-blowing may have both short- and long-term consequences for individuals, groups, organizations, and society at large. For example, whistle-blowers may experience retaliation, or they may be ignored. But if whistle-blowing is followed by prompt, corrective action, which may lead to increased organizational effectiveness, it may also engender increased societal trust in organizations.

This is the first book on whistle-blowing that describes and integrates the scholarly literature so it can be understood by a wide variety of readers. Previous books have been aimed at the "trade" audience and consist mostly of case reports or anecdotes. They generally have not incorporated the existing base on knowledge in related fields, such as social psychology. This book also includes a timely discussion of legal issues in whistle-blowing. We attempt to draw implications from the scholarly and legal literature that can guide both researchers and managers, as well as whistle-blowers or individuals who might contemplate blowing the whistle. While prior approaches are valuable and interesting, the present approach builds on what is known in order to gain a better understanding of whistle-blowing and to help organizations become more responsive to whistle-blowers.

Thus, we have written this book for several audiences. First, we summarize research for professors and graduate students in management, industrial relations, personnel and human resources management, organizational behavior, organization theory, and ethics. We hope these groups will be stimulated to do additional research to address the many unanswered questions involving whistle-blowing. Second, undergraduate management or communications students may also be interested in the social science-based and legal research implications. Third, by explicitly spelling out implications based on empirical research and theory, we hope to reach personnel and human resources management practitioners and line managers, as well as all persons who may be faced with a situation that calls for whistle-blowing. It is our hope that this book may help some individuals to take steps to make whistle-blowing unnecessary, by seeing and correcting problems as they occur.

In the chapters that follow, we explore whistle-blowing through a time sequence and identify the individuals and entities that may be involved. We propose a model of the decision process preceding whistle-blowing, followed by its consequences. We then examine the research conducted to date that identifies variables affecting the various stages of whistle-blowing processes. We describe the legal environment pertaining to whistle-blowing. Finally, based on the research described in earlier chapters, we provide tentative recommendations for managing whistle-blowing in organizations, and we offer suggestions for individuals contemplating it.

The legal chapter was contributed by Professor Terry Morehead Dworkin of Indiana University. We would like to acknowledge the cooperation and support given to us by John Palguta of the United States Merit Systems Protection Board, which conducted several surveys that provide the basis for many of our findings. Support for some of the research was also provided by the Institute for Internal Auditors. We would like to thank several research assistants who worked with us on various papers that we describe. Their thinking is reflected in some of the ideas and perspectives taken in the present book. Most notable are the contributions of Janelle Dozier, Linda Ferguson, and Sherry Sullivan. Moreover, the comments of the series editors, Arthur P. Brief and Benjamin Schneider, were very helpful. The encouragement and valuable information given by William C. Bush, who maintains a network for whistle-blowers, is greatly appreciated. Finally, we are indebted to Beth Anderson, Edith Lewis, and Caroline McCarley at Lexington/Macmillan. Of course, we are ultimately responsible for the content of this book.

1

Introduction

Are whistle-blowers heroes—the "corruption fighters" (Julie, 1987) who represent society's last line of defense against organizational misconduct? Or are they—as others believe—company traitors who reveal secrets for their own personal glorification (Petersen & Farrell, 1986)? While a survey of federal employees showed that most individuals view whistle-blowers positively (Merit Systems Protection Board [MSPB], 1981), the term often has "a negative connotation" (Mathews, 1988, p. 1). As evidence, a leading business magazine characterized laws prohibiting discrimination against whistle-blowers as "rat protection" (Seligman, 1981). Many persons believe that organizations should be free to discipline and retaliate against members who reveal questionable practices. But others argue that corporations "have no natural rights to be left alone where the public interest and welfare are at issue" (Galbraith, 1973, p. 7, cited in Mathews, 1987).

In this book, we examine the phenomenon of whistle-blowing. One purpose of this book is to address the questions of why and how whistle-blowers decide to take action. A second purpose is to explore decisions concerning the form of opposition. For example, why do some whistle-blowers act in concert with other organization members, while other whistle-blowers act alone? What are the predictors of anonymous whistle-blowing? A third purpose is to examine what happens after a report is made. Whistle-blowing may have both short-term and long-term consequences for individuals, groups, organizations, and society at large. For example, whistle-blowers may experience retaliation, or they may be ignored. But if whistle-blowing is followed by prompt corrective action, which may lead to increased organizational effectiveness, it may also engender increased societal trust in organizations.

In examining whistle-blowing, we take a different approach than do authors of most other books on the subject. Previous authors have tended to compile and describe cases involving whistle-blowing, whereas, for reasons explored in some depth later in this chapter, we will focus on research results directly and indirectly pertaining to whistle-blowing, though we acknowledge the limitations of the current research literature.

In this introductory chapter, we discuss the costs and benefits of whistle-blowing, and the costs and benefits of ignoring organizational wrongdoing—for individuals, organizations, and society as a whole. We offer a definition of whistle-blowing and its various forms and describe in some depth the rationale for the definition we have derived. Finally, we show how whistle-blowing can be classified as an organizational behavior so that it can be better understood. As will be explained later, because whistle-blowing occurs in organizations, it can be examined from the perspectives of the research literature on organizational behaviors that are conceptually similar to whistle-blowing in some ways. Before beginning our examination, it is useful to consider why whistle-blowing is worthy of investigation.

The Increasing Incidence of Whistle-blowing

Whistle-blowing incidents are frequently in the public eye. On January 31, 1983, CBS News's "60 Minutes" featured several whistle-blowing cases (Kennedy, 1987). More recently, a whistle-blower notified the public of the diversion of profits from Iranian arms sales to the Nicaraguan Contras. In this case, the whistle-blower was Charles Allen, who was national intelligence officer for terrorism for the Central Intelligence Agency ("CIA whistle-blower . . . ," 1987).

There is no government body that monitors the number of whistle-blowing cases. Therefore, it is impossible to say how many cases occur. However, there are indications that whistle-blowing occurs frequently. According to Finney and Lesieur (1982, p. 256), organizational wrongdoing is "extremely common and much more costly than common crime." An opportunity for whistle-blowing occurs with every questionable activity; therefore, the potential for whistle-blowing is widespread. Also, a well-known reporter has stated that "over the years, we have based hundreds of exclusive stories on tips and testimony by employees who were appalled at the incompetence or outright criminality of their bosses" (Anderson & VanAtta, 1987, p. 4A). For every case reported to the media, there are many more instances of whistle-blowing to other parties (MSPB, 1981).

There is evidence that whistle-blowing is on the increase (Ewing, 1983). In the past decade, employment litigation has moved away from proceedings under the National Labor Relations Act and toward wrongful discharge, discrimination, and other issues. Lawsuits under statutes protecting employee rights now constitute the largest single group of civil filings in federal courts (Feinstein, 1988a, 1988b). While this litigation does not always involve whistle-blowing, this trend suggests that employees, many of whom may be lone whistle-blowers, increasingly are using alternatives to unions to voice their concerns.

Whistle-blowing may reflect a general trend toward greater recognition of employee rights and responsibilities in the workplace. There are many factors influencing this developing trend (Osigweh, 1988). One is that the shortage of entry level workers has forced employers to be more responsive to their needs (Finney, 1988a). This factor and a "consumer rights" attitude toward workplace rights have resulted in a greater propensity for employees to blow the whistle (Ewing, 1983).

Further, as entry-level workers obtain "special concessions," higher-level workers will demand an "equal share of the rights pie" or they will leave (Finney, 1988a). Theory suggests that providing additional protections to one group of employees will have a "trickle up" effect on other employees. Economists (for example, Thurow, 1975) have discussed this process as involving interdependency of utilities, and social psychologists have discussed the notions of distributive justice and equity and relative deprivation (for example, Adams, 1965; Martin, 1981). These researchers maintain that individuals calculate the net rewards, or outcomes they receive in relation to their contributions, or inputs. Individuals compare this ratio with the perceived rewards relative to contributions for other individuals. If the ratio for others increases (for example, if a group of comparison persons receives more voice in the workplace and the individual views this greater voice as a net positive outcome), the focal individual will feel underrewarded and may demand similar treatment.

According to Finney (1988a, p. 40), the employee rights emphasis is shifting from protecting the individual at the workplace to "using employment to protect the interests of society as a whole." Because whistle-blowing frequently serves to protect society's interests, this suggests that, in the future, society and organizations will devote even greater attention to it.

For all of these reasons, it is clear that whistle-blowing is not uncommon and that it is occurring with greater frequency. As such, it is deserving of serious scholarly attention as well as enlightened organizational practice. But it is a complex phenomenon. Because the whistle-blower often stands as a lone individual against the larger and more powerful organization, this confrontation may be analogous to that of David and Goliath (Julie, 1987; Near & Miceli, 1987). As such, it raises some interesting and important questions. For example, why does anyone undertake the role of David? How does "Goliath"—the organization—respond to the whistle-blower's challenge? Can "David" be victorious and escape serious injury? How can organizations respond to concerns when first voiced, and ultimately operate so that serious challenges are unnecessary? To shed light on these questions, we begin by identifying the potential consequences of (a) whistle-blowing and (b) refraining from or failing to take action when wrongdoing is encountered.

Consequences of Whistle-blowing and of Not Blowing the Whistle

Whistle-blowing can have several consequences for organizations, and for other parties, such as the public in general. Likewise, refusing to blow the whistle or to take any other action when one encounters wrongdoing can have consequences. These consequences are summarized in table 1–1.

We do not mean to equate whistle-blowing to action and not blowing the whistle to inaction. In response to wrongdoing, individuals can take action that does not constitute whistle-blowing.

TABLE 1–1

Potential Costs and Benefits of Whistle-blowing and Inaction

Target of the Cost, Benefits	Outcomes of Whistle-blowing and Inaction	
	Costs	Benefits
Inaction		
Observer's organization	Employee withdrawal, risk to long-term organizational survival, escalation of wrongdoing	Smooth organizational functioning, avoidance of frivolous complaints
Society at large	Citizens' rights, privileges, and safety jeopardized	Avoidance of frivolous complaints (e.g., lawsuits)
Whistle-blowing		
Observer's organization	Challenge to authority structure, threats to organizational viability, limits on control, unpredictability of organization member actions	Increased safety and well-being of organization members, support for codes of ethics, reduction of waste and mismanagement, improved morale, maintenance of good will and avoidance of damage claims, avoidance of legal regulation
Society at large	Court logjams	Increased safety and well-being of societal members, reduction of taxes and increases in services, less regulation, support for codes of ethics

For example, they can discuss a problem with, or confront, the perceived wrongdoer. They can express concern in other ways, such as sabotage or strikes. Although we will discuss these alternative actions to some extent later in this chapter, they are not the primary focus of this book and they are also quite varied in their form and likely consequences. Therefore, we omit them from table 1–1 and other chapters in this book. To understand the need for whistle-blowing we first consider the potential costs and benefits of inaction.

Potential Costs and Benefits of Not Blowing the Whistle

Whistle-blowers act in order to stop, or modify, a particular activity (or correct an omission) that is wrongful (Near & Miceli, 1985). The costs of tolerating wrongdoing can be severe (Glazer & Glazer, 1987). The tragedy involving NASA's Challenger space shuttle, in which all crew members were killed as the event was observed by millions of television viewers (Near, 1989), provides a recent example.

POTENTIAL COSTS TO THE EMPLOYING ORGANIZATION. According to Blackburn (1988, p. 9), organization members' "staying silent has negative implications for the organization." Individuals may withdraw psychologically while remaining on the job; they may not devote energies to work and organizational effectiveness may consequently suffer. Drawing on cognitive dissonance theory (Adams, 1965; Festinger, 1957), Ewing's (1983) work on employee concerns, and research on employee alienation (Hackman & Oldham, 1980), Blackburn examined the withdrawal process. She noted the withdrawal process occurs as a way to compensate for disparity in what employees want and what they experience in terms of involvement, satisfaction, meaningful work, and humane treatment.

Over time, organizations whose managers commit wrongdoing may suffer other problems. Organizations in which wrongdoing is committed are likely to experience it again (Baucus & Near, 1991). At least, they may continue their reliance on the wrongdoing and perhaps come to depend on it for their short-term survival (Near & Miceli, 1987). However, such dependence may cause them ultimately to fail. Recent evidence suggests that firms engage in criminal wrongdoing because of an opportunity for gain, not out of a sense of desperation (Baucus & Near, 1991), although as discussed later, other research has shown that poor financial performance is frequently linked with organizational crime. If the wrongdoing is not checked, it may escalate, proving even more costly (for example, in the case of lawsuits) when it is finally detected (Ewing,

1983). If allowed to continue over a long period, the wrongdoing may eventually cost the organization its life, as in the instance of some recent product liability cases.

POTENTIAL BENEFITS TO THE EMPLOYING ORGANIZATION. As shown in table 1–1, organizations can realize two benefits of avoiding whistle-blowing, if one assumes (a) no wrongdoing has occurred, or (b) alternatives to whistle-blowing exist in the organization, that is, managers' timely recognition and correction of wrongdoing. First, the operation of bureaucratic structures depends on the legal-rational basis for their leaders' authority (Weber, 1947; Weinstein, 1979). Thus, employees who accept authority support the structure and hence the operation of the organization by their obedience. Conflict is reduced, and disruption is minimized. So long as leaders implement decisions that are humane and work to the benefit of organization members as well as the organization's constituency and the society as a whole, unquestioned obedience may facilitate the smooth functioning of organizations.

A second benefit concerns the avoidance of frivolous complaints. Organizations may be forced to investigate complaints, costing them time, and to settle complaints that are baseless, costing them valuable resources. Organizations may be forced to retain "curmudgeons" who pretend to use whistle-blowing in order to avoid termination (Seligman, 1981). Consistent with this perspective, one objection voiced by Reagan administration officials at hearings concerning the Whistle-blower Protection Act of 1987 was that protections for federal whistle-blowers would "interfere with legitimate disciplinary actions" (Anderson & VanAtta, 1987). However, we know of no evidence that poor performing employees abuse such protections to any great extent. In fact, some evidence suggests that whistle-blower protections do not inhibit supervisory discretion. Since 1978, the Civil Service Reform Act has protected federal employees, and in 1983 the Merit Systems Protection Board conducted a survey concerning these protections. Our secondary analysis revealed that more than 84 percent of the federal managers who responded believed that the possibility of a "whistle-blower complaint" would *not* pose an obstacle to their taking disciplinary action or would do so only "to a little extent."

POTENTIAL COSTS TO SOCIETY AT LARGE. Employees' remaining silent in the face of serious wrongdoing sometimes jeopardizes the public's rights and privileges. Anecdotal evidence of dangers posed by tolerance of environmental hazards is abundant, and as another example, the rights of citizens to privacy were compromised when police officers refused to report their colleagues' engaging in illegal wiretapping of citizens' telephones (Ruth, 1989). Unfortunately, in this book we must limit our focus to American society. Laws defining the nature of wrongdoing and perceptions of what constitutes legitimate behavior vary across societies. Protections for or sanctions against whistle-blowers also differ in different societies. In countries where whistle-blowers receive more support than in the United States, the costs of not blowing the whistle or of ignoring a whistle-blowers's allegations may be greater than in the United States. This depends on a country's interpretation of the employment-at-will doctrine, which argues that an employer is free to fire an employee for any reason, including whistle-blowing behavior; in countries such as the United States, where this doctrine still dominates, the costs of whistle-blowing are relatively high, thereby increasing the likelihood of inaction, and—ironically—the costs associated with inaction.

POTENTIAL BENEFITS TO SOCIETY AT LARGE. Some managers may become more conservative in their decision making if they feel their subordinates are constantly second guessing them. They might then avoid the type of risky, innovative decisions most needed by their organizations, through fear that potential whistle-blowers would view their actions as misguided or illegitimate. The benefit, then, to society—as to its organizations—is the avoidance of costs associated with frivolous whistle-blowing. These costs include the tangible fees associated with legal actions and the more intangible cost of conservative managerial decision making.

This is a more critical issue than it first appears because managers who fear whistle-blowers may develop a defensive posture such that they avoid decision making in cases that involve any risk. In other words, in order to cover themselves, they may avoid the difficult choices—even when they seem to be the right choices—because they fear the possibility of whistle-blowing (Near, 1989). This type of defensive mentality would obviously be detrimental to the quality of organizational decision making and could exacerbate what some observers consider a dangerous trend toward risk-averse behavior among American executives.

Potential Costs and Benefits of Whistle-blowing

We have discussed the potential costs and benefits of *not* taking action to stop organizational wrongdoing; the potential costs can frequently outweigh the benefits, or the costs may be intolerable regardless of the benefits. This suggests that we should examine whistle-blowing as a means of reducing or eliminating the costs. Previous authors have claimed that whistle-blowers can benefit organizations by suggesting solutions to organizational problems (for instance, Graham, 1983; Mathews, 1988; Parmerlee, Near & Jensen, 1982). They have claimed that some whistle-blowers intend to help the organization and that whistle-blowing begets further prosocial behavior (Brief & Motowidlo, 1986; Dozier & Miceli, 1984, 1985; Gaerte, 1990; Graham, 1983, 1986). However, whistle-blowers may impose costs as well as promise benefits.

POTENTIAL COSTS TO THE EMPLOYING ORGANIZATION

Challenge to Authority Structure. As noted earlier, whistle-blowers may be distressing to individuals within an organization because they may threaten the authority structure (Weinstein, 1979). Many managers believe that membership in a bureaucracy requires obedience (Glazer & Glazer, 1987).

Whistle-blowing may weaken the chain of command. Supervisors may view whistle-blowers as having "gone behind their backs" or "over their heads," which undermines legitimate control in organizations. Understandably, some parties may view this as a cost. But this cost is not inevitable in every whistle-blowing instance. Thus, we now agree only partly with Weinstein (1979). Whistle-blowing sometimes poses a challenge to the authority structure, but organizations that specifically encourage reporting and specify a channel for doing so may not experience authority challenges. Whistle-blowing in these organizations may not be viewed as a violation of the chain of command principle, but rather as an alternative form of upward communication. The wrongdoer in such instances may view whistle-blowing as an authority challenge or unwelcome attempt to limit his or her control, but the wrongdoer is not always the organization or its top management.

Threats to Organizational Viability. Whistle-blowers may provoke controversy because other organization members perceive that they might damage the profits of the organization. It sometimes may be cost-effective to break the law, if by doing so the organization keeps costs low and pays minimal penalties for doing so. Where this is true, whistle-blowers pose a threat to the organization's profitability or effectiveness, because they reduce the organization's freedom to use illegal means to compete for resources. According to Davidson and Worrell (1988, p. 198), "ethical issues aside, from a shareholder's standpoint, illegal acts may be worthwhile if their expected benefits outweigh their expected costs. In addition, some investors may view managerial attempts to test the legal waters as preferable to always proceeding in a risk-averse manner. Wealth-maximizing shareholders may consider it desirable for managers to occasionally get caught trying to cheat."

Limitations on Control. A third reason why whistle-blowers' presence may be unsettling is that they may appear to limit others' discretion. Anyone who has ever sipped cola at a cocktail party has probably experienced a fellow partygoer who derisively calls attention to the cola drinker's choice. Like the cola drinker, the whistle-blower, by not going along with the crowd, prevents others from "letting go." In the case of the whistle-blower, however, others' negative reactions may be more understandable, because the whistle-blower is making a statement of condemnation; not only does he or she choose not to take part in the activities, he or she attempts to keep others from doing so.

Unpredictability of Organization Member Actions. There may also be a genuine concern on the part of organization members that one never knows when another member may decide to blow the whistle, and that an unjustified complaint may lead to interference with one's professional activities (Koshland, 1988). A great deal of professional insurance has been sold to faculty members who fear that someday a student may raise complaints of unfair grading, discrimination, or harassment. While few would dispute students' rights to pursue justified complaints, an unfortunate outcome is that conscientious faculty members may be concerned that they will be a target of complaints that may be more likely in a climate that reinforces assertiveness or activism. Such accusations, whether justified or not, may lead to increased turnover among those accused of committing wrongdoing.

POTENTIAL BENEFITS TO THE EMPLOYING ORGANIZATION

Increased Safety and Well-being of Organization Members. Whistle-blowers may warn organization leaders of problems that threaten the personal or economic well-being of their members. As an example, for over five decades medical personnel and individuals employed in the asbestos industry were aware that prolonged exposure to asbestos causes asbestosis, a serious disease. During the time that silence prevailed, thousands of construction workers and others contracted the disease (Glazer & Glazer, 1987). Whistle-blowing in nuclear energy producing plants, pharmaceutical firms, automobile manufacturers, and many other organizations obviously can have consequences that could preserve life or its quality. Although not every event that could trigger whistle-blowing is as dramatic as these examples (that is, not every incident of wrong-doing threatens human life) certainly any unnecessary loss is too great.

With the increased incidence of organizations concerned with "normal accidents" (Perrow, 1984)—that is, organizations that daily operate with the threat of catastrophic consequences in the event of mistakes—whistle-blowing could be particularly important as an early alarm signal if things run amuck. In nuclear plants or NASA facilities, the effects of error are especially serious, as witnessed most graphically in the Challenger accident. In those instances, whistle-blowers may be the first line of defense against egregious errors.

Support for Codes of Ethics. Organizations interested in maintaining climates that encourage ethical behavior may adopt or revise codes of ethics. However, research suggests that such codes are not sufficient to insure that ethical behavior will follow. A study by

Mathews (1987, p. 125) concluded that there existed "little relationship between codes of conduct and [civil and administrative] corporate violations, contrary to the notion that the codes serve as an effective form of self-regulation." Whistle-blowing may serve to support codes of ethics or other mechanisms to encourage dissent, enabling responsive organization leaders to learn of and correct misconduct. The individual benefits from seeing the enactment of professed standards and exercising the freedom to behave in a manner consistent with ethical values.

Reduction of Organizational Waste and Mismanagement. Where top management is unaware of a lower level problem and is willing to respond by making appropriate corrections, whistle-blowing can benefit the organization in lowering the costs of doing business which may be passed on in the form of lower prices, thus increasing volume or profits. For example, where managers rely on "old boy" (or "old girl") contacts to hire or promote employees, grant contracts, or make other business decisions that should be influenced by qualifications or efficiency, reduced productivity may be realized. This productivity decline may result in part from the direct costs of using inefficient methods, and in part from the indirect costs of employee withdrawal resulting from the perception of a climate of unfair dealings.

Improved Employee Morale. Successful whistle-blowing shows employees that they have the power to change unethical behavior in the organization and improve their work lives as well as the outcomes for others. Whistle-blowers are more satisfied than persons who observe wrongdoing but do not report it (Miceli & Near, 1988a). Also, maintaining a positive climate for whistle-blowing is associated with enhanced employee satisfaction (Zalkind, 1987). On the other hand, invalid whistle-blowing may produce a witch-hunt type of climate antithetical to the maintenance of a cohesive organization or professional group. Allegations of wrongdoing are usually reported; if these are later found to be erroneous, the fact is often unpublicized (Koshland, 1988). Thus, we conclude that true wrongdoing, if allowed to continue unreported, is likely to reduce the morale and cohesion of an organization—but so are unsubstantiated allegations of wrongdoing.

Maintenance of Good Will and Avoidance of Damage Claims. If the public learns of wrongdoing, for example, they may boycott the organizations' products or services, and thus the "market" will penalize wrongful behavior (Fama, 1980; Meyers & Garrett, 1988). Of course, some may argue that whistle-blowing to outsiders *increases* the likelihood that the public will learn of the wrongdoing. But for two reasons, this may be short-sighted. First, research shows that most whistle-blowers initially inform internal parties (Baker, 1983); organizations may be unresponsive, thereby forcing whistle-blowers to go outside. Therefore, it is the organization, rather than the whistle-blower in most cases, that is responsible for outsiders' knowledge of the activity. Second, in many cases (for instance, unsafe consumer products, such as automobiles or children's toys) the public may eventually learn of the wrongdoing even without whistle-blowers. It is a question of the timing of the disclosure rather than disclosure itself. And by the time the discovery is made, damage is often greater than it might have been had attention been paid to a whistle-blower. According to Mathews (1988, p.13), "both Morton Thiokol's and NASA's reputations suffered greatly from the space shuttle accident. The $1 billion lawsuit filed against Morton Thiokol by one of its engineers received extensive media coverage. The FBI's criminal investigation of Morton Thiokol was a further blow to the corporation's damaged reputation."

Avoidance of Legal Regulation. Legal authorities may impose fines and penalties if organizations are caught in wrongdoing; thus, managers and investors alike would pay a price for corporate wrongdoing (Davidson & Worrell, 1988). Whistle-blowers who first warn managers give them the opportunity to correct wrongdoing before outsiders learn of it. This may avoid immediate penalties, as well as attempts by legislators to introduce new statues or regulatory agencies to promulgate new regulations or increase vigilance over organizational activities.

COSTS TO SOCIETY AT LARGE. The society can also experience costs of whistle-blowing; for example, lawsuits involving less substantial charges can prevent courts from dealing with more critical matters. However, the costs are more readily apparent in terms of the organizational consequences and the consequences for the whistle-blower.

BENEFITS TO SOCIETY AT LARGE

Increased Safety and Well-being of Societal Members. Just as whistle-blowers in responsive organizations can protect other organization members, they may protect individuals outside the organization. For example, investors and potential investors who are warned of financial wrongdoing may avoid the loss of substantial resources by investing in more ethical or better managed organizations. Most importantly, individuals whose safety would be jeopardized by wrongful organizational activity will benefit when a whistle-blower's warning is heeded.

Reduction of Taxes, Increases in Services. This is a theme often heard in federal government: "Today, we are losing the war on waste and one major reason is the lack of whistle-blowers" (Julie, 1987, p. 2). Where government organizations correct wrongdoing, taxpayers may benefit from increased services or lower taxes.

Less Regulation. Whistle-blowers can help industries to monitor themselves. If they are effective, there is less need for legislators to enact new, intrusive regulation, which requires a regulatory agency and trained staff. The management of the agency, of course, will require taxpayer money to operate. To the extent that industries are self-policing and self-correcting, societal resources need not be directed toward controlling organizations.

Support for Codes of Ethics. Society benefits from the activation of the codes and the avoidance of organizational wrongdoing. The reasoning is essentially the same as that concerning less regulation.

IMPORTANCE OF COSTS AND BENEFITS. Our description of the potential benefits and costs whistle-blowing poses suggests that organization leaders—particularly those involved directly with human resource management, who may serve as complaint recipients—should pay a considerable amount of attention to the organization's policies concerning whistle-blowers. As noted earlier, providing a supportive climate may enhance morale and may aid in the attraction and retention of employees (Finney, 1988a).

Further, legislators and regulators may direct increased efforts toward improving protection of rights in the workplace, particularly if organizations do not. The costs of waiting until a problem arises, in terms of financial costs or loss of autonomy over organizational practices, are greater than the costs of taking a proactive approach. As noted by Finney (1988a, p. 40), leaders of such organizations as TRW have emphasized that human resources managers must devise good policies for responding to whistle-blowers: "If they don't do it, it will be done for them, and their worst nightmares are likely to be realized."

Differing views of the relative costs and benefits of whistle-blowing may result to some extent from differing definitions of the term. For this reason, and for many others, it is important for us to clarify our conceptualization of whistle-blowing and provide a working definition.

The Definition of Whistle-blowing

We do not know where the term *whistle-blower* originated, but the analogy is to an official on a playing field, such as a football referee, who can blow the whistle to stop action. Popular usage of the term is probably as confounded as its original source.

In an earlier paper (Near & Miceli, 1985, p. 4), we defined whistle-blowing to mean "the disclosure by organization members (former or current) of illegal, immoral, or illegitimate practices under the control of their employers, to persons or organizations that may be able to effect action." The whistle-blower lacks the power and authority to make the change being sought and therefore must appeal to someone of greater power or authority (Graham, 1983; Near & Miceli, 1987). In the following discussion, we consider the elements of this definition and explain why we have chosen the definition we use. When referring to the individual who may observe wrongdoing, we will use the term "focal member," that is, the member of the organization on whom we focus attention.

Disclosure to Persons or Organizations That May Be Able to Effect Action

According to our definition of whistle-blowing, reporting an activity requires the "voicing" (Hirschman, 1970) of dissent to someone in authority. Therefore, simply taking mental note of the wrongdoing, asking the wrongdoer to desist, discussing the situation with colleagues without seeking their action, or leaving the organization without voicing dissent does not constitute whistle-blowing (see also Kolarska & Aldrich, 1980; Laver, 1976).

Observers of questionable activities may discuss them with co-workers, family, or friends. However, this would not constitute whistle-blowing, if these parties are not expected to correct the problem or lack the power to do so.

Whistle-blowing usually is viewed as a discrete act of disclosure. However, whistle-blowing can also be viewed as a process involving a number of stages (Dozier & Miceli, 1985). Organization members must decide whether to report an activity that was observed earlier. They must also decide whether to follow up on the report and to take further action. They may experience retaliation or other reactions from organization members. And the report or set of reports and outcomes may stimulate significant change in the organization and the group in which the whistle-blower is a member. The entire set of steps can be viewed as a whistle-blowing *process* involving a number of subprocesses. For example, the decision process that may be used by observers of wrongdoing in order to determine whether to report wrongdoing is likely to be an important part of the entire whistle-blowing process.

While multiple usages of terms may sometimes be confusing (that is, whistle-blowing as a discrete event versus whistle-blowing as a process), we are hesitant to coin new terms and add unnecessary jargon that may inhibit communication. Instead, we will try to keep clear which usage we employ throughout our discussion.

Organization Membership

There is general agreement among theorists that the whistle-blower must at some time have been a member of the organization against which the complaint is lodged (Elliston, 1982a). It is not necessary to be a member at the time that the complaint is resolved; some whistle-blowers exit their organizations voluntarily or involuntarily (Elliston, 1982a). For example, a whistle-blower may be fired in retaliation, or she or he may quit in anticipation of firing or after experiencing harassment in other forms.

Illegal, Immoral, or Illegitimate Practices

Although any beginning point is arguably arbitrary, we have decided to begin our observation of whistle-blowing when an event in an organizational context arouses concern in the eyes of at least one member of that organization. We ignore activity that is somehow inherently wrong, or activity an outsider considers wrongful, because our concern is with a *triggering* event. If no organization member has observed the activity and defined it to be questionable, then the activity does not serve as a triggering event for whistle-blowing; that is, there must be someone in the woods to hear the tree falling.

The primary implication of our choice of starting points is that we are interested in the consequences of wrongdoing; we do not explore here the etiology of wrongdoing. Readers interested in those issues may refer to literature that deals more directly with the nature of organizational wrongdoing and its antecedents (for example, Banfield, 1975; Baucus & Near, 1991; Clinard, 1983; Clinard & Yeager, 1980; Davidson & Worrell, 1988; Edelhertz, 1978; Finney & Lesieur, 1982; Hamilton & Sanders, 1981; Mathews, 1987). However, because organization members' perceptions of the wrongdoing and why it has occurred may play an important role in whistle-blowing, these perceptions will be discussed in subsequent sections of this book.

It is important to achieve consensus on what constitutes wrongdoing, because responses to activities that do not constitute wrongdoing are not whistle-blowing. The triggering event is an activity that is considered wrongful, rather than simply an acceptable but not optimal organizational activity. Wrongdoing may constitute corporate crime, which is "any act punishable by the state, regardless of whether it is punished by administrative or civil law, which it usually is, or under the criminal law" (Clinard, 1983, p. 10). However, an act that is legal and not criminal, could still be considered illegitimate (Near & Miceli, 1985, 1987), meaning that the act is perceived by the observer to be beyond the realm of the organization's authority. Thus, illegal dumping or fraudulent accounting practices might trigger whistle-blowing as could a directive to require politically appointed employees to contribute "voluntarily" to political campaigns.

Omissions can also be considered wrongful. For example, a pharmaceutical company may fail to inform customers or regulatory agencies of risks or dangers inherent in a drug they produce. Although technically an omission may not be a discrete event, to avoid redundancy, we will consider the terms *event, practice,* and *activity* to be inclusive of omissions.

An employee may propose a cost-saving idea through an internal suggestion system. But this does not constitute an attempt to correct a wrongful practice, because what has motivated this action is not the wish to change illegal, immoral, or illegitimate activity. Communications do not constitute whistle-blowing if the triggering event is not an activity that is viewed as immoral, illegal, or illegitimate. The importance of this distinction is that if a practice is illegitimate, it must be changed (Near & Miceli, 1987; Weinstein, 1979). However, in some instances, there may be a fine line between practices that whistle-blowers consider merely incorrect or undesirable, that is, technically misguided and potentially harmful, and those that they consider wrong, that is, immoral.

Organization members' perceptions of the wrongfulness of the activity or omission determine whether their action in response to it constitutes whistle-blowing. While the perceptions of persons other than the focal member are conceivably important in influencing his or her propensity to act and are important in the consequences of whistle-blowing (as will be discussed later), others' perceptions do not entirely determine whether the focal member considers an act illegal, immoral, or illegitimate.

Two important implications of this observation can be drawn. First, it is important to determine how individuals view activities in order to predict their responses to the activities. This is not to imply, however, that the determination is entirely subjective, arbitrary, or unpredictable. In many instances, observers who do not have a vested interest in the activity may agree that the activity is wrongful. Researchers must, however, not rely on their own assumptions.

about what might be considered wrongful or expect that all organization members might view the same act in the same way. Further,
operationally defining wrongdoing as measured in the perceptions
of organizational leaders as opposed to the individual who makes
the decision about the activity may obviously result in misleading
conclusions.

Second, those interested in developing appropriate organizational
policies toward—or legal protections for—whistle-blowers must
necessarily focus on the beliefs of the observer of questionable activity in addressing appropriate responses. Organizational leaders
or society may determine that it is justifiable to attempt to change
a practice that one truly believes is illegitimate, but that organizations may justifiably deter change attempts by subordinates who are
unwilling to accept the legitimate decisions of superiors. For example, an individual who does not like an organizational policy of
requiring that uniforms be worn may object simply because he or
she does not like the uniform. But organizational leaders and lawmakers may choose to respond to or protect attempts to change the
policy only to the extent that the employee has a basis for believing
that the requirement is illegal, immoral, or illegitimate (for instance,
if only women and not men are required to wear uniforms, which
might violate sex discrimination statutes). An obvious difficulty in
studying whistle-blowing, then, is in assessing whether the whistle-
blower truly believes that the wrongdoing observed is illegitimate as
opposed to simply incorrect.

Activities Under the Control of the Organization

One additional issue that should be addressed is what constitutes
organizational wrongdoing. It is important to clarify this issue because reactions to wrongdoing, and the consequences of whistle-
blowing, may depend on whether observers believe that the
organization committed the wrongdoing—as opposed to individuals who happen to be members—and for what reasons. As will be
explored in chapters 3 and 4, it is conceivable that reactions to
wrongdoing will depend on the perceptions of the observer with
respect to who is harmed (or helped) by wrongdoing and who
would be harmed or helped by whistle-blowing and the consequent
cessation of wrongdoing (Sheler, 1981). We view any wrongdoing

that occurs in organizations to be potentially the focus of a whistle-blowing complaint.

The organization is composed of persons. Its members may commit wrongdoing ostensibly on behalf of the organization (Braithwaite, 1982). For example, a hospital administrator may take inappropriate risks that jeopardize the safety of the employees, clients, or customers because he or she believes costs will be reduced or that profits will increase. Similarly, the commission of a crime may influence stock prices: "some companies may commit crimes that improve cash flows, such as tax evasion and bribing elected officials, and may thereby increase firm value if they are not caught" (Davidson & Worrell, 1988, p. 196).

Research suggests that poor financial performance is frequently linked with organizational crime (Cochran & Nigh, 1986; Finney & Lesieur, 1982; Staw & Szwajkowski, 1975). This linkage could occur for several reasons. Both financial performance and organizational crime may be related to a third variable, such as a history of poor management and substitution of desperate measures because organization members lack competency. Another possibility is that poor financial performance causes organizational leaders to expect impossible performance improvement—to be obtained through whatever means available. These leaders may then reward (for example, through pay or promotions) those individuals who accomplish the goals even if they were accomplished unethically; thus organizational reward systems sometimes exert pressures on members to behave unethically (Jansen & Von Glinow, 1985). On the other hand, recent research suggests that the relationship between organizational performance and crime is not universal; evidence suggests that wrongdoing may be even more prevalent when financial resources are strong, suggesting a greed impetus rather than a desperation strategy (Baucus & Near, 1991).

Sometimes, organization members commit wrongdoing on their own behalf. For example, federal statistics indicate that in 1984, bank employees stole nine times more money than did bank robbers ("Employees greater threat . . . ," 1986). In this case, observers may believe that the organization would not approve of such activities and that it is in fact victimized by the wrongdoing.

We would emphasize that the organization in which perceived wrongdoing has occurred is not always the same as the party against which the complaint is lodged. If the organization's top management has not authorized or engaged in wrongdoing, there may be an individual wrongdoer against whom a complaint is lodged. Further, the party to whom a complaint is made is not always the same as the organization in which the perceived wrongdoing has occurred. In some, albeit few, cases, whistle-blowers reported wrongdoing only to outsiders (Miceli & Near, 1985).

The preceding discussion implies that it is important not to assume that whistle-blowers are a homogeneous group of persons or that every whistle-blowing act is similar in many ways to every other. Instead, we must consider how to make conceptual distinctions among persons or instances in order to better understand the process.

Distinctions Among Whistle-blowers

Our definition of whistle-blowing is not the same as those employed by other writers. In three important ways, our definition may be broader than many. Nothing in our definition excludes those whistle-blowers who (a) ostensibly are required by their jobs to report wrongdoing; (b) report wrongdoing only to parties (complaint recipients) internal to the organizations; or (c) appear to benefit in some way from whistle-blowing. We next explain why we prefer a broad definition, by examining each of these three issues in turn.

Role Prescriptions

Some observers may argue that individuals who appear to be required by their jobs to report certain types of wrongdoing under certain circumstances cannot be considered whistle-blowers. However, whistle-blowing that is role-prescribed is still whistle-blowing, and operationally—at this time—the distinction is not clear. This is because (a) whistle-blowing is formally role-prescribed in many organizations, for many individuals; (b) there are many potential conflicts in prescriptions sent by parties that may be influential over the whistle-blowing; and (c) whistle-blowing is rarely, if ever, truly role-prescribed *by job*.

THE WIDESPREAD PRACTICE OF FORMALLY PRESCRIBING WHISTLE-BLOWING. Role-prescribed behaviors are organization-ally specified as a part of the individual's role or job (Brief and Motowidlo, 1986). One example of an organizational role prescription for virtually all employees exists in the federal sector. The ninth article of the Code of Ethics for Government Service compels employees to " 'expose corruption wherever discovered' " (Pottmyer, 1987). Additionally, research shows that more than half of the codes of ethics examined specifically provided that if any employee "had questions about legal or ethical policy or wished to report possible illegal or unethical conduct . . . she or he [should] contact the company's legal counsel" (Mathews, 1987, p. 116). Sometimes the circumstances under which whistle-blowing is required, and the process for whistle-blowing, are articulated; sometimes they are not. Whistle-blowing also can be prescribed by professional associations (as for engineers or accountants) whose codes of ethics require members to report observed wrongdoing. For example, in Ohio, physicians are required to report suspicions to the state medical board; whistle-blowing is also prescribed for psychiatrists and therapists ("Therapists' sexual misconduct . . .", 1987) and for many academic scientists (Tangney, 1987). In any event, to the extent that many individuals in the public and private sectors in a variety of occupations are required to report wrongdoing, distinctions based on the role prescription become quite muddled and misleading.

MULTIPLE AND MIXED ROLE PRESCRIPTIONS. The term *role-prescribed whistle-blowing* implies that organizations, managers, other organization members, and outsiders such as professional organizations and their members, would universally support attempts to call attention to wrongdoing. Further, it implies that these parties would be *unsupportive* in the case of whistle-blowers whose observation and reporting of wrongdoing are *not* role-prescribed. But the existence of formal channels for making complaints may imply to everyone—regardless of specific role prescriptions—that the organization would be supportive. There are at least three other reasons why persons whose jobs appear to require them to blow the whistle actually face countervailing pressures—in which some forces may be supportive of the whistle-blower and others oppose it—as do other observers of wrongdoing. These are described below.

Formal and Informal Reward Contingencies. Written prescriptions are not the same as prevailing reward contingencies (Dozier & Miceli, 1985). Obviously, the persons responsible for wrongdoing would prefer that observers ignore the wrongdoing. Informal group or organizational norms may require that certain activities be ignored despite the formal prescriptions (Greenberger, Miceli & Cohen, 1987). The reputation and profits of the organization may suffer dramatically if whistle-blowers feel compelled to make wrongdoing known to authorities, which may lead to organizational resistance against whistle-blowing attempts. In one case, a Defense Department auditor was involuntarily transferred after he reported that a contractor had overcharged the Defense Department for spare parts ("Pratt and Whitney . . .", 1983). Similarly, co-workers may resent whistle-blowing by anyone because their lives may be made miserable with increased tension or probing by authorities or reporters; they may feel betrayed or guilty for not having come forward themselves (Jensen, 1987).

Voluntary Decision Making. Like persons for whom whistle-blowing is rarely or never role-prescribed, many "overseers" believe they have the option to ignore wrongdoing or to expose it. As evidence, one group of internal auditors estimated that about 42 percent of bribery attempts are not reported (Johnson & Pany, 1981). This suggests that a decision process must operate for overseers as well as for persons without role prescriptions for whistle-blowing.

Societal Support Even Where Whistle-blowing is Discouraged by the Organization. Society in general may view valid whistle-blowing favorably; increasing the incidence of valid whistle-blowing is often assumed to be a goal of a well-informed society (Ewing, 1983). Societal members may also consider reporting a moral obligation regardless of job requirements. As evidence, over 90 percent of the respondents to a survey approved of whistle-blowing under certain circumstances (MSPB, 1981). These general views may conflict with norms in the organization in which the whistle-blower may be viewed as a deviant but might be considered to be conforming to the norms and values of the larger society (Mathews, 1987). Perhaps this occurs because societal members usually benefit from whistle-blowing while members of the organization in which wrongdoing occurs may be harmed by whistle-blowing; in any case, the conflict may exist regardless of the job held by the whistle-blower.

WHISTLE-BLOWING IS RARELY ROLE-PRESCRIBED BY JOB. Role prescriptions for whistle-blowing *by job* means that, for all activities one may encounter in a job, whistle-blowing would always be officially and informally required and encouraged, regardless of the individuals involved in the activity, the nature of the activity, or the form the whistle-blowing might take. Although empirical data have not yet been collected on this issue, it seems unlikely to us that all these conditions would be met.

Only a limited subset of whistle-blowing activities may be officially encouraged in jobs that appear to require whistle-blowing. For example, the internal auditing standards established by the Institute of Internal Auditors, the primary professional organization that sets standards for auditing practice, encourages reporting through specified channels (for example, to the audit committee of the company's board of directors) of certain activities (such as "significant fraud"). But reporting other activities that an auditor may consider wrongful (such as safety violations) is not addressed specifically, and reporting to parties external to the organization, such as the media, is *discouraged* (Professional Standards and Responsibilities Committee, 1985). For example, a professional standards bulletin (Professional Standards and Responsibilities Committee, 1985, pp. 3–4) included the following question and answer:

Q Does an internal auditor have a responsibility to notify outside authorities of suspected wrongdoing?

A When an internal auditor's procedures lead to suspicion of some kind of wrongdoing, the auditor should determine the possible effects of the wrongdoing, discuss the matter with the appropriate level of management who (management or the internal auditor) should investigate or otherwise follow up the suspicion. When wrongdoing is suspected, the auditor's responsibility extends to the appropriate level of management within the organization.

This suggests that role prescriptions must be defined specifically with respect to an activity or circumstances.

Therefore, we argue that the role prescriptions distinction deserves more empirical attention but that whistle-blowing that appears to be role-prescribed should not be presumed to be something entirely different from other types of whistle-blowing. In later chapters we explore the extent to which role prescriptions may affect the whistle-blowing process.

Internal Versus External Complaint Recipients

Another issue that arises in attempts to define whistle-blowing is whether it includes reports only to parties within the same organization in which the whistle-blower serves. Philosophers have generally presented "a strong moral case" supporting internal reports (Heacock & McGee, 1989) but support for external reporting may be more mixed. Authors agree that reports to parties outside the organization constitute whistle-blowing, but they disagree about internal complaint recipients (Near & Miceli, 1987). In our definition, the complaint recipient may be a member of the organization, perhaps someone above the whistle-blower (a direct supervisor or above) or someone removed from the hierarchy (such as an ombudsperson). This position is shared by other popular writers, organizational leaders, and researchers (for example, Bowman, Elliston & Lockhart, 1984; Campbell, in MSPB, 1981; Elliston, 1982a; Nader, Petkas & Blackwell, 1972; Sheler, 1981; Westin, 1981). However, some authors (for example, Farrell & Petersen, 1982, 1989; Petersen & Farrell, 1986; Weinstein, 1979) reserve the term *whistle-blowing* for external reports exclusively. For three reasons, we believe that the broader definition is more appropriate, and that internal and external reports represent two categories of a general class of behavior.

CONCEPTUAL SIMILARITIES BETWEEN INTERNAL AND EXTERNAL WHISTLE-BLOWING. First, although each whistle-blowing is unique, there are a number of similarities between incidents that are unaffected by the membership status of the complaint recipient. Both types of acts are initiated by organization members who wish to stop perceived wrongdoing in their organizations. Both represent the use of voice rather than an alternative, such as sabotage, exit, or violence, to bring about organizational change, although these other actions could accompany some whistle-blowing instances. Both types of acts may violate (or maintain) group or organizational norms, which may lead to hostility (or support) from others, including wrongdoers, co-workers, managers, family, friends, professional associates, or the public. For example, in the case of Robert Wityczak, who blew the whistle on Rockwell's practice of charging the government for time spent on other projects, Wityczak experienced considerable retaliation before the complaint was made known to the public (Hanrahan, 1983). The disabled veteran was allegedly forced to work in jobs involving physical labor, even though he had "lost much of his body in the Vietnam War" (Hanrahan, 1983, pp. 17 and 20).

Similarly, Bok (1980) provides some support for viewing internal and external whistle-blowing as closely related phenomena. She defines the elements of whistle-blowing to be dissent, accusation of wrongdoing, and breach of loyalty to the organization. The first two elements clearly would characterize both internal and external protests. But at first glance it appears that internal complaining would not constitute a breach of loyalty. However, Elliston (1982a) argued that internal protests could also constitute a breach of organizational loyalty (as when members report wrongdoing to a corporate attorney or to a higher-level manager other than their supervisors, they may be "disloyal" to their supervisors). Further, Baker (1983) demonstrated that external whistle-blowers often describe themselves as members who initiated whistle-blowing *because of* their loyalty to the organization. Consistent with this, Kolarska and Aldrich (1980) and Hirschman (1970) also noted that loyal, long-term members of organizations may be more likely to blow the whistle than to remain silent because their stakes in the process's outcomes may be higher. Thus, the breach of loyalty difference does not appear to be substantial.

EMPIRICAL EVIDENCE OF THE PROGRESSION OF AN ACTION. A second reason why it is inappropriate to exclude internal whistle-blowing from consideration is that empirical data show that (1) nearly all whistle-blowers who use external channels also reported problems internally (Baker, 1983; Miceli & Near, 1984), and (2) there are many similarities between "externals" and "internals" in their attitudes and beliefs toward whistle-blowing and in the types of wrongdoing they witnessed, retaliation expectancies, and other variables (for example, Miceli & Near, 1985). Such findings strongly suggest that the two reporting behaviors are much more conceptually similar than they are different.

OPERATIONAL ISSUES. A third reason for treating internal and external whistle-blowing as two categories of a general class of behaviors is that certain operational problems are solved by the use of a broader definition. First, in viewing internal whistle-blowing as very different from other whistle-blowing, one may prematurely conclude that certain variables that predict one type are irrelevant to the other. We would prefer that this question be addressed empirically. Second, in many cases, it may be difficult to determine whether a given incident—under an "external only" definition— would represent whistle-blowing. For example, does reporting an unsafe product or work environment to a union steward constitute whistle-blowing? The steward is in some sense both an insider and an outsider. Similarly, federal employees who report agency fraud to a member of Congress, would not, under a narrow definition, be considered whistle-blowers, yet reason compels us to recognize them as such.

Therefore, it seems more appropriate to view the role of the complaint recipient as one that potentially affects how the whistle-blowing process is played out, rather than as one that defines whistle-blowing or serves to exclude internal incidents from consideration.

Altruism and Outcomes That Could Benefit the Whistle-blower

Graham (1983, 1984, 1986) uses the term *principled organizational dissent* to refer to a class of behaviors that is broader in some ways than our view of whistle-blowing. Principled dissent involves dissent concerning a violation of some standard of justice or honesty (Graham, 1986). As Blackburn (1988, p. 3) pointed out, Graham (1983, 1986) "described issues of principle as those resulting in attempts to change the status quo because of conscientious objection to current practice or policy." Dissent conceivably could be expressed in ways other than the reporting of wrongdoing to someone who is powerful enough to stop it, a defining characteristic of whistle-blowing. For example, a work stoppage may constitute principled organizational dissent but not necessarily whistle-blowing.

In other ways, principled organizational dissent appears to exclude cases we consider to constitute whistle-blowing, although we must admit to some confusion in understanding the delimiters of the term. According to Graham (1983, p. 3) the term "does not necessarily describe the ultimate motive of the person who raises [the issue at stake]." However, she later asserts that (p. 20), cases "involving personal benefits to the dissidents . . . do not qualify as principled organizational dissent," an assertion that to us clearly refers to the person's motive as inferred by Graham. According to Graham (1983), an individual who files a complaint of illegal discrimination on the basis of sex or race would not be considered a principled organizational dissenter, because he is presumably not able to act on principle alone but also out of self-concern. But Graham's apparent difficulty in dealing with dissenters' motivations echoes our own. Consequently, we have misgivings about adopting this distinction in our definition of whistle-blower, for four reasons categorized as follows: (a) the co-existence of mixed motives; (b) the far-reaching effects of wrongdoing; (c) the availability of alternatives to whistle-blowing; and (d) the difficulty of measuring "pure altruism."

THE CO-EXISTENCE OF MIXED MOTIVES. Several authors have determined that whistle-blowing can be viewed as a type of prosocial organizational behavior (for example, Brief & Motowidlo, 1986; Dozier & Miceli, 1984, 1985; Graham, 1983, 1986). Prosocial organizational behavior is behavior that is "(a) performed by a member of an organization; (b) directed toward an individual, group, or organization with whom he or she interacts while carrying out his or her organizational role, and (c) performed with the intention of promoting the welfare of the individual, group, or organization toward which it is directed" (Brief & Motowidlo, 1986). Because whistle-blowers are organization members who direct their reporting toward the perceived victims of wrongdoing with the intention of promoting the victims' welfare, it is clear that whistle-blowing satisfies the requirements of the definition.

Researchers of prosocial behavior (such as Brief & Motowidlo, 1986; Staub, 1978) have considered whether the expectation of future rewards for the actor places the actor's behavior outside the realm of prosocial behavior. They have determined that it does not; instead, altruism, which is restricted to behavior engaged in without expectation of future material or social reward, is one particular type of prosocial behavior (Brief & Motowidlo, 1986). In fact, some social psychologists maintain that even altruism allows for selfish benefit. For example, Batson (1983, p. 1981) defined altruism as "a desire within one organism to increase the welfare of another as an end-state goal . . . [although it] excludes acts in which one increases the welfare of another as an intermediate goal toward the ultimate end of increasing one's own welfare (as, for example, when one helps another in order to provoke reciprocity, to obtain social rewards, or to comply with social conventions)." In any event, there appears to be agreement among authors that organization members can be said to engage in prosocial behavior even where they may expect some benefit to themselves.

Whistle-blowers can have both selfish concerns and altruistic concerns; they are not mutually exclusive. They may complain about discrimination to help themselves, but they also intend to benefit others. But clearly, whistle-blowing is still prosocial behavior even where some benefits to the whistle-blower are expected, which suggests that research on prosocial behavior will be relevant to whistle-blowing (Dozier & Miceli, 1985).

THE FAR-REACHING EFFECTS OF WRONGDOING. It is difficult to imagine any instance of organizational wrongdoing that does not in some way harm the observer who reports it and hence the cessation of wrongdoing could conceivably benefit the observer. Most readers would agree that a nuclear worker who reports to the media that equipment is improperly maintained is a whistle-blower. But isn't that worker in danger so long as the equipment poses risks? Perhaps if the observer is also the sole and voluntary perpetrator, the net short-term advantages of the continuation of wrongdoing may outweigh the benefits of cessation, but this party is unlikely to be a whistle-blower. In most other cases, it is possible to identify some potential personal benefit to the successful whistle-blower in the cessation of wrongdoing. Therefore, disqualifying whistle-blowers who may benefit from the cessation of wrongdoing would mean excluding essentially all whistle-blowers.

THE AVAILABILITY OF ALTERNATIVES TO WHISTLE-BLOWING. A third reason why we object to the exclusion of individuals who stand to gain from successful whistle-blowing is that organization members frequently have alternatives to whistle-blowing when they are harmed by an organizational practice. Their choice of blowing the whistle may correct the wrongdoing, but it may also bring about harm to themselves that could have been avoided had they relied on another alternative. Their choice of change alternatives may be motivated by altruism. For example, a race discrimination complainant might instead threaten to sue if a pay raise were not forthcoming. His or her manager might grant the raise or offer a settlement, which might solve the complainant's problem. But by blowing the whistle, the complainant takes additional risks, perhaps "because of the principle of the thing"—he or she wants to ensure that enough attention is given not just to the immediate problem but to the problem of discrimination that may affect others as well.

THE DIFFICULTY OF MEASURING "PURE ALTRUISM." A fourth reason is simply a measurement issue. Even if it is conceivable that some whistle-blowers have purely altruistic motivations, how will this be determined? Even if Graham's distinction between "principled" objection and dissent that benefits the individual makes some intuitive sense, a meaningful distinction cannot be made operationally (Blackburn, 1988). As Batson (1983, p. 1382) pointed out, "determining whether a given act is in any degree altruistically motivated is extremely difficult." Further, it is difficult to know even whether the "net motivations" are prosocial (Brief & Motowidlo, 1986; Dozier & Miceli, 1984, 1985; Staub, 1978).

For all these reasons, we believe that at this time it would be inappropriate—if not impossible—to exclude whistle-blowers who stand to gain in some way. With future research, however, it may be necessary to revise this position.

The Need for Empirical Investigation

All three of the factors described above could conceivably demarcate types of whistle-blowers or represent variables that could affect whistle-blowing or its consequences. Therefore, empirical investigation is needed to determine the role played by each of these factors. This issue is discussed at greater length in later chapters of this book.

Categorizing Whistle-blowing

As might be expected whenever investigation of a behavior or a problem is in its infancy, various authors have viewed whistle-blowing from different perspectives. This probably results from a recognition that, if whistle-blowing is similar in some ways to other types of organizational behaviors, it should be classified in some way to show this relationship. In so doing, several key advantages are realized. First, definitional issues can be clarified, and perhaps, resolved. Second, researchers can avoid "re-inventing the wheel" in attempting to understand the phenomenon. They can build from existing theoretical and empirical frameworks a model of whistle-blowing.

Three important taxonomies that have been identified by researchers appear to hold promise in examining whistle-blowing. These are: (a) employee concerns and the exit, voice, and loyalty framework; (b) political behavior; and (c) prosocial behavior and organizational citizenship.

There are additional theoretical perspectives from which we can draw in examining whistle-blowing. However, in those perspectives (for example, conformity, power) there has been no attempt to determine a classification for whistle-blowing as a particular *type* of behavior. Therefore, the limitations and boundary conditions are not clear; the literature from those perspectives may or may not apply to all types of behaviors including whistle-blowing. We will therefore postpone discussion of these perspectives until later chapters.

Below we discuss each of the three taxonomies and how whistle-blowing might be placed in each. In later chapters, we will draw on the theory and research that suggests predictors of the category of behavior represented by whistle-blowing in building a model of whistle-blowing.

Employee Concerns and the Exit, Voice, and Loyalty (EVL) Framework

Employee concerns include problems, complaints, or dissatisfaction with the organization as felt by an employee (Rowe & Baker, 1984), and the expression of the concern, or any attempt by an employee to resolve a concern related to any aspect of work constitutes "employee dissent" (Blackburn, 1988, p. 4). As noted by Blackburn (1988), Graham's (1983) view of employee concerns is quite similar; it is the perception by one person that some aspect of organizational performance could be improved or should be investigated.

Hirschman's (1970) research on exit, voice, and loyalty (EVL) conceives of the employee as possessing several options when faced with organizational decline of some sort (Blackburn, 1988; Graham, 1986). The essential taxonomy can be integrated together with employee concerns as depicted in table 1–2.

Table 1–2 summarizes the types of employee concerns and responses employees could take in response to concerns. Of course, because observers of perceived wrongdoing may take several actions, their behavior may, at different times, cross several cells appearing in table 1–2.

As shown in table 1–2, whistle-blowing represents one type of employee dissent, if the nature of the perceived activity triggering the employee concern involves activity or omissions that the individual believes to be illegal, immoral, or illegitimate. Whistle-blowing can be separated into internal or external dissent. If whistle-blowing is paired with exit, it can be viewed as an exit with protest. Where the public is informed, it constitutes public protest, though whistle-blowers can inform only insiders during the exit interview.

In contrast, dissatisfaction with the temperature of soft drinks from the vending machine on a given day may be an employee concern, but it does not trigger whistle-blowing, even if it leads to a complaint (dissent), because the activity would not be considered illegal, immoral, or illegitimate. Instead, expression of a complaint of this type to parties who may not have a legitimate right to know about the activity may constitute the revelation of company secrets

TABLE 1–2

Employee Concerns and Employee Dissent[a]

	Nature of the Perceived Activity Triggering the Concern			
	Illegal, Immoral or Illegitimate		Not Illegal, Immoral, or Illegitimate	
Expression of the Concern (Voice)	Exit Dimension			
	Stay	Go	Stay	Go
External dissent to someone who can take action	External whistle-blowing	Exit with public protest[b]	Secret sharing	Exit with secret sharing
Internal dissent to someone who can take action	Internal whistle-blowing	Protest during exit interview[b]	Employee participation, grievance	Explain reason for resignation in exit
Dissent in some other form	Discussion, confrontation with wrongdoer	Exit with notice to wrongdoer	Sabotage, strikes	Sabotage, strikes with exit
No expressed dissent	Inactive observation[c]	Inactive departure	Silent disgruntlement	Silent departure

[a]This is adapted, by permission of the author, from figure 1 in Blackburn (1988), which represents Graham's (1986) typology of responses to organizational decline.
[b]This is also whistle-blowing.
[c]This has traditionally been viewed as "loyalty" (Graham, 1983), but Hirschman (1970) questions that view, as does Farrell (1983) who labels it "neglect."

(Sitkin, 1986), which may or may not be accompanied by employee exit. Expression of employee concerns over activities that are not illegal, immoral, or illegitimate to internal parties may constitute employee participation. Or, employees may use a formal or informal grievance procedure existing in the organization. When paired with exit, the employee may simply state the complaint as a reason for exit, in the hope that the organization can make corrections for future employees or to justify leaving.

As noted earlier, employee dissent may assume some form other than whistle-blowing. Where the triggering event is considered illegal, immoral, or illegitimate, the employee may discuss the event directly with the wrongdoer; or, the employee may confront the wrongdoer and demand change. In the former case, the employee may be unsure of the evidence or may believe that discussion would resolve the problem; in the latter case, the employee would likely believe she or he possessed the power to bring about change. In either case, this action does not constitute whistle-blowing because the triggering event has not been reported to a powerful third party. This type of dissent may accompany exit, in which case notice may be given to the wrongdoer, or the dissenter may exit after making repeated attempts to change the wrongdoer's actions.

Organizations that speed up the work flow may have a legitimate right to do so, but employees may dislike the change and may register their views in the form of sabotage, strikes, or other forms of dissent. These employees may also exit.

Organization members may also remain silent, or refrain from expressing dissent. Where the observed activity is believed to be wrongful, but no steps are taken to correct it, we describe this as "inactive observation," or in the case of employees who exit, "inactive departure." Where the observed activity is dissatisfying, though not necessarily wrongful, employees may remain in silent disgruntlement over the activity. Eventually, of course, they may accept the organizational activity or change their views of it. Other employees may depart in silence.

Table 1–2 does not completely represent all actions potentially available to the individual. For example, there may be other forms of dissent that do not appear in the cells. As another example, individuals who have concerns can express them anonymously or not. They may identify themselves openly, or only to the complaint recipient with the request that the information remain confidential, or they may remain anonymous with respect to everyone. Thus, each category in the dissent rows can be subdivided into three additional categories reflecting the extent to which anonymity is preserved. As a third example, whistle-blowers may decide to take action collectively or alone, and they may decide among several potential complaint recipients within or outside the organization. These issues will be discussed in later chapters.

Political Behavior

Individuals in organizations can engage in political behavior to create change (Farrell & Petersen, 1982). Whether whistle-blowing, a change attempt, constitutes political behavior depends on its definition. Unfortunately, there is no clear consensus at this time as to the definition of political behavior. According to Cavanagh, Moberg, and Velasquez (1981), political behavior is the use of either sanctioned or unsanctioned means to reach (organizationally) unsanctioned ends. For example, aspiring managers may ingratiate themselves with powerful authorities in order to get resources that others may deserve. Using this definition, whistle-blowing is one type of political behavior, because if an action is meant to correct wrongdoing by a person who lacks direct authority to institute that change, then the end is not sanctioned (Near & Miceli, 1987). Unfortunately, Cavanagh et al. (1981) did not propose a taxonomy.

Farrell and Petersen (1982, p. 405) defined political behavior to be "those activities that are not required as part of one's organizational role but that influence, or attempt to influence, the distribution of advantages and disadvantages within the organization." As noted earlier, whistle-blowing may in some cases be role prescribed but in other cases it may not be. It clearly is an influence attempt, and it is probably usually true that relative advantages and disadvantages are a target of the influence attempt. Therefore, using this definition, whistle-blowing would frequently, but not always, be considered political behavior.

Farrell and Petersen proposed that political behaviors can be classified according to three dimensions and that the predictors of the political behaviors are different for each classification. First, political behaviors can be "internal" or "external" depending on "the focus of resources sought by those engaging in political behavior in organizations" (p. 405). Second, they can be "vertical" or "lateral" depending on the location in the hierarchy of the communication recipient. In our view, classifying external parties as vertical or lateral can be problematic; this distinction seems to be more appropriate in the case of internal whistle-blowing. Third, political behaviors can be "legitimate" or "illegitimate" depending on whether the behavior "violates the 'rules of the game' " (p. 406). Although Farrell and Petersen viewed whistle-blowing to be illegitimate and external, for the reasons we put forth earlier, we disagree. Therefore, Farrell's and Petersen's taxonomy suggests that the predictors of whistle-blowing, and conceivably, its consequences, may depend on the specific circumstances of the incident. For example, the predictors of whistle-blowing exclusively to parties within the whistle-blowers's organization may be different from those variables that predict external whistle-blowing.

Other researchers have defined political behavior in ways that appear to exclude whistle-blowing. In a review of the literature, Ferris, Russ, and Fandt (1989, p. 145) characterized organizational politics as "a social influence process in which behavior is strategically designed to maximize short-term or long-term self-interest, which is either consistent with or at the expense of others' interests (where self-interest maximization refers to the attainment of positive outcomes and the prevention of negative outcomes)." In our earlier discussion, we maintained that whistle-blowers may sometimes benefit from whistle-blowing, and they may intend to do so at the outset. However, whistle-blowing is undertaken at least in part to benefit others and only rarely could be said to be designed to maximize self-interest. Therefore, it appears to fall outside the realm of the type of behavior to which Ferris et al. (1989) referred. Hence, in our later discussion, we will rely primarily on predictors of political behavior as suggested by Farrell and Petersen (1982).

Prosocial Behavior and Organizational Citizenship

Brief and Motowidlo (1986) provided a preliminary taxonomy based generally on three distinctions between types of prosocial organizational behaviors (POBs). First, POBs can be functional or dysfunctional for the organization. Second, POBs can be role-prescribed or extra-role. Third, the targets of POBs can be the organization or other parties, such as peers, supervisors, subordinates, consumers, or clients. Thus, both Brief's and Motowidlo's taxonomy and the taxonomy summarized in table 1–2 focus on the expected target of whistle-blowing. However, while the taxonomy summarized in table 1–2 also focused on the form of the action taken by the observer of wrongdoing (that is, whether it was reported externally, reported internally, acted upon without a report, or not acted upon; whether the action or inaction was accompanied by exit), the POB taxonomy seems to focus more on the intentions of the whistle-blower at the time of action, and on the organization's expectations of the whistle-blower (whether whistle-blowing is prescribed).

Brief and Motowidlo identified thirteen categories of prosocial organizational behaviors. A listing of these categories appears in table 1–3.

Brief and Motowidlo did not attempt to classify the thirteen behaviors along the three dimensions they proposed, apparently because "these three distinctions do not necessarily define clearly separable sets of behavior" (p. 712). This point is made clear in the case of whistle-blowing. Whistle-blowing incidents are diverse and they are undertaken under a variety of circumstances. Some may have consequences that are functional for the organization, while others have dysfunctional consequences, and still others may have both types of consequences.

It is not clear to us how Brief and Motowidlo (1986, p. 714) classified whistle-blowing, although they viewed it as "prosocial behavior directed more broadly toward the organization as a whole" (Categories 7–13). They included it as an example of Category 9, "Objecting to improper directives, procedures, or policies" (p. 715).

Others (such as Graham, 1983) have viewed whistle-blowing as a type of organizational citizenship behavior, behavior that is "organizationally functional and extra-role" (Brief & Motowidlo, 1986). But it is unclear whether authors who emphasize the cooperative, socially desirable aspects of citizenship behavior (for example, Organ, 1988), would agree (Graham, 1989). Brief and Motowidlo (1986) consider citizenship to be prosocial behavior (see table 1–3). Thus authors agree that whistle-blowing usually is a type of prosocial behavior but they do not necessarily agree about whether it constitutes organizational citizenship.

We would argue that sometimes whistle-blowers act not to benefit the organization but rather to benefit consumers or co-workers. Further, as noted above, whistle-blowing incidents are diverse, and different incidents may fall into different categories. For example,

TABLE 1–3
Categories of Prosocial Organizational Behaviors[a]

Behaviors Directed Toward Individuals

1. Assisting co-workers with job-related matters. Example: Helps co-workers who have been absent.

2. Assisting co-workers with personal matters. Example: Listens to co-workers who have family problems.

3. Showing leniency in personnel decisions. Example: Gives an undeservedly high performance appraisal rating to a subordinate.

4. Providing services or products to consumers in organizationally *consistent* ways. Example: Answers customer questions pleasantly and thoroughly out of genuine concern for customer.

5. Providing services or products to consumers in organizationally *inconsistent* ways. Example: Offers to sell an item to a customer for less than the authorized price.

6. Helping consumers with personal matters unrelated to organizational services or products. Example: Gives customers directions to another location.

Behaviors Directed Toward Organizations

7. Complying with organizational values, policies, and regulations. Example: Wears clothing appropriate for the job.

8. Suggesting procedural, administrative, or organizational improvements. Example: Submits proposal to reduce waste of materials.

9. Objecting to improper directives, procedures, or policies. Example: Files a whistle-blowing complaint.

10. Putting forth extra effort on the job. Example: Doesn't take extra breaks.

11. Volunteering for additional assignments. Example: Asks to serve on a committee.

12. Staying with the organization despite temporary hardships. Example: Remains with a social service agency that experiences a grant cutback.[b]

13. Representing the organization favorably to outsiders. Example: Speaks well of the organization when interviewing applicants.[b]

[a]Derived from Brief and Motowidlo (1986).
[b]Brief and Motowidlo (1986) consider this "loyal" behavior.

whistle-blowing may be viewed as "putting forth extra effort on the job" where the whistle-blower is an auditor and he or she has convincing evidence of fraud in the organization; police officers who report illegal police wire-tapping may be "providing service or products to consumers in organizationally consistent (or inconsistent, depending on one's perspective) ways."

If we are correct, then the propositions offered by Brief and Motowidlo concerning the predictors and consequences of the thirteen categories of prosocial behaviors may apply to some whistle-blowing episodes, but not to others. This suggests that researchers should attempt to include measures identifying the types of whistle-blowing that have occurred, and consider whether the antecedents and consequences vary by type. Unfortunately, the research on prosocial behavior does not distinguish among categories, and Brief and Motowidlo (1986) generally did not speculate about varying antecedents and consequences. Therefore research is needed to address this issue.

Methodological Issues and the Scientific Investigation of Whistle-blowing

An issue that should be addressed before we describe our model of whistle-blowing concerns the methods used to examine whistle-blowing. Methods can be loosely grouped into case reporting and analysis, hypothetical dilemmas (vignettes), cross-sectional field surveys, laboratory and field experimentation, and longitudinal field surveys.

Case Reporting and Analysis

Most of the books written about whistle-blowers (for instance, Nader et al., 1972; Peters & Branch, 1972; Westin, 1981) and some articles (for instance, Glazer & Glazer, 1987) have described individual cases of whistle-blowing. Generally, the information presented has been compiled by the authors following extensive interviews with the whistle-blowers, and sometimes with their colleagues or other persons involved in the cases. Frequently, the authors attempt to determine similarities across cases and to provide guidance to other would-be whistle-blowers.

While such treatments often provide fascinating reading, they suffer from serious shortcomings. First, well-known cases (or those identified through word-of-mouth referrals) typically comprise the majority of cases examined in such books. But they may not be representative of all or even most whistle-blowing attempts. To the extent that this is true, several problems result. What appear to be common characteristics of whistle-blowing cases may in fact be uncommon, or common only to the most dramatic of cases. For example, while many authors report that severe retaliation is practically inevitable (for instance, Shepherd, 1987b), more carefully controlled survey research of a random sample of organization members (as in MSPB, 1981, 1984) suggests that retaliation in any form is perceived by less than one-quarter of the whistle-blowers surveyed, and that severe retaliation is experienced by a small subset of these persons. We hasten to emphasize that this should *not* imply to the reader that retaliation is an insignificant issue. It should be noted that the surveys to date have been conducted in the federal sector and that persons who left the government, as well as persons who have never worked in that sector, were not included. However, these findings suggest that retaliation is much more likely under certain circumstances than under others, and that by examining a small subset of cases, researchers may gain richness and depth with respect to some cases but may lose perspective on the entire population of whistle-blowing incidents.

A second problem associated with the exclusive reliance on whistle-blowing cases in order to draw conclusions about the motivations and experiences of whistle-blowers is that a behavior, tendency, or trait that appears to be characteristic of whistle-blowers in fact may *not* distinguish them from other organization members who did not blow the whistle. Employees who did not observe wrongdoing, or employees who observed but did not report wrongdoing, may share the same characteristic, such as viewing themselves as highly committed or high performing organization members. To determine whether an observed characteristic distinguishes whistle-blowers, it is necessary to include similarly situated non-whistle-blowers in most investigations.

A third difficulty is that unless authors specifically intend to build theory or modify existing theory when examining cases, their observations may not be well-integrated with prior work or with other observations they may make. Conflicts between observations cannot be understood or reconciled. We must then rely on other authors to translate these observations into testable hypotheses, test them, and provide a framework on which later research can build. Finally, exclusive reliance on researchers' observations is susceptible to problems resulting from observer bias, including failure to recognize variables that are operating. A notable exception to these general statements is provided by Farrell and Petersen (1989).

Because of the difficulties inherent in the approaches based on non-randomly selected whistle-blower cases, alternative methodological approaches are helpful. The first of these alternatives relies on presentation of hypothetical dilemmas (vignettes) to subjects.

Hypothetical Dilemmas (Vignettes)

Hypothetical dilemmas can be used to determine what subjects say they would do if confronted with a particular situation. For example, Ferguson and Near (1987) presented subjects with four scenarios involving wrongdoing and asked subjects whether they would blow the whistle if they observed such situations. The advantage of this technique is that independent variables can be manipulated, allowing greater control of effects. On the other hand, subjects' responses are clearly hypothetical and probably subject to social desirability bias. Subjects who say they would blow the whistle if confronted with a particular situation might not actually do so in a case of true wrongdoing. Thus, the use of hypothetical dilemmas really provides only a sense of what variables people believe would be important in influencing them to blow the whistle. Since the vast majority of subjects have never blown the whistle and may never have observed wrongdoing, their own prediction of their likely actions is probably unreliable at best and consciously distorted, at worst. Such results are useful, then, only to the degree that they produce tentative conclusions which should be validated using other methods.

Cross-Sectional Field Surveys

While cross-sectional surveys of large numbers of organization members have advantages (as already noted), they too are limited.

In such surveys, respondents are typically asked to recall events that occurred in the past and explain how they reacted to them. But individuals' perceptions may not be accurate. Common method variance, in which respondents answer questions similarly because both are assessed with the same instrument (Fiske, 1982; Podsakoff & Organ, 1986) can result. Distortion or forgetting may produce inconsistent or questionable data. Survey research generally has not addressed the impact of dispositional variables on whistle-blowing decisions, yet organization members' characteristics may affect both their perceptions of and their reactions to organizational wrongdoing (Farrell & Petersen, 1982; Kolarska & Aldrich, 1980; Perrucci, Anderson, Schendel & Trachtman, 1980).

Further, the findings do not show whether cause-effect relationships exist. Respondents may rationalize their actions or failures to act because attitudes may sometimes follow from, rather than direct, behavior (for example, Salancik & Pfeffer, 1978). This problem seems especially critical where the observation of wrongdoing is concerned, because one may feel compelled to describe one's behavior in a socially desirable or morally correct—but inaccurate— manner. A person who chooses not to blow the whistle may say that she or he believed whistle-blowing would be futile, when in truth that person didn't want to take the time to make a report. While guaranteeing anonymity may reduce this bias to some extent, it does not address the other problems.

Laboratory and Field Experiments

Laboratory research is often useful, because potential harm or intrusiveness to participants or organizations can be minimized, dispositional characteristics can be measured, and situational conditions can be manipulated independent of the participant. Further, the researcher need not rely upon self-reports as measures of both the independent and dependent variables. Thus memory loss, distortion, and common method variance are not problems for laboratory designs. However, it is very difficult in the laboratory to simulate conditions that organization members may face—in particular, the pressures that weigh on a potential whistle-blower, whether to act or not to act (Gaerte, 1990). For example, group norms and dynamics may be quite different after individuals have worked together for some time. Participants may be suspicious of the experimental manipulations, and they may not feel "loyalty" in the same sense that they might to an organization.

Field experiments are very difficult to employ in this arena. One cannot randomly choose an organization in which to create wrongdoing. Usually, a researcher cannot select organization members to witness manipulated wrongdoing in order to determine which individual or situational characteristics are associated with whistleblowing, although this was done in one study (Miceli, Dozier & Near, 1991). Unfortunately, in that study organization members (students at a university who saw "wrongdoing" committed by a confederate research assistant) generally did not work together, so questions involving group dynamics could not be addressed.

Longitudinal Field Surveys

Unfortunately, designs that are frequently used to examine questions that involve cause-effect issues are probably unworkable with regard to whistle-blowing (Miceli & Near, 1988a). Longitudinal survey designs suffer from some of the shortcomings of cross-sectional data, but the primary reason why they may not be workable is that they require that the respondent be identified by name or by code in order for the experimenter to match data collected at different times. In the case of reactions to organizational wrongdoing, there are many sensitive issues raised that might cause many persons who are reluctant to identify themselves not to respond to the questionnaire. This potentially systematic self-selection bias might render any data collected to be of questionable validity. Finally, there is the issue of the representativeness of organizations that would be willing to sponsor intrusive or longitudinal research on whistle-blowing. Perhaps only relatively "clean" organizations would allow researchers to investigate wrongdoing and whistleblowing.

Designing a Research Program

Because each of the methods available for studying whistle-blowing has serious flaws, we argue for a research program that investigates the same hypothesis with different approaches. For example, survey research results indicate that most observers of organizational wrongdoing do not report it (Near & Miceli, 1987); confidence in this finding is increased by the fact that most observers of wrong-doing in a controlled field experiment also did not report it (Miceli, Dozier & Near, 1991). Repeated testing of research findings using different methods and with different samples will allow us to draw stronger conclusions about the whistle-blowing process, which does not always appear to operate in intuitively obvious ways. Among the more "obvious" assumptions which appear to be false is that retaliation against whistle-blowers deters those individuals from future whistle-blowing activities (Near & Jensen, 1983; Near & Miceli, 1985) or that legal protection for whistle-blowers will result in a greater incidence of whistle-blowing (Dworkin & Near, 1987). These counter-intuitive findings require further investigation before they can be accepted as fact, but obviously the replication of find-ings using diverse methods will prevent the inaccurate interpreta-tions that might result from reliance on data obtained through studies relying on a single method exclusively.

The Organization of This Book

Earlier we described two opposing views of whistle-blowers. From one perspective, the whistle-blower is perceived as a disloyal "rat" whose presence is detrimental to the organization. From another, the whistle-blower is a hero who courageously undertakes battle with the powerful organization. There are other perspectives. The whistle-blower can be viewed as a helpful resource who points out unknown problems, or as a self-interested opportunist who seeks attention. Because of the conflicts that these opposing views imply, the decisions to blow the whistle and to persist in pursuing an unresolved complaint are complex.

In the chapters that follow, we explore whistle-blowing through a time sequence and identify the individuals and entities that may be involved in it. We propose a model of the decision process preceding whistle-blowing, followed by its consequences. We then examine the research conducted to date that identifies variables affecting the various stages of whistle-blowing processes. We describe the legal environment pertaining to whistle-blowing. Finally, based on the research described in earlier chapters, we provide tentative recommendations for managing whistle-blowing in organizations, and we offer suggestions for individuals contemplating whistle-blowing.

Summary

In this introductory chapter, we have tried to identify some of the complex issues surrounding whistle-blowing. Evidence suggests that whistle-blowing occurs frequently and that it is on the increase. Discussions of the costs and benefits of whistle-blowing are often one-sided or they go unquestioned; we have tried to present a more balanced picture. For example, organization leaders sometimes express concerns that whistle-blowing undermines organizational authority structures, and that tolerating it may lead to baseless complaints by poor-performing employees. While undoubtedly this happens under some circumstances, there is preliminary evidence that whistle-blower protections do not inhibit disciplinary actions.

We considered the definition of whistle-blowing at some length because authors have disagreed widely on the usage of the term—and certainly popular definitions used in the press have varied as well. We defined whistle-blowing to be organization members' disclosure of illegal, immoral, or illegitimate practices under the control of their employers to persons or organizations that may be able to take action to stop the wrongdoing. This disclosure can take place as a process, that is, the focal member may reassess the situation after an initial report and decide that a report to another party is needed. The belief of the focal member that the party may be able to stop the wrongdoing is important; thus, chatting casually about a matter with friends or co-workers who lack this power would not constitute whistle-blowing. We take a broad view of organization membership in that former employees who disclose after quitting would also be considered whistle-blowers. However, the consequences of such whistle-blowing may be very different for former rather than current employees, since the organization or its members may have less opportunity to retaliate after the whistle-blower has left the organization.

Whistle-blowing can be distinguished from employee participation in suggestion systems in that, generally speaking, the latter provides input concerning activities that may be less than optimal or inefficient, but which are not necessarily judged wrongful, that is, illegal, immoral, or illegitimate. The question of what constitutes illegal, immoral, or illegitimate practices is clearly a perceptual one; further research is needed to determine the circumstances under which activities, or omissions, are deemed to be illegal, immoral, or illegitimate by different individuals. And wrongdoing can be committed by a variety of persons apparently acting on their own behalf or on behalf of the organization, or both.

Following our identification of the elements of the definition of whistle-blowing, we discussed the implications of this definition, which is broad rather than narrow. Specifically, we provided reasons why persons for whom whistle-blowing is sometimes role-prescribed should not be ruled out as "whistle-blowers." We described evidence in favor of considering as a special category of whistle-blowers, those persons who report wrongdoing only to parties within organizations. Finally, we argued that it is unnecessary to require that organization members possess purely altruistic motives in order to be considered whistle-blowers.

By properly classifying whistle-blowing—or distinguishing it from other related forms of organizational behavior—we can identify potential predictors of the decision to blow the whistle and its consequences. Theoretical perspectives for explaining whistle-blowing have come from three sources primarily. First, whistle-blowing has been considered a form of employee concern expression and viewed from the EVL (exit, voice, and loyalty) framework. Second, whistle-blowing is sometimes viewed as political behavior, at least where it is defined as extra-role influence attempts rather than as behavior that is intended primarily to maximize one's own self-interest. Third, some authors have considered whistle-blowing to be a type of organizational citizenship behavior, which is generally considered a type of prosocial behavior, and this perspective in particular has proven to be fruitful. These perspectives were discussed briefly here, and they (and other theoretical perspectives) will be examined further in subsequent chapters.

Finally, we have sought to clarify the difficulties inherent in research of this type. Study methodology employed in examining whistle-blowing can be classified as (a) case reporting; (b) hypothetical dilemmas (vignettes); (c) cross-sectional field surveys; (d) laboratory and field experiments; and (e) longitudinal field surveys. Unfortunately, we concluded that many of the stronger designs frequently recommended for examining other organizational phenomena are difficult or impossible to employ in examining whistleblowing. Our recommendation to researchers is to view findings with caution and to use a variety of methods in examining whistleblowing in future research, in order to offset each method's weaknesses.

We need a clear picture of the whistle-blowing process because of the obvious contribution this will make to our understanding of behavior overall in organizations. Perhaps as importantly, an improved understanding of whistle-blowing would provide important guidance to policy makers. Since many common sense expectations of the whistle-blowing process seem to be fallacious, this information is particularly critical to informed policy decisions both within organizations and across society at large. This point will become clearer, we hope, in the subsequent chapters of this book.

2

A Preliminary Model of Whistle-blowing and Its Consequences

The purpose of this chapter is twofold: to introduce readers to an overview of the literature relevant to whistle-blowing and to describe a model of whistle-blowing that depicts the stages in the process and the parties that may affect one another in each stage. We would emphasize that this chapter presents merely an outline of the model and the pertinent literature. In later chapters, we will describe specific variables that may affect the processes involved in whistle-blowing and its consequences, and we will review the research that has been conducted to date concerning the events, entities, and persons described in this chapter.

Characteristics of the Whistle-blowing Process

Before discussing our model, we must first identify what we consider to be critical characteristics in the whistle-blowing process. These include characteristics of the individual that affect his or her approach to the whistle-blowing case, the situation (including the content and process of the case), the organization that committed the alleged wrongdoing, and the relative power of the parties over one another as well as their dependence on the wrongdoing itself. Research literatures on theoretical frameworks that have been used to predict the effects of these four elements (that is, the individual, the situation, the organization, and the power relationships) on the whistle-blowing process are summarized briefly. Of course, because the elements are interrelated, in many instances, a body of literature bearing on one element is also relevant to another element. Further,

TABLE 2–1

Characteristics of the Whistle-blowing Process and Relevant Research Literature[a]

Characteristics of:	Theories of:
The individual	• Moral development • Motivation • Organization commitment • Voice

The situation
 • Content of case, e.g.,
  a) Nature of wrongdoing
  b) Credibility of evidence
 • Process of case, e.g.,
  a) Report channels
  b) Number of observers and whistle-blowers
	
	• Justice
	• Escalation of commitment
	
	• Bystander intervention, organizational citizenship behavior, prosocial behavior

The organization • Whistle-blowing culture • Bureaucratic structure • Climate for change	 • Norm development • Communication theory • Hierarchy • Organizational change
Power of • Whistle-blower • Wrongdoer • Complaint Recipient • Wrongdoing	 • Resource dependence • Minority influence • Value congruence

[a]We list each body of literature only once, but some are relevant to more than one characteristic.

as will be described later, the literatures sometimes produce conflicting hypotheses for whistle-blowing.

Characteristics of the Individual

Individual difference variables probably should help to predict who will blow the whistle after observing wrongdoing, although research to date has not been successful in identifying variables that have a strong effect (Miceli & Near, 1984, 1985; Parmerlee et al., 1982).

Theories that have been suggested include: theories of moral development, focusing on Kohlberg's work (for example, Ferguson & Near, 1987; Miceli, Dozier & Near, 1991); theories of motivation (for example, Near & Miceli, 1985); theories of organizational commitment or loyalty (for example, Kolarska & Aldrich, 1980); and theories of voice following Hirschman's (1970) seminal work (Farrell, 1983).

Characteristics of the Situation

Characteristics of the situation focus on the content of the case, including the nature of the wrongdoing and the credibility of the evidence, and the process of the case, including factors such as the choice of internal or external channels for reporting, the use of anonymous reports, and the number of whistle-blowers who decide to report the wrongdoing. The theory of escalation of commitment has been investigated with respect primarily to the content of the case (Schwenk, Miceli & Near, 1989), while justice theories might be used to explore whether the nature of the wrongdoing—and whether it violates the whistle-blower's sense of distributive procedural or interactive justice—affects the potential whistle-blower's actions (Near, Dworkin & Miceli, 1990). Theories of procedural and interactive justice might explain how whistle-blowers enact the process; bystander intervention theory has been explored with regard to the effects of number of observers (for instance, Miceli & Near, 1986b), while theories of prosocial behavior (for instance, Brief & Motowidlo, 1986) or organizational citizenship behavior (Organ, 1988) might also predict the whistle-blower's response to the process of wrongdoing.

Characteristics of the Organization

Characteristics of the organization also influence the whistle-blowing incident, including the degree to which its culture supports whistle-blowing, the extent of its bureaucratic structure, and its overall climate for change in general. Theories of norm development (as in Near, Baucus, & Miceli, 1991) as well as communications (Gaerte, 1990) have been suggested as ways to examine the effects of culture. Bureaucracy (as in Weinstein, 1979) and the duty to obey acts of organizational authority (Kelman & Hamilton, 1989) have been proposed as major deterrents to whistle-blowing. Finally, general theories of organizational change ought to be able to predict whistle-blowing as a specific change incident in the organization's life (Near & Miceli, 1987).

Characteristics of Power Relationships

Of all the four elements, power relationships between the whistle-blower and the organization have been most thoroughly explored. The theories of power used to predict the whistle-blowing case have included the literatures of resource dependence, minority influence, and value congruence (as in Miceli et al., 1991). In particular, propositions from the power literature have been applied to the prediction of retaliation by the organization against the whistle-blower (for example, Miceli & Near, 1989b; Near & Jensen, 1983; Near & Miceli, 1986), and to the prediction of the whistle-blower's level of success in changing the organization (Near & Miceli, 1990, 1991).

Stages in the Whistle-blowing Process: An Overview of Our Model

Whistle-blowing can best be examined from the perspective of the individual because it is the individual who initiates or continues the process. From the perspective of the individual, there appear to be at least four stages in the whistle-blowing process that are initiated following the occurrence of a triggering event. Because there are multiple stages and many variables may be involved in each stage, in this chapter we provide a general overview of the model and identify the theories from which we derive hypotheses. Later in this chapter, we discuss each stage in more depth. However, a discussion of the hypotheses linking specific variables to whistle-blowing, and of most of the empirical work pertaining specifically to whistle-blowing, is deferred until later chapters.

Our model is organized by time. That is, we attempt to follow a whistle-blower's path through the process stage-by-stage and to describe the events, persons, and institutions in the environment faced by the whistle-blower that may play a role in determining the outcomes of each stage in the process. While it might be simplest to focus on the "typical" or "most common" whistle-blowing incident, there may be no such thing as a "typical" whistle-blowing incident. Research to date shows some commonalities, but there is much unexplained variance in the observations. Therefore, we will attempt to describe some variations that may be observed at each stage.

The research to date is not sufficiently developed for us to make firm assertions about the precise sequence of events. Our model is based on our current understanding of whistle-blowing and what we think are reasonable proposals, but we emphasize that research is needed to determine whether the sequence plays out as we have described it or in some other manner. Our purpose is to pull together what we think we understand and to stimulate the generation and acquisition of new knowledge about whistle-blowing. Ultimately, we would like to see the development of a comprehensive theory of whistle-blowing, and we view our preliminary model as a first step in that direction.

One final issue that should be addressed before we describe the model concerns the potential whistle-blower's involvement in the perceived wrongdoing.[a] Many incidents involving the witnessing and potential reporting of wrongdoing also involve the choice of participation in it (see also Kelman & Hamilton, 1989). As anecdotal evidence, consider the famous case of Frank Serpico, who not only faced extensive corruption by fellow police officers but was expected to engage in bribery and other corrupt practices. One can also consider the Watergate affair, which illustrated that anyone who is confronted with a cover-up—which in itself is wrongdoing—must choose to participate in wrongdoing or not, regardless of whether that individual was involved in the *original* wrongdoing triggering the cover-up.

Evidence suggests that these are typical rather than isolated incidents. A recent interview-based study (Glazer & Glazer, 1987, 1989) revealed that whistle-blowers face three choices when they encounter wrongdoing: (1) assimilating the new standards and values of the organization; (2) conforming behaviorally without internalizing a new value; (3) protesting and refusing to comply with the

---

[a] We are indebted to the series editors for raising this issue.

wrongdoing. This observation makes it quite clear that whistle-blowers generally face decisions concerning participation in, as well as reporting of, wrongdoing. And a whistle-blower who was initially a willing participant in the wrongdoing may later view it as wrongful or may have other motivations for reporting the wrongdoing.

Consequently, whistle-blowing will frequently involve both questions of conformity in the form of participation in the wrongdoing as well as the question of when one may choose to report it. Thus, we do not view these issues to be clearly separable. At the same time, our primary interest is not in whether organization members will participate in wrongdoing, but whether they will *report* it when given the opportunity. It remains for future research to clarify how the process may play out, depending on whether the whistle-blower is a participant—unwilling or otherwise—in the wrongdoing. For the purposes of describing our admittedly crude model, we will presume here that the whistle-blower is not a willing participant in the wrongdoing at the time of the triggering event.

An abbreviated representation of our model of whistle-blowing, from the perspective of the organization member, is depicted in figure 2–1.

First, in stage 1, a triggering event occurs that ultimately may cause whistle-blowing by the focal member. This event is an activity or set of activities that may be viewed by the focal member as illegitimate, immoral, or illegal. As noted in chapter 1, organizational errors of omission as well as commission can be triggering events.

These activities or omissions "trigger" a decision-making process that constitutes stage 2 of our model. The focal member judges the activity, decides whether to report the activity, and if so, how to report it. Anecdotal evidence suggests that persons who believe they may have observed wrongdoing frequently raise questions with or talk to co-workers about the problems before making an actual report. For example, in one case, "Mark Price began telling people he worked with that his boss was removing legal documents from case files and destroying evidence to prevent states from winning suits against the Department of Education" (Jones & Pottmyer, 1987, p. 23). Interactions with other individuals may affect the decision process. For example, the focal members may seek addi-

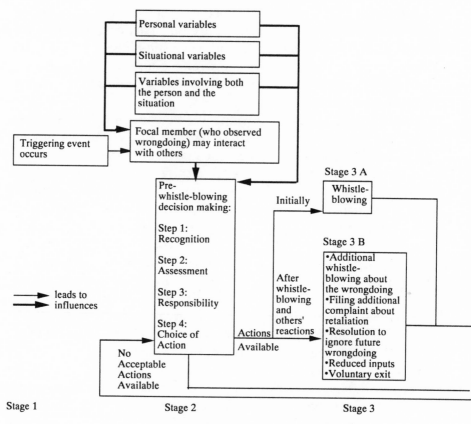

FIGURE 2–1

A Model of Whistle-blowing

tional information to confirm their initial impression that wrong-doing has occurred, or may ask whether their families will be supportive if they choose to blow the whistle. Many variables are believed to affect interactions with others, if these interactions occur, and ultimately, the pre-whistle-blowing decision-making process. These variables, which will be discussed in depth in chapters 3 and 4, can be classified as involving personal variables, situational variables, or variables involving both the person and the situation.

In stage 3, a whistle-blowing report is made, or the individual chooses not to blow the whistle and engages in other actions. We have not listed the alternative actions in figure 2–1, because arguably, a process culminating in an alternative action should not be

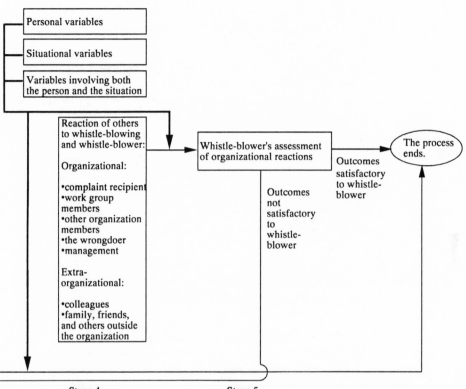

Stage 4	Stage 5

called a whistle-blowing decision process. However, we should describe what we mean by these alternative actions. Whistle-blowers may exit the organization if the situation appears intolerable and whistle-blowing is not judged to be feasible. As another example, the focal member may go directly to the perceived wrongdoer and confront him or her with the evidence of wrongdoing. If no whistle-blowing occurs, then the focal member may monitor the wrongdoing and others' reactions to it. Specifically, she or he may attempt to determine whether the wrongdoing has stopped. Thus, the organization member who initially confronts the wrongdoer does not blow the whistle, but if the confrontation turns out to be unsuccessful, she or he may later blow the whistle.

In figure 2–1, we have designated as stage 3A the whistle-blowing act, which is the outcome of the decision process that occurs in stage

2. But as will be explained below, the consequences of this initial whistle-blowing act may lead to the repetition of at least part of the decision-making process (stage 2). We have designated as stage 3B the outcomes of this repeated decision-making process.

If whistle-blowing occurs, in stage 4, other members of the organization, and certain parties external to the organization, react to the whistle-blowing. The complaint recipient(s) decide how to respond to the complaint and to the complainant. Potential complaint recipients are listed in table 2–2. As shown in table 2–2, there are a variety of parties to whom an individual could report wrongdoing within the organization and for each, there may be a mechanism, or more than one, for filing complaints. Similarly, there are also parties outside the organization to whom wrongdoing can be reported.

Also in stage 4, members of the focal member's work group and organization react, if they are aware of the complaint and the identity of the complainant. Members of the managerial hierarchy and parties external to the organization (such as clients, family, friends, professional associates, the media, and the public) may also respond to the whistle-blowing and whistle-blower.

In stage 5, the whistle-blower assesses the outcomes of the complaint and makes decisions concerning future activities. If the outcome is satisfactory, the process would end. But if the whistle-blower finds the outcomes unsatisfactory, the whistle-blowing process would "loop" back to the latter part of stage 2, where the whistle-blower would make another choice of action. The process would continue until the final outcomes were satisfactory to the whistle-blower, or until no other acceptable actions were perceived to be available. If other acceptable actions are perceived to be available, the process continues to stage 3B.

As indicated in figure 2–1 (stage 3B), there are several actions that might be taken by the whistle-blower in response to the organizational reactions. Whistle-blowers may escalate the complaint to other parties (Graham, 1983). If they experienced retaliation, they may file an additional complaint. They may reduce inputs to the organization; for instance, their performance may suffer or their commitment may drop. They may resolve to ignore future wrongdoing. Whistle-blowers may choose to exit from the organization (involuntary exit would be considered a form of retaliation rather than a reaction to it). Following these reactions, again stages 4 and

TABLE 2–2

Potential Complaint Recipients (Channels for Dissent)[a]

Persons	Mechanisms[b]
Internal to the Organization	
Co-workers (same department)	Employee-initiated communication
Co-workers (other departments)	Employee-initiated communication
Supervisors, "chain of command"(Graham, 1983)	During performance appraisal review or employee-initiated communication
Equal Employment Opportunity (EEO) staff	Internal EEO complaint procedures
Suggestion system coordinator	Suggestion system (Cole, 1981)
Employee relations specialist	Attitude surveys
Employee concerns officer	Employee concerns programs
Ombudspersons	Dispute resolution process (Rowe & Baker, 1984)
Internal auditors	Audit reporting function
Inspectors General (MSPB, 1981)	"Hotline"
External to the Organization	
Members of Congress	Employee-initiated communication
Media	Employee-initiated communication
Regulatory agencies	Employee-initiated communication
Involving Either Internal or External Parties	
Union officials	Grievance procedures
External audit team	Audit reporting function
Members of Board of Directors	Employee-initiated communication (Perrucci et al., 1980)
Officer for "Differing Professional Opinion and Other Ethical Appeals Boards" (Nuclear Regulatory Commission [NRC] 1979)	Employee-initiated communication

[a]Adapted from Blackburn (1988) by permission of the author.
[b]Illustrations of communication mechnisms that may be established are listed; where no formal mechanism exists, employees may initiate a complaint in a variety of ways (e.g., by letter or memorandum, conversations). We refer to these as employee-initiated communication.

5 may be played out. This may occur even if the whistle-blower leaves the organization. That is, others may react to the whistle-blower or to the whistle-blowing complaint, and the whistle-blower may continue to follow the progress of the complaint from outside the organization. The process continues until either the outcomes are satisfactory to the whistle-blower, or no other acceptable actions are perceived to be available.

As suggested in figure 2–1, a wide variety of variables may determine how others react to whistle-blowing and how the whistle-blower assesses and responds to organizational reactions. The categorization of variables affecting stage 2 can also be used to classify those affecting later stages: personal variables, situational variables, or variables involving both the person and the situation.

Because each of these stages is complex, below we will discuss each in greater depth. In chapters 3, 4, and 5, we will discuss the variables that are believed to affect the process at each stage in our model.

Stage 1: The Occurrence of Wrongdoing

As noted in chapter 1, the question of why wrongdoing occurs in organizations is very intriguing, but a comprehensive treatment of such questions is beyond our scope. Therefore, we will simply state here that before whistle-blowing takes place, an activity or omission (a "triggering event") that is perceived by at least one organization member to be questionable must occur.

Stage 2: The Decision Process Preceding Whistle-blowing

The second stage of the whistle-blowing process follows the occurrence of a triggering event. This stage comprises a process of decision making concerning the ultimate response that will be made to the event. This discussion draws largely on research and theory on four important topics: prosocial behavior and bystander intervention; social influence and conformity; motivation; and power. We attempt in our model to integrate these perspectives, and the empirical literature pertinent to each, into a model of decision making preceding whistle-blowing. Specifically, we rely primarily on Dozier's and Miceli's modification of Latané's and Darley's (1968,

1970) model of bystander decision making, which suggested the steps involved in stage 2. As noted in chapter 1, whistle-blowing, like bystander intervention, is a type of prosocial behavior, defined by Staub (1978) to be positive social behavior that is intended to benefit other persons, such as helping, charitable donations, and crime reporting (Dozier & Miceli, 1985). Starting from this view of whistle-blowing as prosocial behavior, we then augment the model with perspectives suggested from the other literatures.

Dozier and Miceli (1985) proposed that at least six decision steps may precede whistle-blowing. However, we have two concerns with this proposition. First, just as we are not certain whether the stages in the whistle-blowing process always play out in the sequence as modeled, we cannot be certain if the hypothesized pre-whistle-blowing decision steps, which comprise private events that are not directly observable, occur in precisely this sequence. According to Graham (1983, p. 74), Latané and his colleagues "do not stipulate a temporal sequence of those intermediate stages, although they are consistently listed in the order shown." Second, we are unsure as to whether there are exactly six steps; this awaits empirical research. In Near and Miceli (1987), we tried, for parsimony's sake, to simplify the model by reducing the number of steps to four. We will continue that attempt here while noting the distinction between this approach and its predecessor.

Figure 2–2 depicts the steps that precede the initial act of whistle-blowing—the first report to a complaint recipient who has some power to take action.

The first step involves *recognition* of wrongdoing: Is the organization (focal) member aware of activity she or he considers wrongdoing? In this step, the member applies her or his standards of what constitutes wrongdoing against her or his perceptions of what has taken place. In step 2, which we called the *assessment* step, the focal member considers whether the triggering event is deserving of action on the part of someone, that is, whether it is intolerable. In step 3, *responsibility,* the focal member considers whether she or he is responsible for taking action. If any of these questions are answered negatively, silence follows and the process terminates.

In step 4, involving *choice of action,* the focal member determines whether any "political behavior alternatives" (here, we use the term in the broadest sense as defined by Cavanagh et al., 1981) are

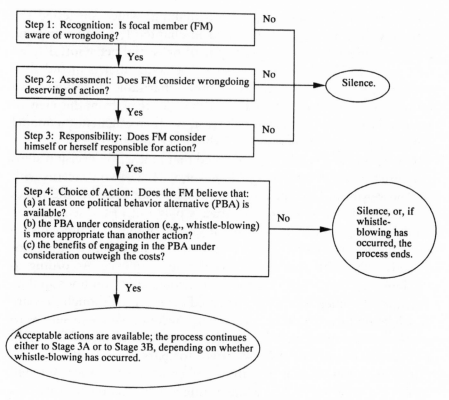

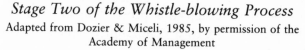

FIGURE 2–2

Stage Two of the Whistle-blowing Process

Adapted from Dozier & Miceli, 1985, by permission of the
Academy of Management

available. By definition, whistle-blowers are not sufficiently powerful to halt the wrongdoing directly, but they can inform others or
exercise other political behavior alternatives, such as sabotage. This
step also involves the focal member's evaluation of the appropriateness of these alternatives, and their expected costs and benefits.
If whistle-blowing is selected, the whistle-blower must consider the
form that the complaint will take and to whom it will be reported.

At this time, little is known about how observers of perceived
wrongdoing generate alternative courses of action, or how they
come to view these alternatives as appropriate. However, in evaluating these alternatives, the focal member may consider the potential costs and benefits of the action. The potential retaliation a

whistle-blower may suffer may be the largest cost (Weinstein, 1979). The benefits to be gained derive primarily from being able to change the organization's actions—the potential to be efficacious in these events (Kolarska & Aldrich, 1980).

If the focal member decides to blow the whistle, at least three choices must be made: whether to report wrongdoing to someone within the organization (versus an outsider), whether to identify oneself, and whether to act with others or to blow the whistle alone. Concerning the first of these, anecdotal and survey evidence suggests that members initiate complaints within the organization before turning to outsiders (for example, Baker, 1983; Graham, 1983), and that whistle-blowers typically report wrongdoing first to their supervisors (Near & Miceli, 1988; Soeken & Soeken, in Pottmyer, 1987). Research also suggests that few whistle-blowers elect to blow the whistle anonymously, even where formal channels exist to encourage anonymous reporting (Miceli & Near, 1989b). Finally, whistle-blowers must consider whether they will join with others in the complaint or act alone. In a recent study (Near & Miceli, 1988), approximately 55 percent of Directors of Internal Auditing who reported perceived wrongdoing joined with others in doing so, while the remaining 45 percent of the respondents acted alone.

If all of the questions raised during the decision process are answered affirmatively, then the process proceeds to stage 3A—if whistle-blowing is the action of choice. As noted earlier, observers of perceived wrongdoing may choose another action, such as to confront the wrongdoer directly, and if no further steps are taken, the process cannot correctly be termed whistle-blowing. On occasion, whistle-blowers may take alternative actions which prove unsuccessful and then, as a result, elect the option of whistle-blowing. If no acceptable alternatives are perceived to be available, however, silence follows and the process ends.

Presuming that whistle-blowing occurs, stage 3A follows. Earlier we noted that the focal member, after blowing the whistle and experiencing consequences, may assess the situation and re-initiate the latter part of the decision process described in stage 2. Whether the focal member takes action following whistle-blowing (for example, whether the whistle-blowing blows the whistle to a second or subsequent complaint recipient) depends on the whistle-blower's assessment of the consequences of the first report and the evaluation of available actions. In some instances, whistle-blowers turn to outsiders when the organization has been unresponsive to an internal complaint (Graham, 1983; Soeken & Soeken, in Pottmyer, 1987). They may warn clients, who presumably would take interest in wrongdoing that adversely affected them, that questionable activities are taking place. For example, in the case of Mark Price (Jones & Pottmyer, 1987), the employee of the U.S. Department of Education decided to share information with the State of Illinois Education Department, which had a case pending before his employer, only after his superiors showed little interest in his reports.

FACTORS THAT AFFECT STAGE 2: AN OVERVIEW. Obviously, our model's reliance on research on prosocial behavior suggests that the processes that bring about prosocial behavior will likely bring about whistle-blowing. Consequently, those processes, and the variables evoking those processes, will be discussed in chapters 3 and 4. But we also noted earlier that perspectives from other literatures contribute to our understanding of whistle-blowing. Below we describe how these perspectives play a role in the decision making that comprises stage 2.

Social Influence. Organizational settings that may evoke whistle-blowing are conceptually similar to other types of settings investigated by social psychologists and other researchers. Whistle-blowers are members of groups as well as members of the larger organization; for example, they are members of work groups, professional associations, or social clubs. Groups exercise influence over their members. Specifically, they develop and enforce norms pertaining to appropriate behavior, because a group's locomotion toward its goals and ultimately its survival may depend on its cohesiveness and the smooth functioning of group activities (Greenberger et al., 1987). Thus, prior to whistle-blowing, when an unusual activity takes place or a member expresses questions about an incident, the group has an opportunity to exercise influence. Therefore, research on conformity and nonconformity to social influence is relevant for understanding whistle-blowing (Greenberger et al., 1987).

Norms conceivably affect each step of the pre-whistle-blowing decision process. Groups may develop and attempt to enforce norms about what constitutes wrongdoing (Greenberger et al., 1987). Thus, co-workers may attempt to influence the focal member when a questionable incident occurs, or when the focal member expresses concern before reporting an incident (Near & Miceli, 1987). In some cases, groups may develop norms that favor whistle-blowing. Perhaps more commonly, groups may develop norms that oppose whistle-blowing. "Tattling" is frequently evaluated negatively even in childhood (Dozier & Miceli, 1985; Elliston, 1982b). Further, suppressing whistle-blowing may be instrumental to the group's survival, particularly where the wrongdoing occurs within the group (Greenberger et al., 1987). Thus, even if survival is temporary, the group may act to discourage whistle-blowing.

Whistle-blowers are members of multiple groups; they may interact frequently with their co-workers or with other members of the larger organization. They may also belong to professional groups, clubs, or religious communities (Greenberger et al., 1987). Obviously, friends and family members may constitute groups to which the whistle-blower belongs. Each of these groups may have developed norms concerning wrongdoing, and the norms of these groups may conflict. Norms may deviate from the formalized rules governing behavior in the organization, such as those appearing in codes of conduct or personnel manuals, or implied by job descriptions or performance appraisals. Sheler (1981) described an instance in which a secretary reported her boss's false expense accounts to top management. The boss was demoted, and later resigned. The secretary "though commended by corporate chiefs, was labeled the 'company fink' by co-workers. Ostracized and humiliated, she, too, ultimately resigned" (Sheler, 1981, p. 81). Norms within the organization may vary from those outside the organization. For example, the professional group may encourage reporting of wrongdoing, while co-workers discourage it.

A model of whistle-blowing should specify which norms will direct the actions of the focal members. We propose that the relative power of these groups will influence the resolution of conflicts as whistle-blowers make decisions about the initial complaint and about persisting in pursuing a resolution. Consequently, indications of power will predict whistle-blowing. Generally, we expect that the norms of the immediate work group will be relatively powerful; therefore, we will focus primarily on the norms of this group.

The work group does not exist in isolation, however, but is part of some larger, usually (at least somewhat) bureaucratic organization. Kelman and Hamilton (1989), in a startling analysis of the effects of authority structures, depicted how so-called crimes of obedience occur in such situations. Although their initial focus was military disasters resulting from obedience (such as the My Lai massacre in Vietnam, in which civilians and children were killed without justification), they readily extended their characterization of such events to organizational wrongdoing.

Specifically, crimes of obedience are more likely to occur in situations involving three characteristics. First, they occur where authority structures absolve the individual of responsibility for moral choices in wrongdoing that appears to be either required or permitted. Second, crimes occur in the presence of routinized decision making, where wrongdoing activities are organized without an opportunity for raising moral questions, thereby resulting in a focus on details of execution of the decision instead of the appropriateness of the decision itself. Third, they occur where targets are dehumanized, so that those who may be victimized by the decision are deprived both of any identity as individuals and community with the actors. A telling example of dehumanization is that of General Motors executives' decision to continue production of the Corvair, knowing it to be unsafe—until some of their own children died in auto accidents while driving Corvairs (Wright, 1979). While obedience may be less "psychologically compelling" in civilian wrongdoing than in the military, Kelman and Hamilton (1989) argued that the presence of these three situational characteristics make disobedience (and, by extension, whistle-blowing) very difficult.

As will be discussed in chapter 4, work group norms may be specific to the type of activity in question. Group norms may depend on who is the victim of wrongdoing and who is the beneficiary, as noted by Kelman and Hamilton (1989). In Sheler's (1981) case just described, top management (and co-worker) reactions might have been different had the activity involved the jeopardizing of employee safety in order to reduce costs. The development and maintenance of norms in the group may depend on the consequences for the group of the cessation of wrongdoing. In chapter 4, we will describe the variables, identified in the literature on social influence, that affect the power relations among groups and their members.

Motivation Theories. A third theoretical perspective that contributes to our understanding of whistle-blowing comprises motivation theories (as in Skinner, 1953; Vroom, 1964), which deal explicitly with rewards and expected rewards of acting. The organizational reward system exerts a powerful influence on employee behavior in general, and on ethical or unethical behavior in particular (Jansen & Von Glinow, 1985).

Observers of wrongdoing may be concerned with the potential efficacy of their actions, and with the level of expected retaliation. Efficacy has been called the perceived ability to influence (Gamson, 1968). Farrell and Petersen (1982, p. 409) stated that "those who perceive their efficacy within the organization to be low will, in the long run, engage in little political behavior." Nader et al. (1972) proposed that observers who expect that they will suffer retaliation from management should be less likely to act than observers who do not. To understand the nature of these predictions, it is useful to draw on motivation theories.

According to expectancy theorists (for example, Vroom, 1964), an individual's force to blow the whistle is a function of the perceived likelihood (expectancy) that outcomes such as managerial attention to the complaint, recognition of the whistle-blower's identity, public attention to the wrongdoing, and so forth, would follow action. Further, the evaluation of the outcomes is a function of the extent to which each is instrumental in achieving other outcomes having desirable or undesirable consequences (valences) for the individual. These outcomes could include the desired changes in managerial practices, as well as retaliation, and support (or lack of it) from family, friends, co-workers, or other observers. For example, some individuals may expect that their blowing the whistle would bring managerial attention to bear on the wrongdoing, and that this attention would lead to the cessation of wrongdoing. They would likely not experience retaliation—presuming that cessation of wrongdoing and avoiding retaliation were desired, we would predict that they would be more likely to blow the whistle than if alternative conditions existed.

In a reinforcement theory framework (for example, Skinner,

1953), the wrongdoing serves as a discriminative stimulus for action when similar wrongdoings (stimuli) have been consistently followed by successful opposition in the past and have been consistently followed by positive managerial reaction. If wrongdoing is tolerated or encouraged, and if previous whistle-blowing attempts have been met with retaliation, the wrongdoing setting serves only to signal "don't act." But what if signals are mixed? It appears that efficaciousness is more important. Near and Jensen (1983) and Miceli, Near, and Jensen (1983) found that perceived efficacy and willingness to file a future complaint was closely related to perceived change in managerial attitudes, but not to retaliation. Further, about 80 percent of the respondents in one large study (MSPB, 1981) said that expected efficacy was one of the two most important factors in motivating whistle-blowing, whereas only 40 percent of the respondents included protection from retaliation as one of these factors. Similar results were reported by Keenan (1990a) in a study of first level managers predominantly from private sector organizations.

These theories suggest that features of the organizational environment are critical in determining whether whistle-blowing will occur, because both reinforcement theory and expectancy theory propose that factors outside the individual, such as those present in the workplace, can affect individuals' motivations to act. They raise the question of what kinds of features may influence perceptions of expected efficacy or retaliation, as well as what other factors may influence whistle-blowing. For example, these theories imply that the climate for whistle-blowing in the organization will be important in determining the extent to which whistle-blowing occurs. These factors will be described in greater depth in chapter 4.

Theories of Power. Finally, theories of power, particularly the resource dependence framework (Pfeffer & Salancik, 1978) and the value congruence view (Enz, 1986, 1988), play a role in examining the decision to blow the whistle. Power, according to Emerson (1962), is defined as the inverse of dependency. Similarly, the resource dependence model (Pfeffer & Salancik, 1978) suggests that organization members depend on their organizations for resources and, conversely, organizations depend on their members for resources (which may be either tangible or intangible). According to power theorists, the criticality of the member's dependence on the organization and the availability of alternative sources of support are determinants of the extent to which dependence exists and will influence the member's action (Near & Miceli, 1985). Since the psychological and financial rewards employers provide are critical to nearly every employee (that is, they need these rewards to survive), the availability of alternative sources of support becomes a very important determinant of dependence. This suggests that whistle-blowing will occur with greater frequency when employment alternatives are perceived to be available and acceptable than when they are not (Farrell & Petersen, 1982).

Contrary to the views expressed by power theorists, however, we propose that the individual's power in the organization is not necessarily inverse to his dependence on the organization. Instead, there may be two dimensions of power pertaining to the extent of resources possessed by the individual or by the organization.

The first dimension of power we will call *influence* in the sense that certain individuals may be able to induce others to act in the organization. Such organization members wield power through providing valued and not easily substitutable characteristics such as personal charisma, position status, unique skills, credibility, or previous performance—characteristics that give rise to varied bases of power (French & Raven, 1959).

The second dimension of power we will call *dependency* in the sense that individuals may be dependent on organizations for resources. Organization members may not be able to find alternative employment (or nonwork relationships) that would provide to them the same levels of rewards, intrinsic or extrinsic, that they currently receive in their organizations.

We contend that identifying two dimensions is necessary for two key reasons. First, it is conceivable to us that a person could possess valued and not easily substitutable characteristics (that is, she or he would be influential) while at the same time be unable to leave the organization (that is, she or he would be dependent). It is also conceivable that organization members may have little influence over others but find it rather easy to obtain alternative employment. Second, if there were only one scale representing a power continuum, then we could not differentiate between persons who were both influential and dependent and those who were neither. In other

Resources Possessed By the Organization	Resources Possessed by the Individual	
	Limited	Considerable
Limited	Individual is relatively uninfluential and independent, e.g., a counter clerk in a fast food restaurant, a bookkeeper for a local boutique *Cell 1*	Individual is relatively influential and independent; e.g., a top manager who has been relatively mobile throughout his or her career, a high performing insurance salesperson *Cell 2*
Considerable	Individual is relatively uninfluential and dependent; e.g., a secretary in a large pharmaceutical company, a steelworker *Cell 3*	Individual is relatively influential and dependent; e.g., a computer systems engineer with unique knowledge of a patented product, a surgeon with a rare specialty in a hospital with matching facilities *Cell 4*

FIGURE 2–3

Resource-based Power Relations Between Individuals and Organizations

words, these two groups of persons would score in the middle of a dependency-power scale that would be anchored at each end by (a) the uninfluential and dependent group, and (b) the influential and independent group, respectively. But we would *not* necessarily predict that these two groups would respond to perceived wrongdoing in the same way, nor would we predict that the organization would respond in the same way to whistle-blowing by members of the two groups. Therefore, it is critical to separate these dimensions. These points are clarified in the discussion that follows.

Figure 2–3 depicts four possible power relationships the individual may encounter in the organization. In the first cell, both organizations and individuals possess limited resources that the other needs. For example, a counter clerk in a fast food restaurant probably doesn't wield much influence because he or she possesses few critical resources, but the notoriously high turnover rates in such organizations attests to the low dependence of the clerks on them. Similarly, the bookkeeper in a local boutique may not be critical to the organization's success but she or he may be able to match or exceed his or her salary (as well as other extrinsic, and intrinsic, rewards) elsewhere without too much difficulty. Thus these individuals are relatively uninfluential and simultaneously rather independent of the organization.

The second cell contains a category of organization members who are both influential and independent. These individuals are highly powerful relative to the organization. Examples would include a top manager who has been willing to move frequently and who has acquired skills and knowledge that are applicable in many industries. In contrast, a manager who has spent her or his life at IBM may have risen to a high position, may be highly respected and possess important knowledge that IBM values, but the knowledge and reputation may be of lesser value to another organization. He or she will lose his or her extensive benefits, pension, and so forth, as well as intangible rewards (such as friendships) if she or he leaves. As a second example of the highly powerful individual, a supersalesperson for an insurance company is likely to be in demand because the skills are transferable not only to other insurance companies, but potentially to other industries, though there may be some retooling necessary. As a high performer, the supersalesperson may be highly credible and the organization may not want this individual to be dissatisfied.

In the third cell are individuals who do not possess valued resources and who work for organizations whose rewards would be hard to match. Hence, they are relatively uninfluential and highly dependent. A secretary who works for a large, high-paying pharmaceutical company may represent this category, particularly when he or she has acquired substantial, forfeitable benefits attributable to years of service and is not particularly well regarded by other members of the organization. Interestingly, these years of service may also convey credibility or allow for the development of friendships, which may *increase* power in the organization. Thus, seniority can render organization members both dependent and influential at the same time. Hence, as will be discussed in later chapters, it is not surprising that the findings concerning the role of seniority in whistle-blowing is unclear. As another example, a steelworker may be highly dependent because his or her skills are not in great demand in the declining industry and may not be transferable across industries. Lacking charisma or some other power base, this individual's low-position status would keep him or her from wielding much influence.

In the fourth cell, individuals possess influence because of their expertise, charisma, or other bases of power, but they do not have many employment alternatives that would match the current reward level. The most obvious examples of individual influence and dependence probably exist in internal labor markets (Doeringer & Piore, 1971). For example, a personal computer manufacturer may be highly dependent on a computer systems engineer who has unique product development knowledge. However, if the product is patented, the engineer may not be as valuable to other organizations, and hence she or he may be dependent on the organization. As another example, a surgeon with a unique speciality may need to be at a particular hospital with the appropriate technical facilities. So she or he is dependent. But this surgeon may also be very influential because of her or his expert power. Conceivably, dependence could also be a function of family ties, for instance, members of dual career couples may be more dependent on their organizations than are single earners because of the difficulty of finding alternative employment for a trailing spouse or partner. Other employees may be reluctant to uproot children.

Hence, power relationships between potential whistle-blowers and their organizations are determined by their relative power over one another. The implications of power relationships for whistle-blowing are important. The potential whistle-blower who depends more on the organization than it depends on him or her may think twice before taking action, because the expected costs of acting may be extensive. On the other hand, the whistle-blower who is highly skilled may both be quite independent of the organization (that is, marketable) and valuable to it; this individual may feel that he or she can blow the whistle with impunity because the organization cannot afford to offend him or her by inattention or retaliation. In essence, we are suggesting that the potential whistle-blowers consider their power relationships with the organization before taking action. Members on whom the organization depends, however, may believe that they do not risk retaliation to the extent that dispensable members feel they do (Near & Miceli, 1985, 1987).

Whether organization members who are uninfluential and independent (such as the counter clerks) or those who are influential and dependent (such as the engineer with patent product knowledge) will be more or less likely to blow the whistle is less clear and remains for future research to determine. The former group are probably unlikely to blow the whistle—why should they do so? They are unlikely to bring about change and if conditions are distressing they can easily leave, thus exercising Hirschman's (1970) voice option. The latter group may be likely to blow the whistle because they are likely to be more successful than are uninfluential members, even though they may experience retaliation because of their dependence; as noted earlier, expected efficacy is a more important determinant of the motivation to blow the whistle than is expected retaliation.

While the resource-dependence perspective provides important insights into whistle-blowing, it may be incomplete. The value congruence perspective suggests that organization members who share the values of top management will gain power in the organization (Enz, 1988). Such individuals may feel more free to blow the whistle, as described above (Miceli, Near & Schwenk, 1991), but they may also be less likely to observe wrongdoing precisely because they share top management's views (assuming that top management creates the wrongdoing). That is, they may not recognize wrongdoing committed by top management, because they agree with top management that the activity does not constitute wrongdoing. This self-censorship represents a more insidious exercise of power that is hard to detect and measure empirically. For example, results of a recent study of whistle-blowing in science laboratories indicated that only 10 percent of the sample of graduate students had observed wrongdoing (here, misrepresentation of data) in their labs during the past year (Ferguson & Near, 1987). Unfortunately, it is impossible to determine whether the level of wrongdoing was in fact this low or whether these well-socialized students had simply not attended to cases of wrongdoing, because doing so would have contradicted their value schema of scientific standards.

Stage 3: Actions Taken by the Focal Member

In stage 3A, the whistle-blower takes action by reporting the perceived wrongdoing to at least one party—the complaint recipient. Several reports may take place simultaneously: A whistle-blower could prepare a letter detailing allegations and send it to his or her supervisor, a union official, and to the personnel office. Here we must emphasize that the term *report* does not refer to a casual conversation with a co-worker or an attempt intended only to obtain information. Instead, the whistle-blower reports activities for which he or she is seeking corrective action.

In stage 3B, which takes place after whistle-blowing has occurred and the consequences are judged to be unsatisfactory by the whistle-blower, there are a variety of actions that could take place, and they are not mutual exclusive. For example, the whistle-blower who experienced retaliation could report the wrongdoing that triggered the initial complaint to a news media representative, file a complaint about the retaliation with the organization, and reduce her or his job performance and commitment to the organization. The decision to continue or accelerate whistle-blowing may indicate escalation of commitment (Schwenk et al., 1989). In any case, the variables that affect this outcome presumably do so by influencing the decision process described as stage 2; these will be discussed in chapters 3 and 4.

Stage 4: The Reactions of Others to Whistle-blowing and to the Whistle-blower

Following whistle-blowing, members of the whistle-blower's organization and some outsiders who know of the complaint will react to the whistle-blowing and to the whistle-blower. Presumably, the complaint recipient must respond in some way, even if it is to decide not to do anything about the complaint. As figure 2–1 shows, other parties within the organization may also react: work group members, other organization members, the wrongdoer, and management. Parties outside the organization may also react, notably professional colleagues, such as fellow accountants in other organizations, or family members and friends. We focus here primarily on the reactions of organization members, for three reasons. First, research suggests that family members and friends are generally very supportive of the whistle-blower (White, Parmerlee, Near & Jensen, 1979). Second, members of the organization may have both substantial reason to react negatively to the complaint and power to hurt the whistle-blower professionally or otherwise. Third, as posited by our model, there may be organizational recourse available to the whistle-blower and obviously such recourse would not be available for responses to the reactions of persons outside the organization. We begin our discussion with the complaint recipient.

THE COMPLAINT RECIPIENT. The complaint recipient(s) decide how to respond to the complaint and to the complainant. No research has yet addressed the role of the complaint recipient in the whistle-blowing process. Because the actions of the complaint recipients may be viewed as potentially "helping" whistle-blowers to bring about prosocial change, the decision process used by complaint recipients may be similar to that used by whistle-blowers, as described earlier. The primary difference appears to be that the complaint recipient may possess the power to change the wrongdoing, particularly if the recipient is a high-level manager or someone who is in another position that allows greater influence in reporting organizational wrongdoing (such as internal auditors). The essential similarity suggests that many of the same variables will affect the complaint recipient's response as affected the whistle-blower's. These variables will be discussed in chapter 5. Next, we will discuss the hypothesized decision process of the complaint recipient and how she or he may react to whistle-blowing.

Before doing so, however, we must clarify what we mean by *reactions*. The complaint recipient's private reactions may be quite different from the public reactions. For example, she or he may be asked to investigate a safety concern by a complainant whom she or he believes complains frequently about trivial issues or submits charges that lack validity. Her or his private reaction may be that the complainant should be disciplined and that investigation is a waste of time. But she or he may be forced to investigate, by procedures, directives from the supervisor, formal role prescriptions (such as in the case of internal auditors), or by a concern that other would-be whistle-blowers with legitimate concerns would be discouraged from reporting if the present complainant were ignored.

We are primarily concerned with the public reactions that are manifested in the complaint recipient's actions and hence, unless otherwise indicated, our comments below pertain to public reactions.

Since the whistle-blower often presents the complaint recipient with information simultaneously concerning the wrongdoing and possible solutions, it is conceivable that the complaint recipient does not follow a sequential process in deciding how to respond. But seemingly, the complaint recipient must decide whether or not to investigate the complaint. He or she must decide whether wrongdoing has occurred, whether it is deserving of action, whether he or she is responsible for acting, and whether efficacious responses are available.

In determining whether wrongdoing has occurred, the complaint recipient may have to decide whether the whistle-blower has presented comprehensive evidence of wrongdoing or if additional information is needed. If the latter, is it likely that the investigation will produce evidence of wrongdoing? If so, the complaint recipient must determine how the investigation should proceed. The organization may have prescribed procedures to follow. There may be legal issues to consider.

If he or she will investigate, the complaint recipient must also decide from whom to seek additional information, and may wish to contact the whistle-blower first. But if the whistle-blower remains anonymous by filing a report without signing it, or gives the complaint recipient incriminating evidence with no indication of its source, obviously the complaint recipient cannot seek additional information from the whistle-blower unless that person's identity is somehow evident.

Whistle-blowers who are anonymous to everyone, including the complaint recipient, take less of a risk of retaliation than do other whistle-blowers. At the same time, they risk their effectiveness for at least three reasons. First, organization members may dismiss the concerns of whistle-blowers who aren't willing to "face" the target of their accusations, and presumably, give the accused an opportunity to confront them (Elliston, 1982a). Second, if whistle-blowers would be viewed as credible complainants because of their characteristics, remaining anonymous reduces their credibility, because the complaint recipient does not have the opportunity to assess it. Third, as implied earlier, if they do not provide sufficient evidence of wrongdoing, the complaint recipient is unable to contact them for additional information.

Another way of remaining anonymous, however, is for whistle-blowers to identify themselves to complaint recipients, but request that their identity not be revealed to others. Identifying oneself while requesting that this information not be revealed to others may increase credibility and facilitate the complaint recipient's investigation, for example, if further information is required, the recipient will know whom to contact. However, the complaint recipient may not respect the wishes of the whistle-blower who asks to remain anonymous. As described by Bernstein and Woodward (1974), the reporters who investigated the Watergate scandal, the information provided by the whistle-blower "Deep Throat" was critical to their investigation. But when the story broke, pressures to reveal the informant's identity were strong. Some persons probably wished to assess the credibility of the source. Others were simply intrigued by the mystery. But still others may have intended to retaliate against Deep Throat and thereby make an example of him or her for more would-be "disloyal" individuals. Fortunately for Deep Throat, and perhaps for the reporters, the whistle-blower's identity was never revealed to others. Complaint recipients may realize that once a confidence is betrayed, they lose access to future informants who cannot trust that their identities would be protected. This is particularly true for official complaint recipients, such as ombudspersons or internal auditors (Near & Miceli, 1988).

When whistle-blowers trust the complaint recipients' willingness and ability to keep their identities confidential, whistle-blowers surrender power to complaint recipients. If, at any time, the complaint recipient wishes to influence the whistle-blower, he or she can threaten to betray the confidence. For example, a government informant who blows the whistle on a crime syndicate but asks for protection to avoid retaliation against self or family may be forced to reveal and unwillingly share additional information, or relocate the family to an undesirable location at the direction of the government agency. Thus, the whistle-blower who remains anonymous can be very vulnerable except with respect to the complaint recipient. The Supreme Court confirmation hearings for Justice Clarence Thomas, in which allegations involving sexual harassment were raised, provides a case in point. Professor Anita Hill had originally provided confidential information, but her identity was leaked and she was forced to "go public" and provide additional information. For this reason, the degree of trust that members of the organization have that the complaint recipient would not reveal their identities is very important, as is the propensity of the complaint recipient to be trustworthy.

Thus, whether the whistle-blower remains anonymous may affect the determination of whether wrongdoing has occurred and whether it is deserving of action. The complaint recipient must also determine if he or she is responsible for acting and if so, whether he or she alone has the power to change the wrongdoing. If not, the complaint recipient must determine whether any efficacious actions are available to him or her. In assessing the costs and benefits to himself or herself, the complaint recipient may consider who is harmed by the wrongdoing.

The complaint recipient must decide whether to share the complaint with others. One reason why information would be shared is that the complaint recipient may decide that she or he lacks the power or authority to take corrective action. Others who are more powerful could be informed of the wrongdoing. This decision would likely be a function of the perceived efficacy of the available actions, based on environmental cues and previous experience with similar complaints.

A second reason why the complaint recipient may share information is that laws or organizational contracts may have such a requirement, or he or she may judge that external law enforcement authorities should be given the opportunity to prosecute. For example, employees who embezzle funds could be reported to the police and to insurance companies. Union contracts may require that officials be informed of safety issues or possible disciplinary actions. The Securities and Exchange Commission or the Internal Revenue Service must be informed of certain organizational activities.

Ultimately, an overt action occurs as a consequence of the complaint recipient's decisions. Ideally for the whistle-blower, a powerful complaint recipient quickly terminates the wrongdoing or takes steps to do so. To encourage future whistle-blowing, the complaint recipient can commend the whistle-blower. This may take the form of employee recognition or, in some organizations such as in the federal government, employees may be eligible for cash awards based on the money saved because of the report. Since the resolution of the complaint itself is reinforcing to the whistle-blower, recognition may be unnecessary (or even embarrassing to the whistle-blower). To send the message to other employees that whistle-blowing is encouraged without identifying the whistle-blower, however, the complaint recipient can arrange publicity about the report and how the problem was resolved through the employee newsletter, bulletin boards, or other communication mechanisms.

Alternatively, the complaint recipient may respond only to the complaint but make no overt action toward the whistle-blower. Or, retaliation may be directed at the whistle-blower by the complaint recipient.

The complaint recipient plays a role in the long-term whistle-blowing process as well as in the immediate response to the complaint at hand and to the complainant. Complaint recipients such as ombudspersons may be given a budget for publicizing their availability, and they may be held accountable for encouraging and effectively processing employee concerns. Therefore, their activities will include not only responding to cases but helping the organization establish and maintain a climate for internal whistle-blowing. Their characteristics and behaviors thus may affect not only what happens to the whistle-blower but also the propensity of other observers of wrongdoing to report concerns internally.

FACTORS THAT AFFECT STAGE FOUR: AN OVERVIEW. Two additional theoretical perspectives that provide information that may be useful in adapting the model are provided by the communication literature and the attribution literature.

Organizations that actively promote participation in decision making may provide more potential complaint recipients as well as create a climate for upward communication of complaints through processes such as suggestions, compliments, and grievances. When the organizations promote participation by designating certain persons to be communication recipients, they are prescribing certain behaviors for persons holding such roles. Thus, the response of the complaint recipient may depend on the position held by the complaint recipient. As noted earlier, complaint recipients inside the organization frequently are supervisors of the whistle-blower (Soeken & Soeken, 1987). But particularly where whistle-blowers believe that the supervisor would not respond favorably to a report, they may seek out other organization members. Managers above the whistle-blower's supervisor may be contacted. Whistle-blowers may write to the editor of the organization's newsletter or the coordinator of the suggestion system. Personnel and human resources representatives or heads of departments in which the wrongdoing is taking place (if not the whistle-blowers' group) may be approached. As Mathews's (1987) study of codes of ethics revealed, it is commonly suggested in large organizations that employees with ethical questions or concerns contact the legal department in the organization. Internal auditors may also receive complaints from informants. And some organizations designate an ombudsperson or other official specifically to accept reports; additionally, they may develop procedures to encourage anonymous reporting (Sheler, 1981).

Responses to others depend on attributions made about their behaviors (Fiske & Taylor, 1984). Therefore, the complaint recipient's attributions about the whistle-blower may be critical. The complaint recipient must have developed a schemata about the whistle-blower—based on prior experience, other sources of information, and the like—which then forms the basis for attributions about the whistle-blower (as in Green & Mitchell, 1979). For example, the complaint recipient may perceive the whistle-blower to be a chronic complainer whose actions are motivated by disgruntlement over perfectly legitimate organizational policies, such as the fact that the whistle-blower is not well paid because he or she truly is a poor performer. The complaint recipient may also be influenced by other procedures used by the whistle-blower. For example, if the whistle-blower did not "use proper channels" as defined by the complaint recipient, such as first notifying the whistle-blower's supervisor, the complaint recipient may attribute this action to nefarious motives on the part of the whistle-blower, because many individuals believe that the accused should have the opportunity to be notified in order to correct the wrongdoing before a third party is involved (Elliston, 1982a). This suggests that characteristics of the complainant, such as her or his credibility, and characteristics of the complaint, such as the seriousness of the wrongdoing reported, may affect these attributions. These characteristics are discussed in chapter 5.

REACTIONS OF OTHERS WITHIN THE ORGANIZATION. If a whistle-blower anonymously reports wrongdoing to one powerful and trustworthy complaint recipient, the process from the individual's perspective may end there. However, if others inside and outside the organization become aware of the complaint and the identity of the complainant, they may respond to the whistle-blowing and whistle-blower. Organization members may react to the whistle-blower with support and encouragement, with hostility and retaliation, or with a reaction falling between those extremes. And a variety or organization members may respond, in different ways. As noted earlier, the complaint recipient may retaliate; retaliation also may be caused by co-workers, managers, or the wrongdoer. Organization members (or outsiders) may derogate the victim in order to restore their vision of a "just world" (Zuckerman, 1975); it may be difficult for them to accept that an organization would retaliate against someone without good cause, so it must be that the whistle-blower deserved the abuse. Thus, these members might not support the whistle-blower. Obviously, the wrongdoer has reason to try to discourage the whistle-blower and may threaten or carry out retaliation. Finally, members of the managerial hierarchy may view the complaint as a questioning of the authority structure and may respond in order to punish the whistle-blower (Weinstein, 1979).

It may be easy to get away with retaliation in many organizations, because the whistle-blower has the burden of proving that retaliation resulted from whistle-blowing. For example, under current law in the federal government, "whistle-blowers must prove that there is a direct connection between retaliation or harassment and the fact that they made a disclosure" (Shepherd, 1987b, p. A6). This issue is explored in greater depth in chapter 6.

Retaliation may take a variety of forms, and more than one type of retaliation may be directed at the whistle-blower (Parmerlee et al., 1982). A wide variety of forms of retaliatory harassment has been reported in the media. For example, Kennedy (1987, p. B1) reported that whistle-blowers in the U.S. Department of Defense are "routinely" ordered by their superiors to undergo psychiatric examinations as a form of harassment. Such retaliation is possible because employees in general are subject to orders from their superiors to undergo these examinations, and their superiors generally lack the training in psychology or psychiatry to make determinations as to which employees should be seen. It is easy to imagine how this abuse might be possible in other organizations, such as those with Employee Assistance Programs, which examine and refer employees who have been asked by their supervisors to seek counseling.

Retaliation may recur in a series of events and it may escalate if the desired outcome of discouraging the whistle-blower is not accomplished (Shepherd, 1987b). According to Shirley Stoll, who blew the whistle on patient abuse in a medical center, "first thing they do is demote or reassign you. They isolate you and if you're not gone, they actively go after you" (Shepherd, 1987b, p. A6). Consistent with this anecdotal information, O'Day (1972) suggested that retaliation normally progresses in four stages. The first stage, "nullification" of the complaint, is characterized by extralegal pressure on the complainant to desist from blowing the whistle; verbally pressuring the whistle-blower to drop the complaint or criticizing his or her job performance would seem to fall into this category. The second stage of retaliatory activities, "isolation," involves attempts to isolate the complainant from others, restrict her or his activities, reduce her or his allocation of organizational resources, or transfer the complainant to a less visible position. The third stage "defamation" of character, may be followed by a fourth stage, "expulsion" from the organization. Parmerlee et al. (1982) provided preliminary empirical evidence in support of this view of how retaliation plays out in organizations.

The question of the extent to which retaliation, as opposed to more supportive reactions, is prevalent has not yet been fully resolved, because so few systematic, empirically sound studies have been completed on this topic. However, based on data provided by the MSPB (Miceli & Near, 1989a) and by private sector directors of internal auditing (Near & Miceli, 1988), it is probably fair to say that retaliation does not occur in the majority of cases, contrary to the view portrayed by the extreme cases that tend to be reported in the media. More commonly, the whistle-blower receives neither organizational support and encouragement *nor* retaliation. However, this is not to deny that retaliation occurs or to minimize its devastating impact where it does occur. It can be argued that *any* retaliation against a whistle-blower who is acting in good faith is too much retaliation (Miceli & Near, 1989a). Moreover, it is entirely possible that certain types of cases are more likely to provoke negative reactions, an issue that will be explored in chapter 5.

Reactions of the Work Group. Work group members may respond by retaliating against whistle-blowers. If whistle-blowing violates group norms, and the threat involves an important challenge to group cohesiveness, then the group members will pressure the deviant to drop the complaint or to avoid complaining to another party.

Conformity and obedience generally are highly valued by organizations and groups. There are many reasons for this; one is that "conformity introduces order into the group process and provides for the coordination of individual behaviors" (Shaw, 1981, p. 289). While our purpose is not to review the considerable literature on reactions to deviance (as in Levine, 1980; Maass & Clark, 1984), the whistle-blower can be viewed as a deviant in groups where norms oppose whistle-blowing. As such, the literature on reactions to deviance, and on minority influence, may provide insight into the consequences of whistle-blowing (Greenberger et al., 1987).

Here we are concerned primarily with the reactions of co-workers of the whistle-blower—those people with whom the whistle-blower has the closest regular contact within the organization. Not every whistle-blower is involved with such a group; some may spend most of their work days in isolation. In these cases, there may be little concern with predicting the reactions of co-workers. However, in most instances, it is likely that the reactions of co-workers are important. We make the presumption that group norms would oppose whistle-blowing. Obviously, where they do not, the process would play out differently. The whistle-blower would not be viewed as a deviant, and hence no conformity pressure would be expected.

When whistle-blowing destabilizes the work group, changes in group structure, composition, and attitudes may follow (Greenberger et al., 1987). The group attempts to restore itself to balance and homogeneity by changing the behavior of the whistle-blower, rejecting the whistle-blower, or by altering its own behavior and attitudes. While rejecting the whistle-blower may not squelch the complaint itself, it may achieve the group's objective of restoring harmony among members. It may also follow unsuccessful attempts to change the behavior of the whistle-blower.

Changing the behavior and rejecting the whistle-blower essentially represent a strategy of attempting to maintain and enforce group norms in resisting the whistle-blower's influence attempt, while a self-alteration by the group represents an accommodation of the whistle-blower's views. The literature on deviance has developed in two streams that approximate these opposing directions. We find puzzling the names given to these directions—"functionalist" and "genetic," respectively (Moscovici, 1976). Because we are building a model of whistle-blowing, we will exercise our discretion to give them new names. We will call attempts to maintain and enforce group norms a *resistance strategy,* and the alternative we will call an *accommodation strategy.* Our use of the term *strategy* is not intended to imply that groups always make conscious strategic decisions to react in certain ways. Instead, we mean simply that groups' reactions are purposeful and may be predictable. We next examine each of these strategies.

The following discussion of the resistance strategy is drawn largely from Greenberger et al. (1987). According to Moscovici (1976), the resistance strategy emphasizes social control and individual submission to reestablishing uniformity in the group (Greenberger et al., 1987). It is based on Festinger's (1950) model and empirical studies with Schachter (Festinger et al., 1950; Schacter, 1951). This perspective views social influence as asymmetrical; a deviant is the target, not an agent, of influence (Levine, 1980).

Research on the behavior of conforming group members (as by Levine & Ranelli, 1978; Moscovici, 1976; Sampson & Brandon, 1964) suggests that co-workers would dislike whistle-blowers, and they see themselves as more similar to each other than to the whistle-blower. Yet attempts will be made to bring deviants back into the fold before rejecting them (Maass & Clark, 1984; Nemeth, 1986). Research suggests that group members who expressed extreme opinions received the most communication from majority members (Festinger & Thibaut, 1951).

If the whistle-blower refuses to withdraw the complaint or informs other parties, communication may grow more forceful; ultimately, majority members may socially reject the whistle-blower. For example, a pilot's relations with fellow employees changed dramatically after he blew the whistle on a serious defect in a wide-body aircraft; some co-workers tried to avoid working on his flights (Gellert, 1981).

In contrast to the resistance strategy, the accommodation strategy emphasizes social change and individual innovation (Greenberger et al., 1987). It is based on the work of Moscovici and his colleagues (Moscovici, 1976; Moscovici & Faucheux, 1972; Moscovici & Nemeth, 1974), who propose that stability is reestablished by altering group norms. The reason why some groups allow whistle-blowers to change them rather than exert influence is essentially that co-workers agree that the whistle-blower is right and the norms are not. According to these and other researchers (such as Levine, 1980), group members evaluate the reasons why an individual deviates. The more credible, confident, competent, and objective the whistle-blower appears to be, the greater the potential influence she or he will have on the group (Greenberger et al., 1987).

Accommodation and resistance *as outcomes* can perhaps be viewed as opposite ends of a continuum. However, we want to emphasize that there may be multiple reasons why relatively more accommodation (resistance) occurs. From the resistance *process* perspective, the group may lack the power to change the whistle-blower or it may not feel sufficiently threatened by the complaint to reassert itself, that is, it may not be sufficiently cohesive. But norms may not change, and the reason why the group does not influence the whistle-blower is quite different from that proposed from the accommodation perspective. From that perspective, the group is responsive to the whistle-blower who "presents a good case." The group may be unresponsive when the whistle-blower does not have a good case, but may be powerful in either case.

As noted earlier, a group may have norms that affect many stages in the whistle-blowing process. Whistle-blowing may appear to violate some but not all norms. This observation, in combination with the recognition that accommodation and resistance are not all-or-nothing phenomena, suggests at least three situations in which groups having some norms that are violated by the whistle-blower may not uniformly and strongly resist whistle-blowing.

First, a group could change its norms somewhat and resist to some extent. For example, a whistle-blower could complain to a federal safety inspector that goggles and helmets were not being worn as required. Group members could convince the whistle-blower to drop the complaint and not to call outsiders in the future. At the same time, they may recognize that he or she went to an outsider because internal attempts were thwarted, so they may be more open to future internal whistle-blowing attempts, and may even join the whistle-blower in voicing future concerns to internal complaint recipients. They also may take greater care to maintain safety standards.

Second, not every member of the group may react in the same way; some could accommodate, while others resist. For example, in response to a complaint of sex discrimination, some members may endeavor to make a work environment less sexist; other co-workers may try to convince the whistle-blower that there is no discrimination and that whistle-blowing is not appropriate.

Third, groups may oppose whistle-blowing as a change strategy, but they may agree that the complaint is valid (or vice versa). In such cases, they may attempt to punish the reporting behavior while correcting the problem that led to the complaint. This may create mixed signals to the unwary member.

The implications of the coexistence of resistance and accommodation strategies are twofold. First, obviously, predicting group reactions is a complex process. Second, rather than viewing the two strategies as distinct theories of group reactions, researchers attempting to understand their contribution to whistle-blowing should try to integrate them. Consequently, in chapter 5, when we discuss the variables that are suggested as predictors by these approaches, we will not treat them as arising from unrelated perspectives.

Reactions of Management. Anecdotal evidence of managerial hostility toward whistle-blowers is abundant (for example, Colt, 1981). However, as noted earlier, management retaliation is not inevitable, but because it does occur, it is important for us to consider the reactions of management and their potential implications for whistle-blowers.

Whether supportive or hostile reactions occur may depend on the power relationships between whistle-blowers and their managers.

The typical organization member is dependent on the organization to some extent. The organization may also depend on the whistle-blower, however. As noted earlier, in some cases, both of these occur simultaneously. Near and Miceli (1985) predicted that organizations would be less likely to retaliate against whistle-blowers who have power within the organization and on whom the organization depends greatly.

In addition to responding to the whistle-blower, managers must respond to the complaint itself, by making statements to organization members and sometimes to outsiders. It should be noted that this response may be communicated through the complaint recipient, but because it represents a managerial response, we chose to discuss it here.

The question of why all organizations do not simply rectify the problem identified by the whistle-blower is interesting. Meyers and Garrett (1988) proposed that organizations' election to manage and thereby to resist change rather than to adapt occurs for several reasons. First, this tactic maintains organizational stability (Giddens, 1984). Second, organizations must behave similarly from day to day in order to meet societal expectations that they be reliable and accountable (Hannan & Freeman, 1977). To ensure reliability, organizations must reproduce the structures of roles, authority, and communication that affect behavior (Hannan & Freeman, 1977). This pressure for accountability also requires that organizations either must communicate their justification of their current position, or "be considered guilty" (Meyers and Garrett, 1988, p. 8). A third reason, we would propose, is that in some instances, organizational leaders believe (perhaps correctly!) that the complaint is not justified, that no wrongdoing has occurred, or that it does not warrant concern. Fourth, organizations may be dependent on a questioned practice (Near & Miceli, 1985, 1987); thus leaders may believe that change would be disastrous in terms of reduced profits or decreased effectiveness, if implemented. Finally, managers may resist effort at change because they were initiated by a lower-level organization member and thus represent a challenge to the continued viability of the organization's authority structure (Weinstein, 1979). Like the deposed captain in *The Caine Mutiny* (Wouk, 1951), they may consider the proposal of change—no matter how reasonable or useful—tantamount to rebellion.

The developing literature on issues management (IM) may shed light on how organizations respond to whistle-blowing attempts. IM has been defined as "the process by which the corporation can identify, evaluate, and respond to those social and political issues which may impact significantly upon it" (Johnson, 1983). According to Meyers and Garrett (1988) and Wartick and Rude (1986), IM has two primary purposes: first, to analyze the environment and prepare the organization for changes; and second, to develop and communicate an organizational response that delineates the organization's stance and response to the changes. The second of these purposes is relevant to whistle-blowing, particularly where reports are made to parties outside the organization, such as the media, regulators, or lawmakers.

Meyers and Garrett (1988) proposed that issues to be managed are generated where structural processes of opposition arise in organizations. Tension between ethics and profit concerns occurs commonly, they maintain, and this tension may produce issues requiring attention. One outcome is the "environmental surprise" or "jolt," which refers to the "transient perturbations whose occurrences are difficult to foresee and whose impacts on organizations are disruptive and potentially inimical" (Meyer, 1982; p. 515). These events are often the foci of public protest or interest; they include lawsuits and boycotts (Meyers & Garrett, 1988) and presumably, whistle-blowing.

Research has shown that "organizations often refuse to meet protest agents' demands for change" (Garrett, 1987, cited in Meyers & Garrett, 1988, p. 6). Frequently, issues never become "solved" in the sense of elimination of the cause of the conflict; rather, they become "resolved" or "managed" (Cheney & Vibbert, 1987, p. 173). If so, the issues manager is primarily concerned with minimizing the damage. One means by which this strategy is effected is communicating with internal and external constituencies in a manner that reinforces the status quo (Meyers & Garrett, 1988). The organization responding in this manner can be said to be "reproducing its structure" rather than adapting to the "jolt" imposed by the vocal protestors (Meyers & Garrett, 1988). Such a view is consistent with Weinstein (1979) who, following a Weberian (1947) rationale, argued that the primary response of any organization to whistle-blowing is to maintain the status quo. Therefore, as noted before, whistle-blowing tends to be punished in order to symbolize the sanctity of the authority structure and to deter future whistle-blowers from attempting to disturb the stability of the organization.

Research that identifies the types of communication strategies through which organizations resist adaptation would be valuable because it may be possible to identify the causes and consequences of each strategy. Such research may enable whistle-blowers to prepare for potential organizational reactions. It may also interest organizational leaders who must respond to whistle-blowers' complaints which the organization considers invalid.

Meyers and Garrett (1988) performed a qualitative analysis of organizational communications reflecting the various ways that public relations officials and other organizational representatives "reproduced organizational structures" in responding to thirty of the thirty-eight consumer and employee boycotts known to occur in North America since 1981. Their analysis revealed that two broad categories of strategies could be identified: first, the "enhancement of self" strategies, and second, strategies involving "derogation of the accusers." Using the first category (pp. 11–14), organizations may emphasize that (a) they must remain independent of special interest groups; (b) their current policy is "fair and just"; or (c) that they attempted to communicate with the accusers. With derogation strategies (pp. 14–16), managers maintain that (a) the accusers' allegations are untrue; (b) the accusers don't understand the business; (c) their organization has been unfairly singled out; or (d) the accusers' motivations were devious. All of these are likely to be common responses to whistle-blowers as well.

Finally, the developing literature on procedural and interactional justice (such as Bies, 1987; Greenberg, 1987) suggests that managerial reactions may affect the choice of communication strategies, as well as reactions of organization members and others to it. According to Bies (1987), managers may provide social accounts, which serve to explain, justify, or apologize for their actions, in order to reduce perceived damage as harmdoers. For example, using an "appeal to superordinate goals," a manager may argue that the wrongdoing was necessary because corporate survival depended on it, while another manager may use a "referential account" and state that the wrongdoing wasn't as bad as what occurs in other organizations or that the observer is naive about business.

The literatures on minority influence, resource dependence, and issues management suggest a number of factors that will affect the reactions of other organization members to the whistle-blowing complaint and to the whistle-blower. These factors are discussed in chapter 5.

Stage 5: Assessment of the Reactions of Others

Obviously, the organization's response to the whistle-blower may not represent the final step in the whistle-blowing process. Whistle-blowers themselves may be satisfied or dissatisfied with the outcome, and register this response through various behaviors. The whistle-blower makes decisions concerning future activities; if the wrongdoing was not corrected, she or he may make another report or take further action.

If organizations represent systems that offer inducements in return for contributions by their members (Barnard, 1938; March & Simon, 1958), then the experience of retaliation would certainly seem to reduce inducements for members to remain and to perform their jobs well. Instead, whistle-blowers may exit, because their contributions no longer seem valued. Retaliation may serve as a deterrent to future whistle-blowing, because the withdrawal of inducements may signify that such contributions are not wanted. Finally, the whistle-blowers may complain about the experienced retaliation. Alternatively, it may dissuade them from further protests of any kind; a rationale can be provided for either response.

Preliminary research evidence suggests that a primary factor influencing the assessment that the outcome has been satisfactory is whether the whistle-blower believes that a change in managerial behavior has been brought about (Near & Jensen, 1983). Therefore, if assessment results in the view that the outcomes are not satisfactory, the whistle-blower either still believes that the wrongdoing is occurring and that she or he is responsible for acting on it, or that the wrongdoing has been corrected but retaliation or some other negative outcome has occurred. Therefore, we propose that following this assessment, the whistle-blower should again consider whether there are any available actions (stage 2). Because this stage was discussed previously, we will not reiterate the discussion here.

Ending the Process of Whistle-blowing

In one sense, the process of whistle-blowing has no finite ending. If the whistle-blower has been successful at terminating the wrongdoing, then substantial procedural and structural change may have taken place or may have been initiated in the organization and may evolve over time. But in another sense, the whistle-blowing process can be said to end when the outcomes are judged to be satisfactory to the whistle-blower. It can also be described as ending when the whistle-blower who is dissatisfied with the outcomes considers further action, but finds that none of the actions perceived to be available are acceptable in terms of feasibility, likely success, or likely risk. Interestingly, the organization's view as to whether the matter has been resolved may be of little importance, since the whistle-blower is the primary assessor of whether the situation has been rectified.

Our model thus concludes at this step. It is obviously an exploratory model, in that research on whistle-blowing certainly has not developed to the point of testing all its implications, and in that the model has evolved as the empirical work has appeared. At this point, however, it may be helpful to compare the model to the only other known comprehensive model of a phenomenon closely related to whistle-blowing.

Comparisons with Graham's Model of Principled Dissent

Since Graham (1983, 1986) proposed a model of principled dissent that is in some ways similar to the model of whistle-blowing we propose here, it is helpful to compare the two and clarify differences. One key difference is that Graham does not view reporting of wrongdoing "through channels" to be whistle-blowing, while we do, for reasons described in the first chapter of this book. She (1983, p. 75) observed that a "typical whistle-blowing case" involved an "initial reporting of wrongdoing through channels."

However, it is not clear if reporting through channels comprises reporting to one's supervisor or other parties, such as the personnel department.

A second key difference in the models concerns the specification of why individuals blow the whistle to someone "outside channels." Graham proposed that, following an "insufficient response to reporting," the individual would blow the whistle. This appears quite reasonable, though at this time we have no empirical evidence as to whether insufficient response triggers more activity. But we would argue that insufficient response may be only one factor that may determine future action. In our model, the factors that affect the initial reporting decision may also affect the decision to make a complaint either outside the chain of command or to pursue subsequent complaints. Retaliation may also play a role. Personal relationships may affect this decision; a whistle-blower may know a trusted or influential party outside the chain of command and feel more comfortable sharing information with this person than with others. The escalation of commitment phenomenon (as in Staw, 1981) may occur when the whistle-blower considers pressing a complaint further. The other difficulty that we have with the sequence proposed by Graham is that the sequence of events may not occur as specified, for example, one may blow the whistle to someone outside channels at approximately the same time as someone within channels is notified.

Summary

In this chapter, we proposed a preliminary model of whistle-blowing, and this model takes the perspective of the whistle-blower. Essentially, we follow an incident of whistle-blowing through a series of stages. First, a triggering event—an act or omission that could be perceived as wrongful—may occur. Next, the focal organization member judges the activity, decides whether to report the activity, and if so, how to report it. Third, the act of whistle-blowing occurs or the focal member engages in other actions, or no action. Fourth, if whistle-blowing occurs, other parties who are aware of the complaint and the identity of the complainant (the complaint recipient, co-workers, management, and persons external to the organization) react to the whistle-blowing. Fifth, the whistle-blower assesses these reactions and may escalate the complaint or take other steps. The process may loop back to the second stage until the whistle-blower decides to stop acting.

The decision process of the whistle-blower (stage 2) was addressed in some depth in this chapter. Research on prosocial behavior (as by Latané & Darley, 1968) has provided the basis for a preliminary model of the decision process that may precede whistle-blowing. The parallels between bystander intervention in emergencies, such as crime reporting, and the reporting of organizational wrongdoing, have been noted by several authors cited in this chapter. The authors argue that the observer of wrongdoing must decide whether wrongdoing deserving of action has occurred, whether she or he is responsible for taking action, and whether potentially corrective actions might be available. Then the whistle-blower considers the likely outcomes of whistle-blowing (or alternative actions), including the expectation that benefits will outweigh costs. It is only when the outcomes of all of these decisions are affirmative that whistle-blowing is expected to occur; hence it is not difficult to understand why observers of wrongdoing often choose not to blow the whistle.

Consideration of our model of the whistle-blowing process illustrates the difficulty of finding a single theory to explain each step of the whistle-blowing process. Thus, a wide variety of literatures has been used to attempt to explain why and how whistle-blowing occurs. Some of those identified in this chapter concern research on prosocial behavior, obedience to authority, conformity and minority influence, motivation, power and dependency relations, issues management, and justice in organizations. We described each of the bodies of research briefly and tried to describe how they inform our understanding of whistle-blowing. In the case of power relationships, for example, we suggested that power and dependency are not necessarily opposite ends of the same continuum: An organization member, such as a computer systems engineer, in an industry or occupation dominated by internal labor markets may find it difficult to leave the organization and find comparable employment, perhaps because of unique skills or because of other forces that operate in internal labor markets. Thus, the engineer is dependent on the organization, but may also be powerful and influential because of valuable knowledge based on years of firm-specific experience. Obviously, further research is needed to test this proposition and others we put forth in this chapter.

Other research traditions not included here may also offer perspectives useful in understanding whistle-blowing; for the time being, however, none of the literatures thus far suggested has been examined adequately as a framework for predicting or explaining whistle-blowing. Part of the reason for this is that the whistle-blowing process itself is composed of multiple, interrelated steps, thereby complicating attempts to explain the process through use of any single model of organizational behavior.

As we noted earlier, this chapter served to provide merely a skeletal framework concerning the whistle-blowing process and the many variables that may affect it. In later chapters, we consider several sets of variables derived from the research literature identified here. We deal specifically with variables pertaining to the individual, to the situation, to the organization, and to the power relationships between individuals and organizations. We consider how these variables may affect the whistle-blowing process in different ways at each step of the process. We review the existing empirical literature on whistle-blowing and related topics in order to summarize what is known about whistle-blowing and to stimulate further research on this topic.

3

Is There a Whistle-blowing "Personality"?

A national survey of psychiatrists recently revealed that two-thirds of the respondents had treated patients who were sexually involved with other therapists. However, respondents said they reported this unethical behavior in less than 10 percent of these cases ("Therapists' sexual misconduct . . . ," 1987). The reason for the failure to report was *not* that the therapists believed that no wrongdoing had occurred: 87 percent of them said that they thought these encounters were harmful for the patients. Nor was the reason that the professional standards for psychiatrists opposed whistle-blowing. According to the chairman of the American Psychiatric Association ethics committee, "our position is to strongly encourage people to report" such incidents ("Therapists' sexual misconduct . . . ," 1987, p. 2B).

Such findings raise an obvious question: Why don't all observers of clear wrongdoing report it? Or, if whistle-blowing is rare, perhaps we should ask, why does anyone blow the whistle? In addition, we are interested in knowing why whistle-blowers may choose to identify themselves or to remain anonymous, and why they might report wrongdoing only to parties within the organization.

In this chapter and in chapter 4, we examine some of the variables that may influence stage 2 of the model developed in chapter 2. This stage involves the decision making that we believe precedes whistle-blowing. We describe specific hypotheses suggested by the model and by research conducted in whistle-blowing contexts. Also, many studies have investigated phenomena that are conceptually similar to whistle-blowing. These studies are included, because they may suggest predictors of whistle-blowing that future research should examine. We describe the outcomes and implications of the research. In this chapter, we focus on personal variables, as opposed to situational variables, that may be associated with whistle-blowing.

An Overview of the Studies Predicting Whistle-blowing

Before we begin our examination of the factors that may cause whistle-blowing, it would be helpful to describe briefly those studies that (a) deal specifically with whistle-blowing, and (b) present quantitative data pertaining to the numbers of persons who observed and reported wrongdoing. Unlike reports relying solely on anecdotal evidence, these studies, listed in table 3–1, provide comparative data that can show the prevalence of whistle-blowing of different types.

Characteristics of the Samples

Generally, we have omitted from table 3–1 those studies with participants who were exclusively whistle-blowers or which for other reasons did not provide data concerning who blows the whistle and who does not. Among those omitted studies are Glazer and Glazer (1987), Keenan (1989, 1990b), Parmerlee et al. (1982), Terpstra and Baker (1988), and Zalkind (1987). However, findings or theoretical contributions from these studies are included where appropriate in the discussion of the factors associated with whistle-blowing, later in this chapter, in chapter 4, and in chapter 5.

The remaining studies, which are listed in table 3–1, have relied primarily on single-administration questionnaires to gather data, with the exception of three experimental studies using college students (Brabeck, 1984; Dozier, 1988; Miceli, Dozier & Near, 1991). We have separated the studies into samples taken in the public sector, in the private sector, and in both sectors, where the responses according to sector could not be separated. In the next few pages, we describe briefly some characteristics of the samples and methodology employed in the survey-based studies, because this information may be helpful in understanding differences in the findings.

The United States Merit Systems Protection Board (MSPB) surveys (1981 and 1984) were mailed to the homes of randomly selected U.S. federal employees in a variety of locations. The survey described in the 1981 report, which focused exclusively on whistle-blowing, was distributed to members of fifteen civilian organizations. Three years later, a shorter version of the survey was distributed to members of twenty-two organizations, including the military and several large agencies omitted from the previous study (such as Department of the Treasury). The later survey systematically oversampled persons at higher hierarchical levels and focused on a number of other issues besides whistle-blowing, for example, the pay systems covering federal employees. Both surveys elicited high response rates (more than half of the persons to whom surveys were sent responded). These surveys provided the data used in secondary analyses by Miceli and Near and their colleagues in many of their publications.

The Near and Miceli (1988) survey of Directors of Internal Auditing was sent to approximately 3,500 members of the Institute of Internal Auditors in the United States and Canada. About 30 percent of the members completed the lengthy (25-page) questionnaire. Percentages of respondents in each 4-digit Standard Industry Classification (SIC) industry code category correlated closely with those of the membership (r (54) = .96, p < .001); respondents predominantly represented private sector organizations, but not-for-profit organizations and public sector organizations were also represented. The sample was predominantly male (86.3 percent), married (85 percent), well-educated (90 percent held college degrees, with 34 percent holding graduate degrees), and managerial (61.1 percent in middle management positions and 30 percent in top management). Respondents' mean age was 41.2 years, with a mean of 9.3 years of service with their employers and average annual salaries between $50,000 and $60,000.

We also compared the demographics with those obtained in an earlier survey of members of the same professional association (Mautz, Tiessen & Colson, 1984). Although this early survey was concerned with career development issues, which obviously were very different from issues covered in the present survey, the demographic characteristics of the two groups of respondents were remarkably similar. Mautz et al. (1984) reported age, service, and education medians for their respondents; respondents were 41 years

TABLE 3-1

Observation of Perceived Wrongdoing and Whistle-blowing in Organizations[a]

Study	Percentages of Nonobservers, Inactive Observers, Whistle-blowers of All Types, Anonymous Whistle-blowers, and External Whistle-blowers[b]					
	NO	IO	WB/P	WB/O	A	E
Questionnaires—Public Sector						
MSPB (1981); n=8,296 fed. employees	57%	30%	13%	30%	28%	14%
MSPB (1984); n=1,944 fed. employees	80%	12%	8%	40%	40%	NA
Near and Miceli (1988); n=119 directors of internal auditing	19%	8%	73%	90%	4%	28%
Questionnaires—Private Sector						
Keenan (1988a, b; 1990a); n=143 first-level managers	54%	25%	21%	46%	NA	NA
Near and Miceli (1988); n=892 directors of internal auditing	18%	7%	75%	91%	2%	48%
Blackburn (1988); n=1,212 employees in nuclear industry	69%	13%	18%	58%	NA	None[c]
Questionnaires—Both Sectors or Indeterminate						
Gartrell ("Therapists . . . ," 1987); n=1,423 psychiatrists	33%	63%	3%	10%	NA	NA
Soeken and Soeken (1987); n=87 whistle-blowers[d]	NA	NA	NA	NA	21%	80%
Tangney (1987); n=245 science professors[e]	68%	>16%	<16%	<50%	NA	NA
	86%	4%	10%	74%	NA	NA

Experimental Studies

Brabeck (1984); $n=25$ psychology students	NA[f]	68%	32%	32%	All were anonymous internal
Dozier (1988); $n=241$ business students	40%	42%	20%	31%	90% NA
Miceli, Dozier & Near (1991); $n=295$ business students	NA[f]	68%	32%	32%	All were anonymous internal

[a] All questionnaire studies except Gartrell ("Therapists . . . ," 1987), Soeken and Soeken (1987), and Tangney (1987) asked about wrongdoing that may have occurred in the preceding twelve-month period. NA = data not available.

[b] NO = Nonobserver participants as a proportion of all participants in the study; IO = Inactive observer participants as a proportion of all participants in the study; WB/P = Whistle-blower participants as a proportion of all participants in the study; WB/O = Whistle-blower participants as a proportion of all observers of wrongdoing in the study; A = Anonymous whistle-blower participants as a proportion of whistle-blowers in the study; E = External whistle-blower participants as a proportion of whistle-blowers in the study.

[c] Blackburn (1988, p. 51) measured only internal whistle-blowing, that is, whether employees had "voiced a concern to an appropriate person." She defined employee concerns more broadly than did other authors shown here (p. 4).

[d] Soeken and Soeken surveyed only whistle-blowers. Therefore, the numbers of nonobservers and inactive observers cannot be calculated. Respondents' names were obtained from support groups and from other whistle-blowers. Therefore, external whistle-blowers are likely to be overrepresented. For this study, the external whistle-blower percentage represents the proportion of respondents who reported internally before going outside the organization.

[e] The first row refers to wrongdoing that occurred anywhere; the second row refers to wrongdoing involving the scientist's own assistant.

[f] Wrongdoing was presented to all subjects.

97

of age, with 10 years of service with their employers and 5 years in the present positions. In addition, 89 percent of the respondents had college degrees, with 28 percent holding graduate degrees. These comparisons provide evidence that the Near and Miceli (1988) sample was representative of the population of internal auditors who are members of the Institute of Internal Auditing.

The data generated in the Near and Miceli (1988) study were analyzed in four manuscripts to which we will refer throughout this chapter, chapter 4, and chapter 5. The first (Miceli & Near, 1988b) examined the predictors of retaliation, while the second (Miceli, Near & Schwenk, 1991) examined the predictors of whistle-blowing and the choice of whistle-blowing channels. The third (Schwenk et al., 1989) investigated the correlates of escalation of whistle-blowing (to multiple complaint recipients over time), and the fourth (Near & Miceli, 1990, 1991) examined the effectiveness of whistle-blowing.

Keenan (1988b, p. 8) asked managers enrolled in "a basic management certificate program at a large midwestern university" to complete anonymous surveys. No response rate was reported, but 143 first-level managers voluntarily completed the surveys. Approximately 75 percent were male, with 64 percent employed in the manufacturing sector and the remainder in the service sector. Most participants were in their 30s, with several years of experience in their present positions; 40 percent had college degrees or graduate training.

Blackburn (1988) administered confidential surveys to randomly selected groups of employees on work time, and she achieved a response rate of 78 percent. Employees were selected from several locations with varying numbers of union and nonunion, professional, and craft employees. Specific demographics were not reported; the author indicated that pilot testing revealed that participants objected to demographic questions.

The three studies shown in table 3–1 that did not separate responses by sector also did not provide response rates or demographic information. Participants in Gartrell's ("Therapists . . . ," 1987) and Soeken and Soeken's (1987) studies represented all areas of the country; Tangney's (1987) science professors were drawn from a university ranked in the top ten in attracting external research funding.

Frequencies of Observing and Reporting Wrongdoing

In general, table 3–1 shows that at least some persons in every sample said they did not observe wrongdoing in their organizations during the relevant time period, generally the preceding twelve-month period. However, these percentages vary widely, from fewer than 20 percent of the study participants (Near & Miceli, 1988) to more than 80 percent of them (Tangney, 1987). As will be explored in our following discussion of the predictors of whistle-blowing, one possible reason for this variation is that where the position held by the whistle-blower appears to prescribe observation of wrong-doing (for example, in the Near & Miceli study, participants were directors of internal auditing, who are formally expected to search for and act on wrongdoing), observation is more like to occur.

Table 3–1 also shows that, in every sample, some persons who observed wrongdoing reported it, while others did not. The proportion of observers who reported wrongdoing was not constant across studies; it ranged from 10 percent to 90 percent. Interestingly, the proportion was fairly consistent across the experimental studies, where the type of wrongdoing was held constant within studies and the nature of participants was similar across studies.

Finally, table 3–1 indicates that, in the field, anonymous whistle-blowing is less common than is whistle-blowing in which the reporter is identified. Higher rates of anonymous whistle-blowing occurred in the experimental studies, which did not permit identified whistle-blowing or made anonymous whistle-blowing easy or attractive, in part because of ethical concerns regarding the treatment of human subjects. Further, the data show that most whistle-blowers do not report wrongdoing through any channels external to the organization. The study by Soeken and Soeken (1987) reported a relatively high proportion of external whistle-blowers, but this may be attributable to the sampling method used, which relied on known cases of whistle-blowing. Whistle-blowers whose complaints are reported only to internal parties may not be known outside the organization and generally cannot be reached by researchers employing this type of sampling method.

These findings suggest strongly that observation of and reactions to wrongdoing varies widely across persons and situations. Consequently, it would be valuable to consider which personal and situational variables are associated with the observation of and reactions to wrongdoing.

Identifying Variables That May Affect Whistle-blowing

As noted earlier, stage 2 (figure 2–2) comprises at least four steps: recognition of wrongdoing, assessment, responsibility, and choice of action. In examining each step, we can identify variables that may affect the outcome of that step. However, a problem arises. Research on whistle-blowers generally has not examined the predictors and outcomes of *each step*, primarily because this model has evolved as a consequence of the research rather than as a guide for the research. Instead, the empirical research predicting whistle-blowing has tended to examine whether the final outcome—whistle-blowing—depends on certain predictors. Therefore, rather than discuss each step separately, we will discuss variables hypothesized to affect any point of the decision process, but we will describe the decision step(s) that each variable is thought to affect.

We have attempted to group variables into categories familiar to many researchers. Included in the first category are personal characteristics of the focal member, including dispositional variables, values, and beliefs; demographic characteristics; and variables pertaining to the occupational choice of, or position held by, the focal member. These variables are discussed in some depth in this chapter. A second category comprises situational variables, including variables pertaining to the perceived wrongdoing and its context, as well as to the group and the organization to which the individual belongs, and the organizational environment. In our third category, we have placed variables that seem to represent combinations of conditions involving both personal and situational variables. The variables in the second and third categories are discussed in chapter 4.

Figure 3–1 presents an abbreviated version of the pre-whistle-blowing decision process, and the first of the three categories of factors believed to affect at least some part of this process. Thus, it depicts the personal variables that may affect whistle-blowing.

Before reviewing the literature, we want to clarify three points. First, we do not consider in this chapter the question of why individuals may choose to blow the whistle more than once concerning

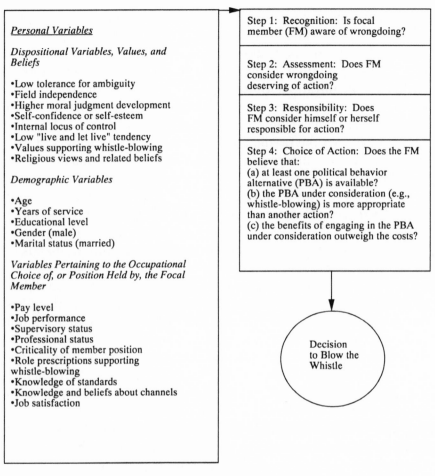

FIGURE 3–1

Personal Variables Hypothesized to Affect the Decision to Blow the Whistle

the same incident of wrongdoing. That is, some whistle-blowers may be dissatisfied with the consequences of the first report and report the wrongdoing to other parties, perhaps at higher levels in the organization. We will address that issue specifically in chapter 5, which deals with the aftermath of whistle-blowing. However, many of the findings discussed next, particularly those dealing with external whistle-blowing (meaning whistle-blowing to complaint recipients outside the organization), are likely to reflect relationships with subsequent reporting rather than initial reporting. As noted in chapter 2, some research shows that external whistle-blowing usually occurs *after* attempts have been made to correct wrongdoing within an organization. Unfortunately, in most of the research to date, no data have been collected concerning the order in which reports were made. Thus, it is often difficult to make a clear distinction between the prediction of initial whistle-blowing and prediction of whistle-blowing concurrent with or subsequent to that initial report.

Second, ideally we would like to make clear distinctions between variables that are *shown* to be related to whistle-blowing and those that have not yet been examined or which have been shown *not* to have an impact. But we cannot, because the literature to date is in its developmental stages. As described in the following sections, most variables have been examined in only one study and frequently, those variables that have been examined in several studies have not been measured the same way in each study or have not been shown to have consistent effects. Consequently, in figure 3–1, we attempted to show the direction of the relationships proposed in the research literature, but we will provide more detail as to whether the research is supportive of the hypothesized relationship of each variable to whistle-blowing.

Third, the literature generally has not demonstrated cause-effect relations between variables expected to cause whistle-blowing and the decision to blow the whistle (or any part of the decision process). As shown in figure 3–1, we will identify personal variables that are expected to affect the decision to blow the whistle and the form it may take. But it is conceivable that many of these variables are affected by whistle-blowing. For example, one's job satisfaction may cause whistle-blowing, but one may become more, or less, satisfied following whistle-blowing and its organizational consequences, such as retaliation or correction of the problem. Therefore, while we focus on variables that cause whistle-blowing in this chapter, we do not wish to imply that it is a one-way process. We now turn our attention to the first category of potential predictors of whistle-blowing: personal variables.

Personal Variables That May Affect Whistle-blowing

The characteristics of organization members and their positions, and some of the values and beliefs they hold, will affect their assessment of questionable activity and their evaluation of whistle-blowing as a potential response. Because some of these variables are likely to be partly a function of current environmental events, they are not completely independent of outside influence, yet they are probably more properly classified as personal rather than situational variables.

Dispositional Variables, Values, and Beliefs

There is some anecdotal evidence that whistle-blowers may be more adept than other organization members at detecting wrongdoing. For example, Powell (1990, p. 10) reported that Bill McInnis, a NASA whistle-blower, "had a knack for simply noticing things that others didn't." This suggests one reason why dispositional or other personal variables may differentiate whistle-blowers from other organization members. Some of the dispositional variables, values, and beliefs that may lead to whistle-blowing follow.

DISPOSITIONAL VARIABLES

Tolerance for Ambiguity. Tolerance for ambiguity may affect step 1 of the decision process, in which the individual may become aware of wrongdoing. Detecting wrongdoing such as fraud is essentially a problem finding task (Pincus, in press). Perpetrators may deliberately attempt to mislead potential whistle-blowers, and the information that may lead one to the wrongdoing is often qualitative and ambiguous (Pincus, in press). Thus, individual differences in cognitive style or information processing may lead to differences in the likelihood of organization members' observing and interpreting wrongdoing.

Because individuals with a high tolerance for ambiguity seek out ambiguity and excel in the performance of ambiguous tasks (MacDonald, 1970) and because recognition of wrongdoing may involve ambiguous cues, ambiguity tolerant auditors would be likely to recognize clues that fraud might exist and to reach an accurate conclusion about the existence of fraud (Pincus, in press). Contrary to this reasoning, however, in a study of 119 auditors who were given a case modeled from an actual audit where material undetected fraud existed (that is, involving substantial sums of money), ambiguity *intolerant* auditors were more successful than were ambiguity tolerant auditors at recognizing clues that fraud might exist and in decision accuracy (that is, whether their beliefs that ultimately fraud did exist matched reality). This was true even when differences in the auditors' ability, motivation, and experience were controlled (Pincus, in press).

As Pincus (in press) noted, auditors who have a low tolerance for ambiguity may cope with ambiguity not by ignoring or denying it, but rather by making an active attempt to resolve it. They may be more vigilant in pursuing signals indicating potential wrongdoing than are individuals who have a high tolerance for ambiguity. Because some research (cited by Pincus) indicates that the passive coping method may predominate, Pincus speculated that the training of auditors (through the application of general accepted auditing standards) may encourage an active approach to resolving ambiguities.

Thus, this research suggests that tolerance for ambiguity may predict—alone or in combination with organizational prescriptions or training concerning the reporting of wrongdoing—the recognition of wrongdoing and, ultimately, whistle-blowing. However, because no research dealing in particular with whistle-blowing and tolerance for ambiguity has been undertaken, we have no information concerning their relationship. Consequently, more research is needed in this area.

Field Dependence. Another cognitive style variable that may be related to the recognition of wrongdoing is field dependence (Witkin & Goodenough, 1977, 1981; Witkin, Goodenough & Oltman, 1979). In the same study of fraud detection among auditors described previously, Pincus (in press, p. 6) argued that success would depend on the ability of the auditor "to separate the individual fraud clues from the complex background of the information set in which they occur." This suggested that field dependence, which refers to "the ease with which a person can disembed a single piece of information from a complex field" (ibid., p. 7), may be related to recognition of wrongdoing.

Pincus hypothesized that field-independent auditors, who perceive patterns in data that are relatively independent of their context rather than view the information set as a whole, would be likely to detect fraud clues because of their ability to separate single pieces of information. Consistent with this reasoning, she found field-independent auditors to be more successful than field-dependent auditors at recognizing clues that fraud might exist and in decision accuracy (when differences in ability, motivation, and experience were controlled). This research suggests that field-independent organization members in general may be more likely to recognize wrongdoing, and potentially to blow the whistle, than are other parties, but again, research is needed to test this proposition.

Moral Judgment Development. It is frequently suggested in the popular literature that whistle-blowers may have different moral standards than do non-whistle-blowers. Researchers (such as Dozier & Miceli, 1984; Graham, 1983, 1986) have also speculated about the relationship between moral standards and whistle-blowing. Specifically, they have considered whether Kohlberg's (1969) six stages of moral reasoning, or moral judgment development, may be related to whistle-blowing.

Moral judgment development (MJD) could affect all of the steps in the whistle-blowing decision process. Higher MJD could heighten the awareness and assessment of wrongdoing; it could increase the observer's propensity to judge himself or herself responsible for action; and it could affect the way observers generate and evaluate action alternatives. For example, the high MJD may view whistle-blowing as morally justified or even necessary, while the low MJD may want to take action but believes that whistle-blowing is not appropriate. Also, individuals with high levels of MJD may highly value the termination of wrongdoing. Therefore, even if they expect to incur costs—they may have to spend a great deal of time pursuing a complaint or experience severe retaliation—they will blow the whistle because their moral disposition does not permit inaction. It may be easier for organization members will lower levels of MJD to ignore or redefine wrongdoing in order to avoid potential costs of reporting it (Near & Miceli, 1987).

Several researchers have developed tests of MJD (Kohlerg, 1969; Piaget, 1932; Rest, 1979), although the tests' construct validity has been questioned (Emler, Renwick & Malone, 1983; Kurtines & Greif, 1974; Nassi, Abramowitz & Youmans, 1983). The literature on prosocial behavior, which generally relies on these tests, shows that "the higher the individual's level of moral judgement is, the more altuistically he or she behaves" (Rushton, 1980, pp. 83–84). Research suggests that individuals with strong prosocial tendencies have internalized higher and more universal standards of justice, social responsibility, and modes of moral reasoning (Brief & Motowidlo, 1986; Rushton, 1984), particularly where situational conditions support prosocial intervention (Staub, 1974).

Forsyth (1985) classified persons according to two dimensions: (a) idealism, reflecting the extent to which the individual believes that good consequences can always be obtained and that one should strive to achieve it; and (b) relativism, reflecting the extent to which the individual questions whether universal moral values are important. He found that high idealists used a different model of judging situations that did low idealists. Relativists may be more sensitive to situations in determining whether wrongdoing deserves action, and in the use of cues indicating action. Some support for this logic was found by Fritzsche and Becker (1984). Subjects read vignettes of ethical dilemmas; some individuals relied on "rights" criteria (for example, the right of the public to safe cars, which might be comparable to the "idealistic" view) while others relied on "act utilitarian" criteria (such as the risks to consumers versus the costs, to the individual of whistle-blowing, which might be comparable to the "relativist" view). Those who relied on "rights" criteria, which may represent higher levels of moral reasoning than reliance on utilitarian criteria, were more likely to say they would blow the whistle. However, individuals' statements of intentions to blow the whistle may not be related to their actually doing so.

Consistent with these results, one laboratory investigation of whistle-blowing (Brabeck, 1984) demonstrated that "highly moral" (as defined by the Rest [1979] scale) individuals were more inclined than others to point out a possibly unintentional error in a manuscript in response to a specific request by the manuscript writer. However, this study was not definitive. Subjects may have viewed error identification to be purely "helpful," because the public, the organization, and the "error-maker"—who may not have been viewed as a wrongdoer—would be helped. In most instances of successful whistle-blowing, however, the public would be helped, but the wrongdoer (and perhaps, the organization) would likely be hurt. Situational conditions, which in Brabeck's study seemed supportive of whistle-blowing but which were not manipulated, would be particularly important in settings that evoke moral conflict—or in those which call for behavior that is not entirely altruistic (Brief & Motowidlo, 1986). If the situation did *not* suggest that blowing the whistle would be viewed as clearly helpful, MJD may be unrelated to whistle-blowing, because the hypothesized underlying psychological process is that helping and not hurting is caused by higher moral development.

On the other hand, the experimenter (Brabeck herself) could have been expected to know that her manuscript was in error—it misstated basic information concerning the "Little Albert's conditioned fear of rabbits" study that is covered in introductory psychology classes. She had power over the whistle-blowers, and could have reacted negatively to attempts to correct her. In many whistle-blowing contexts in organizations, "management" may be viewed as a monolith, even though wrongdoing may be committed only by some members of management. Therefore, internal whistle-blowing in the form of reporting to any member of management may be viewed as the same type of response as Brabeck observed.

Consequently, Miceli, Dozier, and Near (1991) attempted to provide a setting with somewhat greater opportunity for moral conflict perhaps more analogous to whistle-blowing. A confederate "Research Assistant" (RA) asked subjects to complete a "managerial hiring decision" task, but before the subjects did so, he explained that "the study wasn't going as hoped" and asked them to "fudge" the data. An opportunity to blow the whistle anonymously to an authority who appeared not to be connected to the study was provided. In that study, whistle-blowing was associated with *lower* rather than higher levels of moral judgment development, but there was no interaction effect with the threat of retaliation.

This finding was surprising, because it appeared to be contrary both to findings from Brabeck's (1984) study and to predictions based on a prosocial perspective—that is, moral judgment development was thought to increase the likelihood that an immoral event is viewed as wrongful and or that has a moral obligation to intervene to stop wrongdoing where the situation suggests that whistle-blowing is appropriate. However, the findings can be reconciled with prior empirical research and theory in two ways.

First, Brabeck's "whistle-blowers" were asked by the "wrong-doer" to find manuscript errors. Little moral conflict would be generated by such a request. In the present study, and probably in most "real world" cases of whistle-blowing, more moral conflict would be evoked. The wrongdoer obviously acted wrongfully, and reporting was done not at his request, but to a powerful third party who could punish him. Clearly the wrongdoer would not appreciate reports of his wrongdoing. Further, research shows that norms against "finking" are well-established in childhood (Dozier & Miceli, 1985). Consequently, the observer may wonder if the ends justify the means. Where moral conflict exists, highly moral subjects may be less likely than "low moral" subjects to define whistle-blowing as an appropriate solution.

Second, in Miceli, Dozier, and Near (1991), the costs and benefits of action versus inaction may have been weighed differently by persons with differing MJD scores. The costs of inaction may have been perceived by everyone as rather low, since the harm of an inaccurate, published article is less tangible and dramatic than the consequences of other types of wrongdoing (such as exposure to radiation or other safety hazards). Perhaps the "low moral" subjects experienced reactance at the control attempt by the RA; in response, they may have tried to gain a benefit —"even the score"—by reporting the RA. The "high moral" subjects might have been more concerned with the negative consequences to the RA. Thus, future researchers may want to identify conditions under which moral judgment development will either increase or decrease whistle-blowing and explore the reasons why. It may also be that the relationship is not linear. Graham (1983) suggested that individuals in the third stage of moral judgment development would be more likely to use voice than would other individuals (Blackburn, 1988). This stage is characterized as commitment to an internalized definition of good and bad (Andrews, 1981).

Perhaps characteristics of the situation and the person interact to determine whether whistle-blowing is viewed as a "morally correct" action. Individuals with higher levels of MJD may be more likely than lower MJD counterparts to view some situations as warranting reporting, while the reverse would be true for other situations.

If so, it would be important to determine whether observers viewed themselves to be morally compelled to take action *concerning the particular activity observed.*

In a survey investigation of directors of internal auditing (Miceli, Near & Schwenk, 1991), we found more whistle-blowing where the situation was viewed as more morally compelling than where it is not. The finding that moral compulsion plays a role is interesting, because it underscores the discretionary nature of whistle-blowing, even when it might appear that one's job would require the reporting of wrongdoing. That is, even where whistle-blowing would appear to be required by the job, it is less likely to occur if the observer does not also believe that whistle-blowing is morally required. Future research should examine whether the extent to which an observer of wrongdoing feels compelled to blow the whistle is a function of personal variables, situational variables, or both. For example, it may be that whistle-blowers feel a greater need to control their environments, particularly when their own ethical standards have been violated. This may cause them to feel compelled to report the same activity that another onlooker would ignore or accept. This issue is discussed later, in the section describing the potential role of an extended sense of responsibility, as opposed to a "live and let live" tendency.

Self-confidence or Self-esteem. Several researchers (such as Farrell & Petersen, 1982; Near & Miceli, 1985) have proposed that self-confidence or self-esteem may be positively related to whistle-blowing for several reasons. First, organization members who have low self-esteem may be apathetic about most organizational activities or may withdraw from situations; thus, they may be less likely to blow the whistle than would persons with higher levels of self-esteem (Kolarska & Aldrich, 1980). In terms of our model, withdrawal caused by low self-esteem may lead to lower probabilities that wrongdoing will be recognized or assessed to be deserving of action. The apathetic organization member may not consider himself or herself responsible for action.

Second, Graham (1986) proposed that individuals with low self-esteem are unlikely to perceive themselves as generally effective and are therefore less likely to engage in dissent. This reasoning suggests that step 4 of our model would be affected: Higher self-esteem individuals may be more aware of potentially appropriate, cost-effective actions that can be taken.

It may be that a more specific, situational confidence will be related to whistle-blowing. Blackburn (1988) proposed that one's confidence in himself or herself as a change agent may lead to more dissent. This is consistent with the social influence literature (for example, Levine, 1980; Moscovici & Nemeth, 1974), which suggests that the more credible, confident, competent, and objective the member is, the greater the potential influence he or she will have in a group. It is also consistent with the literature on prosocial intervention (Dozier & Miceli, 1985), which shows that perceived instrumental competence is associated with helping (Senneker & Hendrick, 1983). Thus, organization members who believe they have some expertise either in judging organizational actions or in bringing about change may feel that what appears to be wrongdoing has been accurately assessed, and that if they choose to blow the whistle, they will be effective in getting wrongdoing stopped. Unfortunately, no research has directly tested these propositions.

Locus of Control. One dispositional variable that may be closely related to self-confidence or self-esteem may be locus of control, at least with respect to its potential relationship to whistle-blowing. According to Rotter (1966), individuals with an *internal* locus of control ("internal LOCs") believe themselves to be largely in control of their outcomes, while individuals with an *external* locus of control ("external LOCs") believe that fate, luck, or chance determines much of what happens to them. Research shows that internal LOCs are more inclined than are external LOCs to engage in prosocial behavior, such as helping and crime reporting (see Spector, 1982, for a review). However, there are three possible explanations for this relationship.

First, because internal LOCs believe that they control the events that affect them, they may have a stronger "action orientation" than do external LOCs (Spector, 1982). This implies that step 3, in which one's responsibility for action is considered, would be viewed differently depending on the degree of internality.

Second, internal LOCs may feel more personally competent than do external LOCs, which may affect step 4, in which actions are chosen. As noted earlier, felt personal competence to deal with an emergency was prominent in distinguishing intervenors (as in Shotland & Heinold, 1985). Thus, internal LOCs may believe that they will be able to stop the objectionable practice, while external LOCs may believe that the questionable activity is controlled by forces or parties too powerful to stop. Other evidence (cited by Spector, 1982) suggests that internals outperform externals in organizations, which may lead to a general feeling of competence within the organization. Similarly, research on whistle-blowing suggests that whistle-blowers tend to be high performers (Miceli & Near, 1988a). Competent individuals may believe they will exert greater minority influence over other organization members, enabling them to expect to avoid retaliation or to bring about the cessation of wrongdoing (Near & Miceli, 1987).

Third, Glauser (1982) proposed that internal LOCs would engage in more upward communication than would external LOCs, presumably because of their belief in their ability to control events. This suggests that internal LOCs may be more likely to choose internal channels when expressing dissent.

Similarly, internal LOCs are less conforming and compliant to authority than are external LOCs, and they may be less affected by influence attempts (such as threatened retaliation), especially where the pressure seems strong (Spector, 1982). Internal LOCs may experience greater psychological reactance (Brehm, 1972) in response to influence attempts (Biondo & MacDonald, 1971). To the extent that organizational norms oppose whistle-blowing, this research suggests that external LOCs would be reluctant to report wrongdoing, particularly within the organization. Finally, internal LOCs may be more likely to take personal responsibility for the consequences of ethical behavior and to be less affected by external forces (such as, attempts to dissuade the observer from blowing the whistle) than by personal ethical standards (Trevino, 1986).

In the only known investigation of these propositions (Miceli, Dozier & Near, 1991), locus of control had no main effect on students' propensity to report apparent wrongdoing by a "research assistant" to their university's "research committee" representative. Locus of control did not interact with threatened retaliation. In this study, whistle-blowing was anonymous and the only channel available was an internal one. The extent to which locus of control might affect other types of whistle-blowing decisions is not known. But we know of no theoretical reason why locus of control should affect identified actions to a greater extent than anonymous actions, and as noted before, we expect internal locus of control to increase internal whistle-blowing. Clearly, more research is needed.

"Live and Let Live" Tendency. A picture that emerges from a review of the literature on whistle-blowing, including the case reports, is that whistle-blowers may have had a need or a wish to control their environments to a greater extent than the average organization member. As will be seen in the review of situational factors, many inactive observers, like whistle-blowers, faced conditions that would be expected to produce whistle-blowing—that is, they were powerful, there were available complaint recipients, the wrongdoing was serious—yet they did not act. This implies to us that whistle-blowers may have a strong need or wish to change a situation in the workplace, while their inactive counterparts may be comfortable to "live and let live"—without interfering in the situation. Whistle-blowers may then have a greater propensity to act when situations requiring change arise. This may in some sense be viewed as an extended sense of responsibility.

Thus, there may be a dispositional characteristic common to many whistle-blowers for which a measure has not yet been developed. At one extreme manifestation of this characteristic—the "interference" end of the continuum—organization members may believe it is appropriate to interfere in the actions of others in the organization, even when the actions are normatively viewed or organizationally prescribed to be legitimate or appropriately under the control of the others. For example, an accountant may tell a peer (who has not sought the accountant's advice) that she or he thinks written memos are an ineffective communication device and the peer should always communicate verbally. Extreme scorers may favor the imposition and enforcement of extensive rules. At the opposite end of the continuum—the "live and let live" end—the organization member does not wish to get involved in organizational activities outside the narrowest confines of the job description, even when involvement would appear appropriate or essential. For example, a supervisor may ignore employees' blatant and persistent personal use of the telephone for long distance calls even when the bills are enormous. In the middle of the continuum, appropriateness of intervention is not clear to the individual. For example, faculty members may be reluctant to confront certain political behaviors, such as an attempt to manipulate a hiring decision, on the part of other faculty members.

It is our speculation that whistle-blowers may tend to fall between the middle of the continuum and the interference end of the continuum. This is because we view both extremes to represent "illegitimate" or at least "inappropriate" degrees of control that need expression, whereas whistle-blowing is certainly appropriate under certain circumstances. In contrast, inactive observers generally may prefer to "live and let live." Presumably, this construct would affect steps 3 and 4: "Live and let live" individuals would not see themselves as responsible for action, and they would not believe that whistle-blowing is appropriate. They would not blow the whistle. However, this is not to say that all inactive observers would possess "live and let live" personality types; many individuals may have an extended sense of responsibility, but because there are many other factors that influence whistle-blowing, other factors may depress their willingness to act.

We would distinguish the hypothesized construct from locus of control (Rotter, 1966) in that locus of control refers to individuals' beliefs about *what affects their own* behavior or outcomes rather than *what would they be likely to do* concerning *others'* behavior or outcomes, which may have only tangential connection to the individual's outcomes. The propensity not to "live and let live" can also be distinguished from Greenberger's and Strasser's concept of personal control (Greenberger & Strasser, 1986; Greenberger, Strasser & Lee, 1988; Greenberger, Strasser, Cummings & Dunham, 1989). According to these authors, individuals have varying levels of desire for control, and of how much control they possess, over what happens to them in the present work situations, and both of these variables can be a function of both dispositional and situational factors. When control desired is much greater than control possessed, individuals will attempt to restore their freedom before becoming helpless. Thus, the personal control construct focuses on *events that directly affect the individual*, whereas the hypothesized "live and let live" construct focuses on how the individual views *controlling others' actions or outcomes*. The hypothesized construct is conceived to be a dispositional variable that may affect personal control perceptions or reactions to insufficient personal control (Greenberger, Porter, Miceli & Strasser, 1991). Obviously, research is needed to examine all of these propositions.

VALUES AND BELIEFS

Values Concerning Whistle-blowing. As noted in chapter 1, individuals differ with respect to their values concerning the justification of whistle-blowing. Research suggests that whistle-blowers are more likely to believe that whistle-blowing, in general, is more desirable than are (a) organization members who observe wrongdoing but do not blow the whistle, or (b) those who do not observe wrongdoing (Miceli & Near, 1984).

Unfortunately, we cannot be certain whether the beliefs preceded action, were influenced by action, or both, because data on both variables were collected after whistle-blowing occurred. Inactive observers may have rationalized their nonintervention by saying they didn't approve of whistle-blowing. But nonobservers presumably have little reason to distort their views of whistle-blowing. Nonobservers could say they didn't observe wrongdoing (even if they did) to absolve themselves of the responsibility of reporting, but this would allow them to express support for whistle-blowing and maintain attitudinal and behavioral consistency. The fact that they—like the inactive observers—were less supportive than whistle-blowers suggests that views precede action, but empirical testing is needed to confirm this. The issue may be of little practical importance, however. While values or beliefs predict whistle-blowing, their effects, in general, are weaker than are those of situational variables concerned with the particular incident of wrongdoing (Miceli & Near, 1983, 1984, 1985).

Religious Views and Related Beliefs. Religious institutions may help individuals define what activities are considered wrongful (Glazer & Glazer, 1987). This influence may be manifested in individuals' values; hence in that sense it may be viewed as a "personal" variable. These beliefs may also affect whether wrongdoing should be corrected by certain individuals, and how correction should be initiated, thus affecting all the decision steps. For example, it is easy to imagine how a belief that there will be a final, higher accounting for one's actions would enable an observer of wrongdoing to downplay concerns about potential retaliation: The focal member may believe that "I may suffer now, but I will get a higher reward; the wrong-doers may win the earthly battle, but will be held accountable for their sins against others and against me."

There is some anecdotal evidence that religious views may be related to whistle-blowing. The typical whistle-blower studied by Soeken and Soeken (Pottmyer, 1987, p. 30) described himself or herself as "moderately religious" though it is not clear how this might differ from the self-description of people in general. In another study, some whistle-blowers described their religious faith as contributing to their decision to blow the whistle; however, religious belief alone may be insufficient to cause whistle-blowing (Glazer & Glazer, 1987). Instead, an action orientation may be necessary.

However, it is certainly conceivable that individuals who have varying levels or types of religious beliefs, as well as individuals who are nonreligious, will hold such values. At this time there is no comparative empirical evidence as to whether religious views bear any direct relationship to whistle-blowing or to the decisions that may lead to whistle-blowing, with or without an action orientation.

Demographic Variables

As in the case of dispositional characteristics, values, and beliefs that organization members may possess, demographic variables may be associated with whistle-blowing. Some research has considered the respective roles of age, years of service, educational level, gender, and marital status.

AGE. Although the age of an organization member and his or her years of service with an organization are likely to be correlated, here we will deal with each separately. We will describe the expected effects of age with service "controlled"—that is, apart from the effects that service is likely to have as it increases with member age.

It is difficult to predict whether younger members will be more or less likely to blow the whistle than older members. On the other hand, young members may be unsure about what constitutes wrong-doing and may err on the side of judging wrongful acts to be acceptable, thus affecting steps 1 and 2 of the decision model. They may be less likely to believe that they are responsible for acting. Also, younger organization members often have career aspirations that may affect their decisions about engaging in behavior that could alienate members of the managerial hierarchy (Hacker, 1978). Further, they may be viewed as "young turks" who do not have good judgment and hence their credibility may be low. Thus, younger workers may lack influence in the organization and knowing this, they see few benefits and high costs of action (step 4). Consequently, they may be reluctant to blow the whistle.

On the other hand, young workers may apply a higher, rather than lower, set of standards for defining wrongdoing than do older workers, or they may find it more difficult to tolerate situations they find objectionable (steps 1, 2, and 3). Further, research shows that organizational members who have "high mobility aspirations" communicate more frequently with their superiors and they "are more precise and accurate about important task matters" than are other organization members (Glauser, 1982, p. 8). This, along with our other reasoning, seems to suggest that younger organization members would be *more* likely to report wrongdoing internally. However, Glauser (1982, p. 9) also reported that research conducted in nonorganizational settings suggests that subordinates would "tend to withhold and/or distort information which is bad news for the superior." Since the superior may punish the subordinate who reports the bad news of perceived wrongdoing by thwarting the subordinate's career progress, this second finding would appear to be particularly relevant for the "fast track" young employee. Such an organization member is rather powerless relative to persons without high aspirations. Thus, there appears to be somewhat more reason to predict that younger persons would be *less* likely to blow the whistle than would older employees—without regard to the effects of years of service.

Parmerlee et al. (1982) found that female whistle-blowers (alleging complaints of sex discrimination) were younger than the average worker in the female work force. But Soeken and Soeken (1987) found that respondents, predominantly male, were somewhat older than the typical worker (mean = 47 years). Neither of these two studies employed random sampling techniques, so it is difficult to interpret their different findings, nor did they control for service effects. In a secondary analysis of the 1980 MSPB survey, which used random sampling, Miceli and Near (1984) found that whistle-blowers tended to be supervisors who had high education yet earned low pay. This finding suggested that observers who do not report wrongdoing tend to be "fast trackers" who presumably may have lower ages than whistle-blowers. However, age was not directly measured. The 1983 MSPB survey, which also employed random sampling, asked about respondents' ages, but because of the high correlation with service variables, we combined these variables in our secondary analysis (Miceli & Near, 1988a). Consistent with the earlier findings, the combined age and service variable was associated with whistle-blowing; more-senior organization members were more likely to blow the whistle than were less-senior members.

YEARS OF SERVICE. Years of service may influence whistle-blowing for five reasons, but these reasons may not be consistent in their direction. The first three suggest that more experienced organization members will be *more* likely to report wrongdoing. First, Keenan (1990a) found that first-level managers with lower levels of service believed they had less adequate information about where to report wrongdoing than did more senior first-level managers, suggesting that junior managers might be *less* likely to report wrongdoing.

Second, members with many years of service tend to have higher personal investments in their organizations than do newcomers. They have given the organization their productive years. In return, in most organizations in the United States, experienced employees are compensated at higher pay levels than are newcomers, and benefits such as pensions are often contingent on accumulated years of service, thus making exit relatively costly for senior employees. Other, less tangible rewards, such as the development of friendships, may also accrue to these organization members. As noted in chapter 2, it may be difficult to duplicate such rewards if one were to search for a job outside the organization.

Experienced employees' low turnover rate (Porter & Steers, 1973) may attest to this. With greater investment and possibly decreased mobility, the experienced organization member may care to a greater extent about what happens in the organization than do members with lower investments (Kolarska & Aldrich, 1980). If so, she or he may be reluctant to exit after confronting wrongdoing and may be more interested than the newcomer in ridding the workplace of objectionable activity. Instead, the long-term member may wish to reciprocate by "helping" the organization preserve its reputation for honest dealings. At the same time, by reporting wrongdoing rather than remaining silent, she or he may benefit by improving the working environment if the wrongdoing is corrected. Consequently, through affecting steps 2, 3, and 4 (Assessment, Responsibility, and Choice of Action), higher service may lead to reporting wrongdoing, but only to internal parties, so as not to risk harming the organization.

Third, research on "idiosyncrasy credits" (Hollander, 1958) proposes that by demonstrating conformity to group norms over time, members are freer to deviate without being rejected; thus, the costs of action may be lower and the expected benefits (of influencing others and hence stopping the wrongdoing) may be higher (step 4). Like the reciprocation argument, the idiosyncrasy credit argument suggests that experienced individuals will be *more* likely to blow the whistle than newcomers.

The fourth reason why we expect service to be related to whistle-blowing suggests that junior members may be more likely to blow the whistle. In evaluating the potential costs and benefits of action (step 4), organization members may fear that by whistle-blowing, they risk losing their investments in the organization as well as the high levels of rewards the organization provides (Farrell & Petersen, 1982). Thus, *newcomers* may be more likely to blow the whistle, because they have less to lose than more-experienced members (Raelin, 1987).

The fifth rationale linking service and whistle-blowing does not predict a direct effect. More-experienced organization members may be more aware than are newcomers of what constitutes wrongdoing (step 1), at least in the eyes of the managerial hierarchy or a potential complaint recipient. Further, the more-experienced member may have internalized organizational norms to a greater extent and may therefore agree with the organization's likely assessment of the activity. An experienced member who has witnessed wrongdoing that is likely to be judged wrongful may be more likely to recognize it as such and blow the whistle, than will the less-experienced member, who may see the situation as ambiguous or as violating his or her own personal standards but not necessarily those of the organization. But the experienced member who believes that others will not judge the activity to be wrongful may be more likely to view it as not constituting wrongdoing, than will the newcomer. These factors suggest that years of service would not necessarily be directly related to whistle-blowing—whistle-blowing would depend on the extent to which the perceived wrongdoing matched the organizational norms defining wrongdoing.

Unfortunately, preliminary evidence is not consistent in supporting any of these propositions. As noted in chapter 2, Soeken and Soeken (1987) found that whistle-blowers tended to have service levels that were similar to those of the average individual in the work force. We found that *external* whistle-blowers tended to have high pay, low education, and nonsupervisory status (Miceli & Near, 1984), which suggested that they were more-experienced employees than were nonobservers, inactive observers, and internal whistle-blowers. In a later study (Miceli & Near, 1988a, as noted earlier) we found that the combination of age and service was associated with more whistle-blowing, but respondents weren't questioned as to the channel; thus we do not know whether service is associated with whistle-blowing or with only certain types of whistle-blowing. It may be useful to ask respondents about the various decision steps rather than to examine the effect of service on whistle-blowing alone.

EDUCATIONAL LEVEL. Educational level may affect all four decision steps. Higher education may increase or qualitatively affect one's recognition and assessment of wrongdoing, and it may affect the increase in the perceived responsibility for action. Higher educational levels may be associated with higher status in the organization and hence more power to bring about change (step 4). Parmerlee et al. (1982) and Jensen (1979) found that female complainants to employment discrimination enforcement agencies (that is, external whistle-blowers) tended to have higher levels of education than did women in the U.S. work force. But Miceli and Near (1984) found that, when the effects of other variables were controlled, external whistle-blowers tended to be slightly *less*, and internals slightly *more*, highly educated than were other organization members.

Consistent with the findings concerning internal whistle-blowers were those reported by Graham (1989, p. 10). She administered surveys to employees in three organizations and created a citizenship scale, Individual Initiative, that she viewed as encompassing internal whistle-blowing. It comprised items including "communications to others in the workplace [co-workers and superiors] to improve individual and group performance, challenge groupthink, and encourage both innovation and widespread participation in decision making; it may also describe trouble-making and rocking the boat." She found that individuals high in this factor were relatively well educated. Although the findings are limited, they appear to be somewhat consistent in suggesting that education will be positively associated with whistle-blowing, but this effect is not strong.

GENDER. Several years ago, we speculated that men would be more likely to blow the whistle than would women (Near & Miceli, 1985). At least four hypotheses have been proposed as a basis for this speculation.

First, men may tend to occupy positions where more serious wrongdoing is more likely to be observed, because many high-status occupations are sex-segregated (England, 1979). Thus, they may be more likely to be aware of consequential wrongdoing (steps 1 and 2 of the decision process). Also, Crosby (1982, 1984) posited that women in high-prestige jobs may be more sensitized to unfairness than women in low-prestige jobs or than men, because they may have compared their own situations to those of men in comparable positions. Or, they may have learned to complain more stridently because they entered male-dominated occupations (steps 3 and 4). Thus, position, or position and gender, rather than gender alone, may account for any relationship between gender and whistle-blowing.

Second, men may be more likely to be established members of professional groups where whistle-blowing is encouraged as part of a code of ethics (such as, engineers and physicians). Thus, they may feel more morally responsible for correcting perceived wrongdoing (step 3 of the decision process). But in Brabeck's (1984) study, all whistle-blowers were female (though the effects of gender were not statistically significant) and they had higher levels of moral judgment development than did nonwhistle-blowers (which was significant). Thus, moral development rather than gender may have accounted for those findings.

A third hypothesis linking gender and whistle-blowing stems from the observation that men, in general, may have higher levels of self-esteem or initiative (Eagly, 1983). As noted earlier, these characteristics may influence prosocial behavior (Rushton, 1984) and whistle-blowing (Kolarska & Aldrich, 1980), through the choice of action (Step 4).

Fourth, there is some evidence that women tend to conform more to a majority opinion than do men (Costanzo & Shaw, 1966), though the evidence is by no means conclusive (Eagly, 1983). Thus, social influence opposing whistle-blowing during any of the four steps would decrease women's propensity to blow the whistle.

Fifth, women may be less knowledgeable about how to respond to wrongdoing in their organizations. Interestingly, Keenan (1990a) found that male first-level managers believed they had more knowledge of where to report wrongdoing and more adequate information about how to do so than did their female counterparts; however, this did not hold true for upper-level managers (Keenan, 1990b).

Several studies using a variety of research methods have suggested that whistle-blowers are more likely to be male than female (Miceli, Dozier & Near, 1991; Soeken & Soeken, 1987), although the effect in one study was quite small (Miceli & Near, 1988a). Similarly, Gelfand, Hartmann, Walder, and Page (1973) found that women were significantly less likely to report shoplifters than were men. Graham (1989) found that men scored higher than did women in individual initiative (which encompassed internal whistle-blowing). In Miceli, Dozier & Near (1991), an experimental study, the gender effect occurred even when we held constant the opportunity for observation of wrongdoing, the nature of the wrongdoing observed, and the levels of moral judgment development and locus of control. These findings suggest that men and women may view whistle-blowing differently with respect to its appropriateness, costs, and benefits. On the other hand, male marketing managers who read vignettes describing hypothetical wrongdoing were no more likely than female marketing managers to express stronger intentions to blow the whistle (Fritzsche, 1988).

Thus, future research should explore the generalizability of this finding, and determine the reasons why men are more likely to act, if in fact they generally are. One obvious possibility is that observer gender may interact with the gender of the wrongdoer and with the gender of the complaint recipient. Observers may be more comfortable reporting wrongdoing to members of the same gender, particularly if the wrongdoer is of the same gender. In the Miceli, Dozier and Near (1991) study, in which other variables were the primary focus, the gender of the wrongdoer and that of the complaint recipient were held constant to reduce extraneous variance. The wrongdoer was male, and the complaint recipient, represented by a male student member of a faculty committee in a college with about 90 percent male faculty, was probably perceived as male. This may have depressed women's, and increased men's propensity to report wrongdoing. On the other hand, Gelfand's (1973) study suggests that this hypothesis will not be confirmed in future studies of gender and whistle-blowing. In that study, all wrongdoers were women (confederate shoplifters) and although the authors did not report the gender composition of the group of complaint recipients (cashiers at a convenience store), it is likely that at least some of them were women. Yet, as described earlier, the propensity of women and men to report wrongdoing was remarkably similar to the Miceli, Dozier, and Near (1991) results.

A related possibility is raised by a recent study of the use of workplace power strategies (Mainiero, 1986). Mainiero (p. 643) found that, when confronted with a frustrating workplace situation on which they depended, women were more likely than men to use an "acquiescence strategy" in which the "low-power individual accepts the power imbalance and decides that nothing else can be done in the situation." Mainiero identified two perspectives that predicted this finding: (a) that structural segregation (into less powerful organization positions) has caused women to be less likely to exert power forcefully, and (b) that early socialization shapes men's and women's behavior differently; men are perceived as and rewarded for using "direct aggressive strategies," whereas women are expected to remain powerless. Both the structuralist perspective and the socialization perspective suggest that women may feel less capable of bringing about change in a male-dominated organization. Thus, future resarch should explore whether the gender and other characteristics of the wrongdoers, perceived victims, and complaint recipients affect whistle-blowing directly, or whether these characteristics interact with the characteristics of the observer.

MARITAL STATUS. Marriage may provide a financial or personal support system for potential whistle-blowers (Parmerlee et al., 1982). This may enable observers of wrongdoing to weigh less heavily the expected costs of whistle-blowing to a greater extent than can unmarried observers, and thereby influence the choice of action step in the decision process.

Two studies reported that whistle-blowers are more likely to be married than the average worker (Parmerlee et al., 1982; Soeken & Soeken, 1987). On the other hand, a third study (Jensen, 1979, cited by Parmerlee et al., 1982) suggested that the opposite was true, though no significance tests were reported. However, all of these studies included only nonrandomly selected whistle-blowers (primarily those reporting to external complaint recipients). Consequently, it is not known whether most whistle-blowers as a group tended to be more likely to be married than observers who do not report wrongdoing or those who do not observe wrongdoing.

Variables Pertaining to the Occupational Choice of, or Position Held by, the Focal Member

The perception that organizations are dependent on the observer of wrongdoing, that is, that the whistle-blower would be influential, is likely to affect steps 3 and 4 of the decision process. Potentially influential observers of wrongdoing are likely to view themselves to be responsible for initiating change, and they may believe they will be effective in doing so.

The position held by the focal member may indicate the degree of potential influence. Several variables that may be associated with the position are the pay level, job performance, supervisory or professional status, and criticality of the position.

Similarly, certain incumbents may feel that they would avoid retaliation, because their role makes whistle-blowing more appropriate for them than for others. Individuals who know more about standards for wrongdoing and where to report it may believe whistle-blowing is appropriate when questionable activity is observed. Finally, where organization members are satisfied with their jobs or organizations, they may be more inclined than less-satisfied members to blow the whistle for a variety of reasons discussed below.

VARIABLES SUGGESTING ORGANIZATIONAL PRESTIGE OR POWER

Pay Level. In two studies using the MSPB data (collected in federal agencies), Miceli and Near (1984, 1988a) found that whistle-blowers tended to be more highly paid than were other organization members. In a later private sector study, we again found that whistle-blowers earn somewhat higher salaries than do persons who observe but do not report wrongdoing (Miceli, Near & Schwenk, 1991). These findings suggest that whistle-blowers who earn higher pay levels may feel relatively influential in the organizations and therefore are more likely to challenge the organization's actions.

Job Performance. Anecdotal and interview evidence suggests that whistle-blowers are high performers (for example, Powell, 1990; Glazer & Glazer, 1987). In addition to their influence (possibly based on their value as an important organizational resource), high performers may be influential for other reasons. Whistle-blowers are motivated by their wish to change an organizational practice (Farrell & Petersen, 1982; Near & Miceli, 1985). Their effectiveness in bringing about change may depend on their ability to influence others; as such, whistle-blowing may represent a case of attempted minority influence (Greenberger et al., 1987). The ability of a minority to influence others depends on the minority's credibility (as in Moscovici, 1976). Thus, the observer of wrongdoing may consider the extent in which he or she may be credible to others. Individuals who are viewed as competent or who believe that they are competent have higher credibility (Greenberger et al, 1987). This view is consistent with the earlier discussion of the role of self-esteem and competence in prosocial intervention.

Further, research on "idiosyncrasy credits" (Hollander, 1958) proposes that by demonstrating competence in different situations, members are freer to deviate without being rejected. This research suggests that observers of wrongdoing who are better performers may believe they will be more influential or that they will escape retaliation; therefore, they may be more likely than their lower-performing counterparts to blow the whistle.

Two studies, one in the public sector, and one largely based on private sector data, have found evidence consistent with this proposition. In the first, we found that receipt of performance-based awards within the preceding two years was associated with whistle-blowing (Miceli & Near, 1988). In the second, whistle-blowers considered themselves higher performers than did observers of wrongdoing who did not blow the whistle (Miceli, Near & Schwenk, 1991).

Supervisory Status. Miceli and Near (1984) found that internal whistle-blowers tended to be more likely to hold supervisory positions than did other organization members. This suggests that while supervisors may be more likely to blow the whistle within the organization, perhaps due to greater influence, they are not necessarily more likely to blow the whistle outside the organization, perhaps because as supervisors they may feel an obligation to support the management hierarchy. There is preliminary evidence, however, that hierarchical status above the supervisory rank does not make much difference, despite the greater power possessed by higher-level managers. Fritzsche (1988) found that executives, middle managers, and supervisors did not differ in their stated intentions to blow the whistle when presented with vignettes describing hypothetical wrongdoing.

Professional Status. There are several reasons why professionals might be more likely to blow the whistle. In addition to their potential influence due to relatively prestigious positions in organizations, their membership in professional associations may affect their awareness of wrongdoing and their assessment of whether it deserves their action (steps 1–3). For example, internal auditors follow a guideline of "materiality" to determine whether a particular incident of wrongdoing is serious enough to warrant action. Professional associations may also influence step 4, the choice of action. Leaders of professions maintain that professions are characterized not only by expert knowledge, but also by a code of ethics that includes a commitment to public service and a strong sense of individual responsibility on the part of their practitioners (Freidson, 1972; Glazer & Glazer, 1987). In one instance, a whistle-blower said that "I did what I did because I believed that the ethics of my profession demanded it" (Jones & Pottmyer, 1987).

Thus, observers who are members of professional groups whose norms suport whistle-blowing may feel sufficient support to take action (Perrucci et al, 1980). The expected costs of *not* acting may include the fear that the wrongdoing will be revealed, and by either participating in the wrongdoing or failing to reveal it, the observer of wrongdoing will also be implicated (Glazer & Glazer, 1987). Inaction may risk damage to the observer's professional reputation, delicensure, or criminal charges (Glazer & Glazer, 1987).

However, substantial countervailing pressures of self-interest may also exist for professionals; professionals sometimes restrict access to professional rewards to a small, elite group (Glazer & Glazer, 1987). This suggests that career concerns may cause professionals to view the potential costs of blowing the whistle as greater than those facing nonprofessionals.

The implications of this conflict are that we would not expect professionals to be necessarily any more likely than other organization members to consider a particular activity as deserving of action. Beyond this, there may be individual or situational differences (for instance, one professional may internalize the code of ethics while another views it as merely a piece of paper or an ideal that cannot always bear up under pressures of reality in organizations).

Research on whistle-blowers in the federal sector shows that professionals (that is, people with high pay and high education levels) are not necessarily more likely to blow the whistle (Miceli & Near, 1984), although one study showed a significant but slight positive effect (Miceli & Near, 1988a). The study of Bay Area Rapid Transit engineers, on the other hand, suggested that whistle-blowers involved felt enough support from their professional group to press their allegations of technical inadequacy in the system (Perrucci et al., 1980).

Criticality of Member Position. In a laboratory study (Martin, Brickman & Murray, 1983), subjects assumed the role of inequitably treated employees. Those who were told that their position was critical to the organization were more likely to attempt to fight the inequity than were subjects given other information. This effect occurred regardless of the magnitude of the perceived wrongdoing. However, criticality covaried with other "mobilization resources," so it is not clear whether criticality alone would motivate action. Further, the effect occurred with respect only to "less legitimate" means of fighting, such as work slowdowns. Whether whistle-blowing would be affected is not known.

Role Prescriptions. In chapter 1, we argued that whistle-blowing may sometimes be role-prescribed. Graham (1986) noted that assigned oversight responsibilities, as in auditor or managerial roles, may increase perceptions of personal responsibility, but may or may not increase voice (Blackburn, 1988). Miceli and Near (1984) found that observers of wrongdoing, particularly internal whistle-blowers, were more likely than nonobservers to be inspectors whose jobs required them to observe and report wrongdoing. This suggests that persons whose observations of wrongdoing are role-prescribed are more likely to observe and report wrongdoing (Miceli & Near, 1984) than those whose role is not prescribed.

However, we also argued that whistle-blowing is rarely role-prescribed for all activities witnessed by a particular job holder, but rather the prescriptions may be more specific. Further, informal prescriptions rather than formally assigned prescriptions may be critical. Thus, beliefs about roles held by observers of wrongdoing may be important (Brief & Motowidlo, 1986). Reporting wrongdoing of some types of activity may be viewed as part of one's job, while reporting of other types of activity may not be. Role prescriptions for whistle-blowing may especially encourage internal reporting. In the only study investigating this proposition, internal whistle-blowers were no more likely than other types of whistle-blowers to believe that whistle-blowing concerning the activity witnessed was role-prescribed (Miceli, Near & Schwenk, 1991). However, that belief was powerfully associated with whistle-blowing in general.

RELEVANT KNOWLEDGE

Knowledge of Standards. A variable affecting the perception of wrongdoing is whether incumbents have the knowledge necessary to detect it. To persons lacking knowledge of legal, professional, or other standards of conduct, questionable financial statements may appear proper; safety precautions may appear sufficient; and an act of discrimination or harassment may seem to be acceptable workplace behavior. Knowledge can be gained in a variety of ways, as from prior experience in other jobs or in the present job, from professional training, or from organizationally sponsored training. In some cases, training that is highly technical may be required: "[I]t is extremely rare for a certified public accountant to discover fraud because he [*sic*] is not trained to look for it . . . in order to detect potentially vulnerable areas within a company, one must, in effect, think like a thief" (Schutt, 1982, p. 19). Unfortunately, we know of no study of the linkage between knowledge of standards and whistle-blowing.

Knowledge of Channels. Organization members can be viewed as being dependent on certain forms of corrective action (Near & Miceli, 1985). If they believe that the organization's behavior must be changed and that methods other than whistle-blowing through official channels will be ineffective, they are dependent on official channels. Similarly, if organization members are unaware of alternative methods or they believe that particular methods are more effective than others, they will be more inclined to select the one believed to be effective. If they do not know the procedure for making internal complaints, they may not blow the whistle at all (Kolarska & Aldrich, 1980).

Organization members who have encountered questionable activity may have a greater awareness of potential complaint channels, because they have previously confronted a situation not faced by nonobservers (Miceli & Near, 1984). Further, some observers may not act simply because they do not know where to report wrongdoing (Kolarska & Aldrich, 1980). Miceli and Near (1984) found that whistle-blowers (and, to a lesser extent, nonobservers) believed they had greater knowledge of where to report wrongdoing within their organizations than did inactive observers, who observed but did not report wrongdoing. Because the nonobservers' awareness was similar to the whistle-blowers', these findings provide stronger support for Kolarska's and Aldrich's view than for ours. Alternatively, inactive observers may have rationalized their inaction after the fact. Since the data were retrospective, it remains for future research to answer this question.

JOB SATISFACTION. Some observers, including one federal official once responsible for assisting and protecting whistle-blowers, have expressed the view that whistle-blowers are "malcontents" (Devine & Aplin, 1986). This view raises the interesting question of whether whistle-blowers are generally disgruntled individuals bent on complaining about something, or whether they are generally satisfied with their jobs or organizations but dissatisfied about a specific activity, namely, the wrongdoing.

The literature on prosocial behavior suggests several reasons why and how job satisfaction could be expected to influence whistle-blowing. A considerable body of research has focused on the effects of mood states on prosocial behaviors. It has demonstrated that people in a positive mood are more likely to engage in helping behaviors than are people in a negative mood (as in Isen & Levin, 1972). Staub (1978) proposed that potential helpers engage in *hedonic balancing*. In hedonic balancing, the focal person (for example, the observer of wrongdoing) evaluates his or her well-being as compared to the well-being of the person in need of help. If the discrepancy between the focal person's current and accustomed level of well-being is favorable relative to the discrepancy for the needy person, then the focal person feels he or she has additional resources and is more likely to help than if the discrepancy is unfavorable (Staub, 1978). Consistent with this perspective, Isen (1970) and Berkowitz and Connor (1966) found that subjects who were successful on a task were more likely to help others than were unsuccessful subjects. This research suggests that positive mood states, or job satisfaction, may increase whistle-blowing by increasing the perceived responsibility for action (step 3 in the pre-whistle-blowing decision process).

A second rationale for the prediction that whistle-blowing may be associated with job satisfaction is that negative moods may lead to less helping behavior because they cause the individual to feel less capable of helping. Job dissatisfaction may cause organization members to feel less able to stop wrongdoing, or to be more susceptible to potential retaliation. Thus, this rationale suggests that negative mood states may affect whistle-blowing through the generation and evaluation of choices of action (step 4 in the pre-whistle-blowing decision process).

However, the studies examining mood states and helping have

been performed mostly in the laboratory. Mood states were temporarily manipulated (as by offering cookies or by enabling subjects to discover a dime in a telephone booth), and an emergency or other short-term opportunity to provide help was presented by experimenters. In organizational contexts, job satisfaction may be more stable or complex and more time to process information and choose a course of action may be available. Therefore, examination of research in organizational contexts would be helpful.

Research in organizational contexts has shown that individuals who are satisfied with aspects of their working life or who feel equitably treated by their organizations are more likely to engage in some types of prosocial behavior (Bateman & Organ, 1983; Motowidlo, 1984; Smith, Organ & Near, 983). Similarly, pay satisfaction may lead to whistle-blowing. From a social exchange perspective (Blau, 1964), it could be predicted that whistle-blowing will be more likely to occur when individuals believe they have been fairly rewarded. Individuals who believe they have received satisfying outcomes from the organization may wish to reciprocate by helping the organization correct wrongdoing. Previous research has shown that employees' evaluation of their pay relative to various comparison persons was associated with citizenship behavior (Organ & Konovsky, 1989; Scholl, Cooper & McKenna, 1987). Other research has shown that positive social comparisons are closely related to pay satisfaction (Heneman, 1985). This research suggests that observers of wrongdoing who are satisfied with their pay will be more likely to blow the whistle than will observers who are less satisfied with their pay.

Specifically with respect to whistle-blowing, two field studies have examined the role of variables related to job satisfaction. We (Miceli & Near, 1988a) found that more positive job responses were associated with whistle-blowing. However, whistle-blowers tended to be *less* satisfied with their pay (Miceli, Near & Schwenk, 1991). This was unexpected and seemingly contrary to the social exchange perspective, which suggests that one would help an organization that was munificent. Thus, further research is needed concerning these propositions.

Some General Suggestions for Future Research

At this time, the empirical research relevant to whistle-blowing is quite limited, and consequently, the motivating forces that propel the whistle-blower to take action are very poorly understood. Further, a variety of limitations become apparent as one reviews this body of research. First, some of this research was not designed to examine whistle-blowing, but rather it examined other behaviors (such as bystander intervention), and much of that research has been performed in laboratory settings. Therefore, while the studies often demonstrate careful measurement and suggest cause-effect relations, it is not clear to what extent the findings are applicable to whistle-blowers.

Second, some of the field research on whistle-blowing did not include comparison groups of persons who observed wrongdoing and did not report it, or of persons who did not observe wrongdoing. As a result, it is not clear that the characteristics observed to be common to whistle-blowers or whistle-blowing incidents are characteristic of whistle-blowing; the same characteristics might be observed in the absent comparison groups.

Third, survey research on whistle-blowing has relied on retrospective accounts. It is easy to imagine how both inactive observers of wrongdoing and whistle-blowers could engage in post-decisional justification (Staw, 1980), which might render these results suspect.

Fourth, the limited experimental research specifically dealing with whistle-blowing comprised (a) presentation of vignettes describing ethical dilemmas and (b) laboratory studies. While such studies demonstrate cause-effect relations and remove incentives for distortion of reality, questions of generalizability remain. The generalizability of survey results may also be questionable, because the samples used were probably not representative of American employees in general.

Blackburn (1988) called for more cause-effect research, within the limitations of research designs that reflect the sensitivity of reporting wrongdoing. Unfortunately, field experimental and longitudinal survey designs, which are frequently used to examine questions that involve cause-effect issues, are probably unworkable with regard to whistle-blowing. For example, because of obvious ethical concerns, one cannot randomly select employees to witness manipulated wrongdoing in order to determine which individual or situational characteristics are associated with whistle-blowing. Further, longitudinal survey designs require that the respondent be identified by name or by code in order for the experimeter to match data collected at different times. In the case of reactions to organizational wrongdoing, there are many sensitive issues raised that might cause many persons who are reluctant to identify themselves not to respond to the questionnaire. This potentially systematic self-selection bias might render any data collected to be of questionable validity. Finally, there is the issue of the representativeness of organizations that would be willing to sponsor intrusive or longitudinal research on whistle-blowing. Perhaps only "clean" organizations would allow researchers to investigate wrongdoing and whistle-blowing. Therefore, while research based on existing cross-sectional survey data has serious limitations, such data may be the best available for some time to come.

More importantly, perhaps, many hypotheses suggested before and in prior writings on whistle-blowing have not been tested at all. Because whistle-blowing is such an important phenomenon, we suggest that researchers not be discouraged by the limitations of the various research methods. Rather, we would encourage them to examine whistle-blowing by using a variety of methods.

One other perspective on research directions deserves mention. As noted by Dozier and Miceli (1985), whistle-blowing is an uncommon phenomenon. This may seem odd, because most persons, including managers, express approval of whistle-blowing under certain conditions (Clinard, 1983; Fritzsche & Becker, 1984; MSPB, 1981). To the extent that the decision steps accurately reflect organization members' decision-making processes, however, one can see why so few organization members come forward. There are many points at which one can decide against sticking one's neck out. Consistent with this, Blackburn's (1988) findings, like our own, suggest that inactive observers may be alienated employees. Consequently, she concurred with Ewing's (1983) suggestion that Hackman's and Oldham's (1980) research on employee alienation may yield insights into the process of whistle-blowing decision making. That is, whistle-blowers often were more like the nonobservers in the level of positive perceptions of management and climate, and the inactive observers were often lower. These findings suggest that some mechanism operates to *depress* the propensity to act. If so, perhaps researchers should refocus their attention. We have concentrated on whistle-blowers as exceptional individuals and tried to understand why they act; perhaps instead, we should concentrate on what organizational, situational, and personal factors cause organization members to remain silent.

Finally, research is needed to examine alternatives to whistle-blowing. One recent study of responses to sexual harassment (MSPB, 1988) showed that most organization members who take action against harassment use informal methods of problem resolution. It may be that many of our hypotheses predicting whistle-blowing actually predict the taking of some action—which may not be whistle-blowing. If so, the presence of large numbers of "active non-whistle-blowers" (who would be classified in the prior studies as inactive observers) may account for results that fail to show differences between whistle-blowers and inactive observers.

Summary

In this chapter, we have summarized existing research that may enhance understanding of the decision process that may precede whistle-blowing. A great many personal variables seem conceptually to be related to whistle-blowing. In general, there is evidence that personal characteristics are associated with whistle-blowing, but many variables have been examined in only one study, or not at all. These limitations should be borne in mind in reviewing the following summary of the research findings.

Several dispositional variables, values, and beliefs may be related to whistle-blowing. Research suggests that organization members who have low tolerance for ambiguity and are better able to separate cues from backgrounds may be more acutely aware of wrongdoing. Observers of wrongdoing who have higher moral judgment development may be more likely than other observers to blow the whistle, but experimental research evidence to date is mixed. Field research suggests that moral judgment regarding the particular activity observed, which may be more situationally sensitive than is a dispositional moral judgment measure or which may also capture an action orientation, is associated with whistle-blowing.

Theoretical reasons exist for suggesting that organization members who have higher levels of self-confidence or self-esteem—either in general or with regard to the specific demands of the situation—may be more likely to blow the whistle, but no research has examined this hypothesis. Although there is reason to propose that whistle-blowing would be associated with internal locus of control, the evidence to date has not supported this proposition. We have proposed that an extended sense of responsibility, or a tendency not to "live and let live," may cause whistle-blowing, but research has not examined this possibility. Research suggests that whistle-blowers are more likely than other parties to believe that whistle-blowing, in general, is desirable, but it is not clear that this was true before their whistle-blowing took place. Other authors have proposed, but no research has examined, the hypothesis that religious beliefs, combined with an action orientation, may stimulate whistle-blowing.

Hypotheses linking demographic characteristics and whistle-blowing have also developed in the literature. In general, the observed effects have been statistically significant but not large, and there is reason to believe that situational variables may interact with these personal variables, though investigations have been rare. Although there are theoretical reasons to propose that whistle-blowers may be more likely to be younger or have less service than average employees, there are also theoretical reasons to propose just the opposite. The research conducted to date supports the latter view—that whistle-blowing is slightly, but positively, associated with the age and service of the organization member. Education levels have generally been shown to be positively related to whistle-blowing. Men are somewhat more likely to blow the whistle than are women, but the reasons for this finding are not clear. The findings concerning marital status are ambiguous at this time.

Finally, we considered the role of variables pertaining to the occupational choice of, or position held by, the focal member. In general, we propose that these variables will affect the whistle-blower's perceived expected influence and power to bring about organizational change. The empirical findings generally do not support the view of the whistle-blower as a disgruntled employee (or ex-employee) who would rather complain than do his or her job. Instead, they suggest that whistle-blowers who are more satisfied and who earn higher pay levels in the organization are more likely to challenge the organization's actions. Among the most consistent of all the findings, found in research using a variety of methods, is that whistle-blowers tend to be somewhat higher performers than other organization members. However, generally, these findings have been based on self-reported performance, and thus confirmation with independent measures of performance would be beneficial. Although it can be argued that we should place little confidence in these preliminary findings because whistle-blowers may engage in self-enhancement bias, so might other organization members—and perhaps to the same extent as do whistle-blowers! If so, "puffery" would not account for the findings of a positive relationship between job performance and whistle-blowing.

Evidence suggests that supervisory status, but not necessarily hierarchical level above supervisory level, is associated with internal whistle-blowing. And, while much has been written about the professional as whistle-blower, to the seeming exclusion of the "ordinary" employee, we find little evidence linking this variable to whistle-blowing, although measures in the studies have been imperfect. Perceived role prescriptions supporting the reporting of wrongdoing appear to encourage whistle-blowing, but not necessarily internal whistle-blowing. We know of no research investigating the role of knowledge of standards concerning wrongdoing. However, research shows that whistle-blowers believe they know more about where to report wrongdoing than do other organization members.

Finally, research shows that whistle-blowers are more satisfied with their jobs than are other organization members, though they are not necessarily more satisfied with their pay. But more research is needed to confirm these findings.

In conclusion, it appears that many personal variables may be related to whistle-blowing. However, these variables may have limited effects. Of potentially greater consequence may be situation variables, or variables involving both persons and situations. These variables will be examined in chapter 4.

4

Does the Situation Affect Whistle-blowing?

We have discussed a number of personal variables thought to influence the decision to blow the whistle, but by no means are these the only important ones. As in chapter 3, we will examine some of the variables that may influence the second stage of the model developed in chapter 2. This stage involves the decision making that we believe precedes whistle-blowing. Again, we describe specific hypotheses suggested by the model and by research conducted in whistle-blowing contexts or studies of related phenomena. We describe the outcomes and implications of the research, which of course is limited in the ways described in chapter 3. In this chapter, we will examine additional variables that may affect whistle-blowing.

Figure 4–1 depicts an abbreviated version of the decision process described earlier. In figure 4–1, situational variables that may influence this process also appear; we attempted to show the direction of the relationships proposed in the research literature. More detail as to whether the research is supportive of the hypothesized relationship of each variable to whistle-blowing will follow.

Situational Variables That May Affect Whistle-blowing

Variables Pertaining to the Wrongdoing

Both the quality of evidence concerning wrongdoing and the characteristics of wrongdoing may affect whistle-blowing. In the following pages we discuss their impact.

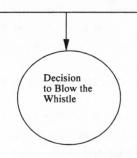

Situational Variables

Variables Pertaining to the Wrongdoing

•More evidence concerning wrongdoing
•More serious wrongdoing
•Illegal wrongdoing
•Prevalence of other types of wrongdoing

Variables Pertaining to the Focal Member's Immediate Work or Social Environment

•Field vs. home office location
•Less role overload
•Group norms and power supporting whistle-blowing
•Low status of the wrongdoer
•High social support outside the organization

Organizational Signals Concerning Likely Reactions to Whistle-blowing

•Potential organizational responsiveness
•Potential responsiveness of complaint recipients
•Potential outcomes benefiting the whistle-blower (e.g., cash awards)
•Low threatened retaliation

Other Organizational and Environmental Characteristics

•Larger organization size and less bureaucracy
•Supportive organization climate and culture
•Organizational codes of ethics encouraging whistle-blowing
•More highly regulated industry
•Organizational environment (less criticality of wrongdoing for organizational survival; societal culture supporting whistle-blowing)

Step 1: Recognition: Is focal member (FM) aware of wrongdoing?

Step 2: Assessment: Does FM consider wrongdoing deserving of action?

Step 3: Responsibility: Does FM consider himself or herself responsible for action?

Step 4: Choice of Action: Does the FM believe that:
(a) at least one political behavior alternative (PBA) is available?
(b) the PBA under consideration (e.g., whistle-blowing) is more appropriate than another action?
(c) the benefits of engaging in the PBA under consideration outweigh the costs?

Decision to Blow the Whistle

FIGURE 4–1

Situational Variables Hypothesized to Affect the Decision to Blow the Whistle

QUALITY OF THE EVIDENCE CONCERNING THE WRONGDOING.
The literature on norm conformity suggests that the quality of the evidence showing wrongdoing has taken place will influence whistle-blowing (Greenberger et al., 1987), primarily through the recognition and assessment steps in the decision model (figure 4–1). Research on conformity suggests that group members may convince the focal member that an activity constituting wrongdoing has not

occurred, particularly where evidence of the stimulus event is ambiguous, because ambiguity may be associated with lower levels of
deviance from norms (Greenberger et al., 1987). Where stimuli are
ambiguous, the group is more powerful in influencing members'
interpretations. But where evidence of wrongdoing is less ambiguous, the group may be less powerful in influencing members to
ignore the activity or define it to be acceptable. On the other hand,
Berry (1990) argued that sometimes highly ambiguous wrongdoing
can be very serious, as in the case of malpractice. Hence, it is important to separate conceptually the nature of the evidence from the
nature of the wrongdoing. That is, if it is clear that an event *occurred,* then the *evidence* is unambiguous, but if it is not clear
whether the event *constitutes wrongdoing,* then the event itself is
ambiguous. We would expect more whistle-blowing where the evidence that wrongdoing has occurred is clear or direct. This result
has been found (Miceli & Near, 1985), although the observed effects were not strong.

CHARACTERISTICS OF THE WRONGDOING

Seriousness of Wrongdoing. The empirical literature on prosocial
behavior reveals that the seriousness of the incident requiring help
is associated with helping (Dozier & Miceli, 1985). Similarly, an
organizational activity with serious consequences, such as the failure to correct a faulty automobile-axle design, may trigger more
decision making concerning whistle-blowing than does a less serious event (Graham, 1984, 1986). Although there may be many
ways to view wrongdoing seriousness, here we refer to the extent to
which a particular wrongful activity recurs or involves substantial
financial consequences. Later, we consider the nature or the type of
wrongdoing.

The seriousness of wrongdoing probably affects all four steps of
the decision process; it may increase the awareness of the wrongdoing and whether it is considered deserving of action; and it may
cause the focal member to believe he or she is responsible for acting
on it. Seriousness may affect the choice of actions (step 4) by suggesting (a) that others will respond to a complaint (Near & Miceli,
1985); (b) that whistle-blowing is justified because of the wrong-

doing's consequences; and (c) that the benefits of problem correction will outweigh its costs. Consistent with this reasoning, empirical evidence suggests that societal and managerial approval of whistle-blowing increases when wrongdoing is serious (Clinard, 1983; Ricklefs, 1984). Also, the relationship between seriousness and managerial approval of whistle-blowing suggests that manifestations of disapproval, that is, retaliation, would be less likely to occur when wrongdoing is serious. This suggests that the more serious the wrongdoing, the more likely it will be reported.

Further, Glauser (1982, p. 19) noted that "relevant and important messages, as perceived by the subordinate, tend to be communicated up the hierarchy more frequently than irrelevant and unimportant messages." These results imply that seriousness of the wrongdoing would be associated with *internal* whistle-blowing in particular.

On the other hand, the seriousness of the perceived wrongdoing may suggest the extent to which the organization may depend on perceived wrongdoing and consequently, its resistance to changing the objectionable practice. This would reduce the perceived efficacy of whistle-blowing and may increase the perceived likelihood of retaliation. Thus, individuals may resolve the conflicting consequences that may result from reporting serious wrongdoing within the organization by reporting it *externally*. Outsiders may be more responsive when wrongdoing is serious than when it is not, because (a) they are not dependent on the wrongdoing and (b) acting on it may be approved of by society (Clinard, 1983; Ricklefs, 1984). Observers may reason that, unlike insiders, outsiders have no greater motivation to retaliate when wrongdoing is serious, and outsiders may be able to offer some protection from internal retaliation by making insiders aware that the public is watching (Parmerlee et al., 1982).

Consistent with this reasoning, Miceli and Near (1985) found that wrongdoing seriousness was associated with whistle-blowing in general, and that the most serious wrongdoing was reported to *external* parties. On the other hand, in a study involving vignettes presented to U.S. marketing managers (Fritzsche, 1988), seriousness was unrelated to respondents' intentions to blow the whistle to external parties.

Finally, one study examined the relationship between seriousness and anonymous whistle-blowing. If a focal member believes that observers are responsible for reporting wrongdoing but that the organization would retaliate against whistle-blowers, these beliefs cause motivational conflicts. Earlier, we stated that one might report externally. But external reporting may lead to even more retaliation, because it may be threatening to the organization. An alternative way to resolve these conflicts is through acting anonymously (Miceli, Roach & Near, 1988). Elliston (1982a) suggested that the moral justification for anonymous whistle-blowing exists when wrongdoing is serious. Despite this, whistle-blowers were *more* likely to identify themselves when the wrongdoing was serious (Miceli et al., 1988). It may be that when one reports wrongdoing anonymously, one jeopardizes the complaint's chances of success, because the complaint recipient cannot obtain additional information from the complainant, or because the complaint loses credibility if the complainant refuses to identify himself or herself. Moreover, in all studies, seriousness was measured primarily in terms of financial consequences, but we do not know how seriousness in terms of environmental damage, personal health, or other consequences might affect whistle-blowing. These empirical questions remain for future research.

The Nature or Type of Wrongdoing. Research shows the public perceives that corporate crimes causing bodily harm are more deserving of severe punishment than are most forms of street crime (for example, Braithwaite, 1982; Mathews, 1987) or financial crime (Spencer & Wokutch, 1984). According to Davidson and Worrell (1988, p. 199), some organizational crimes "may be intrinsically bad and may harm society in general; polluting is an example. Other crimes may be designed as such because the government has been pressured to so label them; antitrust violations are an example." Although one may question how crimes come to be viewed as "intrinsically bad" as opposed to "designated as bad," Davidson's and Worrell's opinions are consistent with the hypothesis that individuals' or society's view of the nature of "badness" may influence how an activity is viewed (step 1 of the decision process) and how individuals define an appropriate response to it (step 4 of the decision process).

Sitkin (1986) has proposed that individuals may be more likely to report "secrets" to parties outside the organization when these individuals view the activities as being legitimate for outsiders to know. For example, it may be illegitimate for an employee of a paint manufacturer to share with outsiders confidential personnel records or patented paint formulas, but if the formulas contain illegal toxins or if the records reveal unfair discrimination, they may not be viewed as legitimate "secrets" deserving of protection from revelation. Likewise, a review of legal protections and a survey of employees suggest that both are more supportive of whistle-blowing when the wrongdoing is illegal as opposed to unethical (Callahan, 1990). Where there are no laws proscribing a particular activity, it may be less clear to parties outside the organization that wrongdoing has occurred. External reporting may seem more justifiable where the wrongdoing is illegal, because society has acted to stop the particular activity, such as discrimination, through the establishment of agencies to receive complaints. This suggests that wrongdoing involving a violation of law (such as involving theft, unsafe products or working conditions, or illegitimate personnel practices) may be more likely than other types of wrongdoing to be reported, particularly outside the organization.

One study has reported results bearing on these propositions. Illegal wrongdoing was no more likely to be reported than was wrongdoing objectionable on other grounds; but external channels were used when the wrongdoing involved theft (Miceli, Near & Schwenk, 1991). There was no relationship between external whistle-blowing and whether the wrongdoing involved other types of illegal activity.

Prevalence of Other Types of Wrongdoing. There is some question as to whether the existence of widespread, varied wrongdoing in the organization would increase whistle-blowing. On the one hand, it may increase the likelihood that any one incident is reported, because members may eventually find that "enough is enough." On the other hand, it may depress whistle-blowing, because it implies that wrongdoing is tolerated.

There is evidence that the extent to which wrongdoing is commonplace in a particular organization varies substantially by organization. Research is consistent in showing that the rate of organizational wrongdoing is partly a function of industry and organization characteristics. Organizational crime rates vary by industry (Baucus & Near, 1991; Cressy, 1976; Mathews, 1987). Mathews (1987) found that the type of industry had a far greater impact on violations than did a code of ethics. Industries with a higher number of violations and a high level of recidivism were those in the food, drug, and medical instrument and supply industries. She speculated that this may have occurred because of closer scrutiny by the Food and Drug Administration, or because there are more issues or more unethical behavior patterns in these industries.

Similarly, survey research in the U.S. federal government sector shows that the incidence of waste, fraud, mismanagement, and related wrongdoing as perceived by employees varies dramatically by agency (MSPB, 1981, 1984). Surveys concerning sexual harassment show similar results (MSPB, 1988).

Where many incidents of wrongdoing occur in certain organizations (or industries), whistle-blowing may be more likely because it may be harder to ignore or redefine multiple wrongdoing incidents (step 2). On the other hand, the prevalence of various types of wrongdoing may convey a norm of acceptability of wrongful behavior, or it may indicate that the organization is dependent on wrongdoing to survive. If so, whistle-blowing may be less likely, at least to parties within the organization (step 4).

Unfortunately, we have little evidence about the effect of rates of organizational wrongdoing on whistle-blowing. We found that a high incidence of perceived wrongdoing, measured at the organizational level as the percentage of all survey respondents who said they observed any wrongdoing, was weakly associated with external whistle-blowing (Miceli & Near, 1985). We also examined this question at the individual level, that is, respondents were asked how many different types of questionable incidents they had observed in the preceding twelve months. Respondents who saw more incidents were more likely to report the one incident they saw as most serious or most directly affecting them than were respondents who saw fewer incidents. This provides some support for the first of the two hypotheses previously described.

Variables Pertaining to the Focal Member's Immediate Work or Social Environment Office Location

Conceivably, being located at a home office, as opposed to a field or regional office, may encourage whistle-blowing, because the communications concerning channels may be more complete there (step 4). To the contrary, Keenan (1990a) found that first-level managers who worked at the home office believed that the organization provided less encouragement of, and less information about, whistle-blowing than did managers located in field or regional offices. However, this study did not examine whether these managers were consequently less likely to blow the whistle.

ROLE OVERLOAD. For focal members to be able to detect wrongdoing, they must have sufficient access to information suggesting that wrongdoing is occurring (step 1). But where members experience role overload, they have a larger number of assigned tasks than time in which to perform them, so scrutiny of their work or their environment may not be as careful as where time resources are plentiful. Thus, wrongdoing may not be detected in "lean" organizations because members may be so busy with their own activities that they cannot attend to wrongdoing or follow up signals that wrongdoing may be occurring. If there is no inducement for members to monitor others' activities or organizational actions, doing so represents a cost in terms of time away from performing rewarded duties (step 4). For all these reasons, we would predict that role overload would be negatively associated with whistle-blowing. Unfortunately, no research examining the proposed linkage between role overload and whistle-blowing has been conducted.

GROUP NORMS AND POWER. Research suggests that the presence and behavior of others, such as co-workers in the organization, may have an impact on whistle-blowing. Where other parties present confirm the observation of wrongdoing and suggest that observers have the responsibility to act, they may exert social influence. Consistent with this view, subjects were more likely to turn in shoplifters (who were confederates) when other shoppers (who also were confederates) commented that they too saw the shoplifter and together they had the responsibility to act (Bickman & Rosenbaum,

1977). Similarly, a confederate clerk's request for confirmation also increased reporting (Dertke, Penner & Ulrich, 1974). Interestingly, these findings suggest that a norm supporting the acceptance of responsibility (step 3) may be made salient by one influence agent's comments, even if that agent has no apparent power over the target. Thus, it would be helpful to examine research on social influence in groups.

That groups develop and attempt to enforce norms about appropriate behavior is well documented (Greenberger et al., 1987). Groups norms may define wrongdoing in ways that differ from the perception that the focal member would form in isolation (apart from the influence of the group) (step 1). For example, using the company's long-distance telephone lines for personal calls (or copier machine for personal letters or recipes) may be defined as a "perquisite" by the individual, but as "embezzlement" by the group. Similarly, groups may vary in the norms they develop. Careless or deliberate incorrect charging of work hours toward one project when they were actually used for another may be acceptable. In another group, these activities may clearly violate norms.

Group norms may interact with the power of the group to enforce norms (and perhaps other variables) to produce or inhibit whistle-blowing (Greenberger et al., 1987). That is, a powerful group that accepts certain wrongdoing may inhibit whistle-blowing; a powerful group that proscribes it may experience infrequent norm violations, but when they occur, whistle-blowing occurs. The norms of a group that is less powerful may be irrelevant to whistle-blowing. Groups are particularly powerful when focal members are highly dependent on them, as when the group provides valued rewards or information, where tasks are interdependent, where the majority is highly credible, and where the focal member feels insecure (Greenberger et al., 1985).

However, in many instances, there may be limited interaction with other organization members who may have observed the same incident of questionable activity observed by the focal member. Early research (for example, Latané & Darley, 1968) suggested that where observers of wrongdoing are aware of other bystanders, they are less likely to intervene than when they believe they are alone, because of the "diffusion of responsibility" for intervention. Research on the "diffusion of responsibility" effect on bystander intervention has shown, generally, that the larger the group of bystanders, the less likely any one bystander is to engage in the prosocial behavior of offering a victim help in an emergency (as in Latané & Darley, 1970).

Such research suggests that whistle-blowing will be more likely to occur where few organization members could have observed wrongdoing (Dozier & Miceli, 1985; Graham, 1986). That is, if others are aware, one may reason that one is less responsible for acting because, conceivably, someone else could intervene (step 3), whereas if one is alone no action will be taken if not by the sole observer.

But preliminary results in whistle-blowing contexts suggest that the *opposite* effect occurs (Miceli & Near, 1988a; Miceli, Dozier & Near, 1991), though this research focused primarily on reporting to parties *internal* to the organization. In these studies, observers of wrongdoing were more likely to blow the whistle when *more*, rather than fewer, other observers were present. The fact that one result was obtained in a controlled experiment suggests that the survey result is not attributable to self-report bias.

It might be argued that, in whistle-blowing contexts, observers were influenced differently than in emergency interventions because the presence of additional others increases the possibility that at least one other person would report the wrongdoing, thus implying that the nonreporting subject is a moral failure. However, this speculation is questionable for at least three reasons. First, the *same* reasoning could be used to suggest that bystanders would be more likely to report crime when more others are present. But this is *opposite* to the effect that has been observed in bystander intervention studies. Second, in Miceli, Dozier, and Near (1991), the subjects were anonymous to the wrongdoer and to the complaint recipient at the time of reporting, and the reporting opportunity was designed so that subjects could not be aware of whether others had reported the wrongdoing, precisely to minimize the social impact. Therefore, no one could learn who had failed to report the wrongdoing, and the nonreporter would be unlikely to fear that someone could identify and humiliate him or her. Third, unlike reporting obvious criminal assault to the police, which most persons would agree is morally correct, as noted earlier, whistle-blowing frequently may raise moral conflicts. Different parties may view it to be appropriate under different circumstances. Thus, a nonreporting subject could believe that others might not condemn his or her refusal to be a "fink." It is therefore unlikely that the fear of potential embarrassment accounted for the whistle-blowing results.

On the other hand, the whistle-blowing results are consistent with Latané's (1981) social impact theory, which views social influence to be a function of the number of sources of influence (and other factors). Unfortunately, this theory does not specify the *direction* of influence: Alone, it is of limited value in predicting reactions to whistle-blowing, because it does not attempt to explain the conditions under which others may influence the observer of wrongdoing to report or to refrain from reporting. However, we can speculate that if (a) the wrongdoer is viewed as an influence agent discouraging whistle-blowing and (b) the other members of the group were influence agents potentially *supporting* whistle-blowing, then the other members' influence would be less powerful in smaller rather than larger groups, because the number of sources is smaller. Or perhaps, observers of wrongdoing fear that their reports would be less easily corroborated when few observers are present, that the foundation for their accusations would be viewed as "your word against his." A third possibility may be that it would be easier for the wrongdoer to identify and retaliate against subjects in smaller groups.

A fourth possibility is consistent with later research on prosocial intervention, which suggested that the existence of other conditions may moderate the diffusion of responsibility effect. Where the observer is a member of either (a) a *large, tightly knit* group of co-workers who observe a serious act, or (b) a small group of relative strangers, the focal member will feel greater personal responsibility for taking action than where other situational conditions prevail (Rutkowski, Gruder & Romer, 1983; Senneker & Hendrick, 1983). Thus, it is possible that where groups are cohesive and supportive of whistle-blowing, the size of the group will be positively associated with whistle-blowing.

One recent study did show some support for the original "diffusion of responsibility" hypothesis, however. More whistle-blowing occurred when there were fewer other observers, particularly to external parties (Miceli, Near & Schwenk, 1991). The present results taken together with prior results suggest that the presence of other observers may affect internal and external whistle-blowing differently; the diffusion of responsibility effect here was more pronounced for external whistle-blowers. More research is needed to determine the precise nature of the relationship between the presence of other observers and whistle-blowing to various parties.

STATUS OF THE WRONGDOER. The research on prosocial behavior reveals that a norm against "finking"—reporting wrongdoing behind the wrongdoer's back—may exist, at least under certain conditions. Harari and McDavid (1969) examined the propensity of children with knowledge about a guilty peer (a confederate) to report wrongdoing when questioned by an adult. Every subject incriminated the wrongdoer-confederate when the latter was present. However, subjects were *less* likely to report when the wrongdoer was of *high* status, and only the authority and an innocent peer were present (Harari & McDavid, 1969). The authors interpreted the results as suggesting that the situation poses moral conflict; "the conflict then becomes not whether or not to be moral—but how to decide between two contending moral principles: not to lie (or to disobey), or not to 'fink' on a peer" (1969, p. 240). The norm against finking on a *high*-status peer behind his or her back may be more compelling than the principle not to lie or disobey (Dozier & Miceli, 1985).

However, the results can be interpreted as a cost-benefit analysis involving expected retaliation rather than a struggle of moral values and norms (Dozier & Miceli, 1985). Retaliation may be directed at whistle-blowers by several parties, including the wrongdoer(s), by co-workers, or by members of the managerial hierarchy. In this case, fear of the wrath of the wrongdoer may have influenced action. Because the authority questioned several children, subjects who were alone with the authority could report without being identified by the wrongdoer. When questioned in the presence of an innocent peer who might tell others of the "finking," some subjects may have been reluctant to take the chance that a high-status wrongdoer might retaliate at some later date. The hazard would be lower when implicating a socially weak, low-status peer.

This interpretation of the results suggests that the status of the wrongdoers or their ability to exact revenge may be weighed by observers of wrongdoing before acting (step 4). If so, then whistle-blowing may be less likely when the wrongdoer is of higher rather than lower status. One study (Miceli, Near & Schwenk, 1991) found support for this notion, but for external whistle-blowing only.

SOCIAL SUPPORT OUTSIDE THE ORGANIZATION. Observers of wrongdoing with social or financial support from family or friends could be expected to blow the whistle at higher rates than those lacking such support (Weinstein, 1979). Where support is provided by spouses or other family members, the dependence of the whistle-blower on the organization is decreased. This support may reduce the cost of whistle-blowing (step 4), or it may strengthen the focal member's belief that she or he has made the right decision at any other step. One study of whistle-blowers found that virtually all had received emotional support from family or friends (Near, Parmerlee, White & Jensen, 1981). However, because no comparative data were available, it is not clear to what extent this is unique to whistle-blowers.

Organizational and Environmental Variables

ORGANIZATION SIGNALS CONCERNING LIKELY REACTIONS TO WHISTLE-BLOWING. These variables can be classified as responses to the wrongdoing—potential organizational responsiveness in terms of correcting wrongdoing in general, and responses more specifically aimed at potential whistle-blowers, that is, incentives and threatened retaliation.

Potential Organizational Responsiveness. Prosocial actions are influenced by the extent to which the actor feels capable of bringing about change (Dozier & Miceli, 1985). Similarly, in organizational settings, if observers of wrongdoing do not believe that powerful authorities—when notified—will be willing and able to correct the wrongdoing, then whistle-blowing is not a feasible or reasonable option for them (step 4). Consistent with this proposition, Miceli and Near (1984) found that observers of wrongdoing, particularly whistle-blowers, were slightly more likely than nonobservers to agree that corrective action would encourage them to blow the whistle.

However, the operationalization of this construct at the individual level can be problematic, because of possible post-decisional justification (Salancik & Pfeffer, 1978). If observers of wrongdoing are asked retrospectively to explain their responses to wrongdoing, whistle-blowers may say that they acted because they knew they could make a difference, while observers who did not blow the whistle may rationalize their inaction by stating that they did not think blowing the whistle would make a difference. This problem can be solved through measurement of inactive observers' perceptions in general. That is, if a high proportion of organization members who observed wrongdoing, but did not act, agree that corrective action would or could not be taken on a variety of problems (rather than select *other* reasons for their inaction), then it is more likely that the perceived intractability of management is real.

We used this method to compare the potential organizational responsiveness among fifteen organizations in the 1980 MSPB data set and among twenty-two agencies in the 1983 MSPB data set. We found that, in both analyses, perceived organizational responsiveness was positively associated with whistle-blowing. Thus, a general, shared perception that organizations would respond to complaints by correcting wrongdoing may lead to a greater propensity to blow the whistle on the part of individual members who observe wrongdoing.

Several recent studies have examined the methods organizations may use to suggest that they would be responsive to internal reporting. Keenan (1990b) surveyed upper-level managers about the policies and practices regarding wrongdoing (for example, whether the organization has a written policy, conducts regular reviews on what actions to take, and has a watchdog department or person concerned with the issue of whistle-blowing). He found that existence of these policies and practices, and lower feared retaliation, was associated with positive perceptions about the adequacy of company encouragement of whistle-blowing. He did not examine whistle-blowing, itself, as a dependent variable, however.

In another survey-based study, Barnett, Cochran, and Taylor (1990) examined the effects of internal dissent policies on internal and external whistle-blowing, as perceived by approximately three hundred personnel executives. Most respondents said their organizations had formal internal dissent policies, in contrast to Keenan (1990b), who found that most upper-level executives said these policies did not exist. Of the Barnett et al. (1990) sample who reported that formal policies existed, most said if employees were to report wrongdoing to a designated office, the policy promised retaliation would not occur, and there was an appeal procedure. About 76 percent of these respondents said policies had been developed since 1980.

There was support for the hypothesis that, in those organizations with developed policies, personnel executives perceived an increase in internal whistle-blowing, and a decrease in external whistle-blowing, following policy implementation. Organizations where there was no such policy were likely to experience lower levels of internal whistle-blowing, but there was no relationship between policy existence and external whistle-blowing. Existence of a policy was related to perceptions of greater managerial responsiveness to complaints, which in turn was related to higher levels of internal whistleblowing. However, responsiveness was unrelated to external whistle-blowing. These findings provide preliminary support for the view that there are actions organizations can take to encourage internal whistle-blowing. As the authors pointed out, future research is needed to address the issue of whether the *manner* in which management responds to a whistle-blower may be as important as the existence of formal policies and procedures. This emphasis on processes, as opposed to an emphasis strictly on the outcomes of the complaint—whether the wrongdoing is terminated and whether the whistle-blower experiences retaliation, is reminiscent of the research on procedural and interactional justice (for example, Bies, 1987). This literature emphasizes the critical effects of not only the actions taken and how they are played out, but how they are communicated to organization members. Clearly, more development of this important topic is needed.

Potential Responsiveness of Complaint Recipients. We classify variables pertaining to the focal member's perceptions of complaint recipients as situational variables, because we believe that these perceptions are largely a function of cues in the environment rather than a "steady state" that may exist in the focal member. Here, also, we are describing perceptions concerning a specific party rather than perceptions about the organization in general.

Both Graham (1986) and we (Near & Miceli, 1985) proposed that perceived protection from retaliation and perceived likelihood of the organization's self-correction would affect whistle-blowing (Blackburn, 1988) (step 4 of the decision model). Presumably, the characteristics of complaint recipients within the organization suggest the extent to which it may be protective and self-correcting. However, research is not entirely consistent with this reasoning. Blackburn (1988) found that employees who expressed concerns believed the complaint recipient was more responsive to concerns than inactive observers did, but they perceived *less* responsiveness than did the nonobservers. Because the data were retrospective, it is difficult to interpret them. It may be that initially, the whistle-blowers thought the recipient would be responsive but were somewhat disappointed after filing a complaint—though not as cynical as the inactive observers.

Perceptions of complaint channels may also affect the decision to remain anonymous while reporting wrongdoing. Frequently, it is not possible to remain anonymous, because the reporter of wrongdoing has information that can be traced to him or her. Although one may question why anyone would assume the risks of identifying themselves if anonymous whistle-blowing *is* possible, whistle-blowers may believe that doing so would increase their efficacy. They may forego the protection of anonymity so that the complaint recipient can seek additional information from them later if necessary. Consistent with this logic, anonymous whistle-blowers who used internal channels had more faith than did identified whistle-blowers that the recipient would take corrective action in response to anonymous complaints (Miceli et al., 1988). Anonymous whistle-blowing may be a function of trust in the complaint recipient's promise of confidentiality, that is, if whistle-blowers believe their identities might be revealed by the complaint recipient. In this case, identifying oneself may represent an appropriate defensive strategy. Presumably, the complaint recipient's history of trustworthiness would play an important role.

One final point is that one can remain anonymous with respect to everyone *except* the complaint recipient, or one can remain anonymous with respect to the complaint recipient also. For example, organization members can usually report wrongdoing to an internal auditor without revealing their identities to other members of the organization. Research is needed to determine the circumstances under which one might choose either of these types of anonymity.

Potential Outcomes Benefiting the Whistle-blower. Earlier it was argued that whistle-blowers, like other prosocial actors, can pursue ends that benefit themselves as well as others. Frequently, whistle-blowers can benefit by the cessation of wrongdoing. It may be that potential personal benefits encourage whistle-blowing because the expected benefits may ultimately outweigh the expected costs (step 4). Consistent with this proposition, Miceli and Near (1985) found some evidence that corrective action benefiting the observer was associated with whistle-blowing. Respondents were considered to have benefited when the problem they exposed had "the greatest impact on me" as opposed to being "the most serious problem" about which they had evidence (MSPB, 1981).

If the organization is dependent on a questionable practice, it may provide cues that whistle-blowing will be met with resistance to changing the questioned practice (Near & Miceli, 1985). On the other hand, if the organization wants to encourage whistle-blowing and wrongdoing correction, it may offer inducements for internal whistle-blowing, for example, in the form of cash incentives. But at this time, there is little evidence that such incentives are effective, primarily because little investigation has been conducted into incentive programs. Federal whistle-blowers have been potentially eligible for such awards for some time (MSPB, 1981). However, a Congressional investigation indicated that only one segment of the federal government that has the incentive program actually paid awards (Kasich, 1988). Ironically, this active program is administered within the Defense Department, which frequently is the subject of news stories reporting scandals involving payments to contractors. Thus, administrative problems or insufficient funding may account for the limited known success of such programs.

On the other hand, other evidence suggests that providing some types of incentives may in fact increase whistle-blowing. Specifically, as discussed in chapter 6, whistle-blowing cases increased following the implementation of a program to allow the whistle-blower to receive a portion of the amounts recovered from wrongdoers.

Some organization members may consider payments inappropriate for "moral" actions such as whistle-blowing. Miceli and Near (1984) found that nonobservers of wrongdoing were more likely than observers to agree that financial incentives were inappropriate. Nonobservers and whistle-blowers were less likely than inactive observers to believe that financial incentives would encourage them to blow the whistle. Keenan (1988a) found that only one of 139 first-level managers sampled indicated that the availability of monetary rewards for whistle-blowing would most encourage him or her to blow the whistle. Other incentives included seeing the problem corrected (selected by 51 percent of the respondents); observing a serious problem (16 percent); being able to blow the whistle anonymously (13 percent); being protected from reprisal (10 percent); and having co-worker approval (10 percent). Clearly, research is needed as to the potential effect of incentives on whistle-blowing.

Threatened Retaliation. If an organization depends on a questionable practice, it may provide cues that whistle-blowing will be met with retaliation to whistle-blowers (Near & Miceli, 1985). Threatened retaliation or other indications that retaliation might follow whistle-blowing may increase the expected costs of acting (Farrell & Petersen, 1982; Dozier, 1988), which are weighed in step 4 of the decision model.

Anecdotal evidence that retaliation—which is sometimes very severe—follows whistle-blowing is abundant and has received a great deal of media attention (as in Nader et al., 1972, Peters & Branch, 1972; Westin, 1981). Consequently, many people (such as Julie, 1987) believe that retaliation invariably occurs. Despite this, whistle-blowing occurs in many organizations and is expected to increase in frequency (Ewing, 1983). Therefore, it is important to consider more fully the relationship between threatened retaliation and whistle-blowing.

Bandura's (1977) research provides one theoretical framework for understanding this concern. It is possible to use other frameworks, such as reinforcement theory (as in Skinner, 1953), but only if reference is made to stimulus control; we refer here to *expected* consequences rather than to the effects of experienced retaliation. We rely on Bandura simply because more readers may be familiar with his propositions than with stimulus control propositions, but the predicted relationships among variables would be the same.

Bandura proposed that if individuals' desire and ability to manipulate the environment, or "self-efficacy," is essential to their well-being, then they will be motivated to perform acts that demonstrate their self-efficacy. "A risk of feared consequences" and "situational uncertainty" can influence efficacy expectations (Bandura, 1977, p. 83). In the case of whistle-blowing, where wrongdoers suggest that they would react unfavorably to it, observers of wrongdoing may be discouraged from acting because such consequences would be punishing ("a risk of feared consequences"), or because it is unclear to them what the appropriate response should be ("situational uncertainty"). Consistent with this idea, previous research (cited by Trevino, 1986) shows that subjects were more likely to behave unethically if it appeared that ethical behavior would be punished. Thus, even if blowing the whistle is viewed as ethical behavior, retaliatory threats should reduce whistle-blowing.

Although the reasoning is straightforward, *not one* previous study of whistle-blowing supports it. The comprehensiveness or severity of perceived actual or threatened retaliation was unrelated to intended future whistle-blowing at the individual level (as in Near & Jensen, 1983; Near & Miceli, 1986). Miceli and Near (1984) found that inactive observers were more likely than nonobservers to perceive that if they were to blow the whistle, retaliation would follow. But whistle-blowers were just as likely to perceive a retaliatory threat as were inactive observers. In another study (Miceli & Near, 1985), a retaliatory climate (as measured by the aggregate perceptions of all respondents within a given organization) was associated with a *greater* propensity to blow the whistle to parties *external* to the organization. Extending the findings of upper-level managers primarily in private sector organizations, Keenan (1989) found that perceptions of retaliatory threats were *not* associated with feeling obliged to blow the whistle if they were to observe wrongdoing. These findings provide evidence that threatened retaliation may not dissuade whistle-blowers from acting.

However, in these survey-based studies, uncontrolled variables may have operated to obscure the relationships, and perceptions may have been distorted. For example, some whistle-blowers unknowingly may have exaggerated perceived threats or harassment.

It is also possible that, in all the cited studies, restriction of range may have attenuated the observed relationship. Self-selection by respondents (following a mailed request for participants) may have excluded many respondents who experienced no retaliation, or those who did not want to relieve a traumatic experience. In some studies, surveys never reached those who left their organizations, perhaps after being fired or experiencing other extreme forms of retaliation. But our controlled field study (Miceli, Dozier & Near, 1991), which was not subject to these design limitations, also produced the same results. This suggests that methodological shortcomings probably did not account for the results.

There is also anecdotal evidence that individual whistle-blowers knew in advance that they would likely experience retaliation but acted anyway (for example, see Glazer & Glazer, 1987). Perhaps in such cases, it is impossible for blowing the whistle to jeopardize one's job security because there is no job security. It would be better to lose one's job over a dearly held principle or over a successful intervention to save other's lives than to be fired for trivial infractions. But without empirical testing of this possibility we cannot know whether the presence or absence of job security plays a role.

Another possibility is that there is a "whistle-blowing personality" that is not dissuaded by threats of retaliation, whereas persons who do not have such a personality will act only if conditions are conducive to reporting—or not at all. Although it is highly speculative to interpret results in this way, Miceli and Near (1984) found that whistle-blowers were less likely than inactive observers and nonobservers to agree that a guarantee of anonymity would encourage them to blow the whistle. This may suggest that whistle-blowers will act regardless of the potential costs (or regardless of the protection offered by anonymity), because their personality compels them to do so—perhaps due to their need to control their environments (discussed earlier), or because of their adherence to principle, or for other reasons.

Finally, it is possible that a number of situational variables may *interact* with threatened retaliation to cause whistle-blowing. For example, if a problem is intolerable and no alternatives to whistle-blowing exist, then one may risk serious retaliation and blow the whistle (Dozier & Miceli, 1985). But if a problem is not viewed as important, or if a less risky means of resolution is available, then threatened retaliation may "chill" whistle-blowing. Thus, more research is needed to determine the role of retaliation.

OTHER ORGANIZATIONAL AND ENVIRONMENTAL CHARACTERISTICS

Organization Size and Structure. The characteristics of the organization, including its size and structure, may affect the responses of its members to wrongdoing (Graham, 1986; Near & Miceli, 1985) for several reasons. The first reason suggests that whistle-blowing may be more likely in smaller organizations (all other factors, such as incidence of wrongdoing, being equal). Large organizations are presumably less dependent on any one individual than are smaller organizations, because it may be easier for large organizations to reassign the responsibilities of an employee who exits. Therefore, individuals in large organizations may feel less influential.

For three reasons, we might expect more *internal* whistle-blowing by members of smaller organizations, all other factors being equal. First, in larger or taller organizations, organization members may be reluctant to communicate upward because communication channels may be impeded (Glauser, 1982). The upward communication literature provides evidence that the distance between parties to a communication and the number of sequential links it must travel inhibit communication flow. Since in larger organizations there may be more distance or sequential links, there may be less internal whistle-blowing in larger than in smaller organizations. Second, it may be more difficult in larger than in smaller organizations for top managers to encourage whistle-blowing by making members aware of established channels for reporting wrongdoing. If so, internal whistle-blowing would be less likely in larger organizations than in smaller organizations. Third, organization members in smaller organizations may feel greater satisfaction than those in larger organizations and therefore may choose to blow the whistle internally, because they believe this action would be less damaging than external whistle-blowing to the organization.

Evidence concerning the role of organization size is limited. The sex discrimination complainants surveyed by Parmerlee et al. (1982) represented a variety of organization types, but no comparative statistics were reported. One study found that, contrary to prediction, whistle-blowers worked in larger organizations than did inactive observers and there were no significant organization size differences between internal and external whistle-blower groups (Miceli & Near, 1985). We can speculate, based on the literature on procedural and interactional justice (such as in Bies, 1987; Greenberg, 1987) that perhaps procedures guaranteeing greater fairness in the whistle-blowing process may be more likely to exist in larger, rather than smaller, organizations. This reasoning suggests that the structure of the organization must be considered.

Organizations that are more hierarchial, bureaucratic, or authoritarian may be less open to whistle-blowing challenges (Baucus, Near & Miceli, 1985; Weinstein, 1979). Whistle-blowing represents a form of organizational dissent (Near & Miceli, 1987) and frequently, deviation from majority views (Greenberger et al., 1987). Bourgeois (1985) argued that in bureaucratic organizations facing performance declines, diversity of views may be suppressed in the belief that unity of views will improve performance. Schwenk (1988) proposed that in rigidly structured organizations where a single view predominates, dissent introduced by "devil's advocates" is likely to be ignored. An intensive study of decision making in eight organizations showed that chief executive officers (CEOs) with authoritarian decision styles were suspicious of open disagreement and regarded it as "foot dragging" (Eisenhardt & Bourgeois, 1988, pp. 743–744). Such decision styles may discourage whistle-blowing.

However, members of bureaucratic organizations who find wrongdoing intolerable may report it to parties outside the organization (to a greater extent than do members of more open organizations), because external parties may be more likely than internal parties to bring about change. In the only known study examining this proposition, Miceli, Near, and Schwenk (1991) found that whistle-blowers of all types perceived their organization to be *less* bureaucratic than did inactive observers.

However, it should be noted that our measure of organizational structure was based solely on the perception of one member of the organization and thus cannot be viewed as necessarily an accurate description of the organization. Nonetheless, it is this perception that influences and is influenced by the whistle-blower's action.

That is, even if the organization is really quite bureaucratic, yet the whistle-blower believes that the organization is actually *less* bureaucratic and *more* open to dissent, he or she may be more willing to engage in whistle-blowing behaviors. In future studies, it would be valuable to include independent measures of the level of bureaucracy or other organizational characteristics.

Organization Climate and Culture. Organizations may establish and maintain climates and cultures that support whistle-blowing, even though they may not do so by design (Near, Baucus & Miceli, 1991; Zalkind, 1988). For example, organizations could communicate that wrongdoing would not be sanctioned by formal or informal norms, that appropriate responses to those few instances of wrongdoing that might occur would be to report them, and that such reports would be taken seriously and lead to corrections without costs to reporters (Near & Miceli, 1987). Merely communicating wishes does not establish a climate or culture; the organization's communication channels and reward system operation would have to be aligned with these communications. These influences would need to work in tandem to produce lower wrongdoing, a higher proportion of reported wrongdoing, and a lower proportion of threatened retaliation. Thus, climates could affect all of the decision steps (figure 4–1).

Some empirical work to date has examined the relationship between organizational climate and the incidence of whistle-blowing. One study found that whistle-blowers who worked in organizations with more encouraging climates for whistle-blowing tended to report wrongdoing only to parties within their organizations (Miceli & Near, 1985). In a study using organizational-level measures, Baucus, Near, and Miceli (1985) found that (a) the incidence and the mean seriousness of wrongdoing, and (b) the frequency of reporting wrongdoing, were at least partly related to the culture of the organization. Furthermore, observers were more likely to report the wrongdoing internally than to remain silent or report it externally, when the culture was more supportive of whistle-blowing—where it was less retaliatory and less tolerant of wrongdoing.

Keenan (1988a) examined the perceptions of first level managers in a variety of organizations with respect to climates and whistle-blowing. He administered the thirty-six-item Communication Climate Inventory (Costigan & Schmeidler, 1984), which is based on Gibb's (1961) theory of communication climate. This theory characterizes supportive climates as oriented toward "provisionalism, empathy, equality, spontaneity, problem orientation, and description," while defensive climates have "evaluation, control, strategy, neutrality, superiority, and certainty" (Keenan, 1988a, p. 247). The two subscales, both of which showed excellent reliability but for which no correlation was reported, were related to perceptions of the likelihood of retaliation and to whistle-blowing. Specifically, less-defensive and more-supportive climates were associated with managers' greater confidence that they would not experience retaliation, were they to blow the whistle. Inactive observers tended to work in climates that were more defensive than those perceived by nonobservers and whistle-blowers, and less supportive than those perceived by nonobservers. There were no differences in climates perceived by nonobservers and whistle-blowers.

Blackburn (1988) and Graham (1986) also proposed that more supportive climates would lead to more whistle-blowing. Blackburn (1988) found that individuals who expressed employee concerns (and nonobservers) had more positive views of management in general than did employees who remained silent; for example, they believed that management was selected on the basis of skills and qualifications, that management cared about employees, and that management could be counted on to do what they said. (She considered this a "climate" variable.) The comparison group of nonobservers were more positive than whistle-blowers concerning management in general.

Blackburn found that employees who voiced concerns viewed top management more positively and perceived a more participatory climate, than did those who were silent. The comparison group of nonobservers were more positive than whistle-blowers concerning management in general and participatory climate, but no different concerning perceptions of top management. These findings are particularly interesting because all the data were gathered in one organization, that is, all were perceiving the same top management. Thus, organizations must concern themselves not only with actual top management behavior but also with employee perceptions of that behavior.

Creating a climate supportive of whistle-blowing as well as of the exercise of other employee rights may have desirable consequences aside from encouraging whistle-blowing. Two studies (Gorden, Infante & Graham, 1988; Zalkind, 1987) found that more favorable climates for whistle-blowing or employee rights led to enhanced satisfaction with the organization.

Organizational Codes of Ethics. One aspect related to the climate that may influence the assessment of wrongdoing and responsibility for action as well as the likelihood of correction (that is, all steps in the decision process) may be reflected in codes of ethics. Organizations may have varied reasons for establishing codes of ethics. First, they may believe that doing so is morally correct. Second, they may believe that encouraging ethical behavior is "good business." According to a recent survey by Touche Ross & Co., two-thirds of the corporate executives questioned believed that high ethical standards improve a company's competitive position ("Ethics pay . . . ," 1987). Third, and perhaps more cynically, organizations may adopt codes of ethics because they want to forestall outsiders' attempts to legislate or regulate their activities. Black (1976) has suggested that regulation varies inversely with other forms of social control, including codes of conduct (Mathews, 1987). In short, codes of ethics may be used to "buy" legitimacy for the organization in its environment.

The cynical perspective, unfortunately, has some empirical support. Mathews (1987) undertook a content analysis of codes of ethics of the most profitable U.S. manufacturing corporations with over $100 million in annual sales. She found (p. 115) that "desirable behavior pertaining to consumers and the general public— product safety, product quality, environmental affairs, relations with consumers, and civic and community affairs—was discussed in the codes much less frequently than was either conduct against the firm or other activities—such as bribery or questionable payments—on behalf of the firm." This raises doubt as to whether many codes of ethics provide a framework for evaluating whether all activities within the organization are ethical. More commonly, they appear to be intended to discourage only those activities that might harm the organization. Perhaps not surprisingly, she found that there was little relationship between codes of conduct and corporate legal violations, contrary to the notion that the codes serve as an effective form of self-regulation.

Top management plays a critical role in encouraging ethical behavior in organizations, that is, in making the codes of ethics meaningful. Organizational policies even where committed to writing will likely have little effect if top managers show through their behavior that ethical behavior will not be reinforced (for example, Baldwin & Baldwin, 1981; Ouchi, 1981). Thus, top managers serve as role models (for example, Bandura, 1977) for other members of the organization (Mathews, 1987). However, there is no research in whistle-blowing contexts concerning the efficacy of codes of ethics or the influence of top management, and so research in these areas would be valuable.

Industry. As noted earlier, levels of wrongdoing may vary by organization or industry. Similarly, the propensity to blow the whistle may also vary, for two reasons. First, as described in chapter 6 of this book, the existence of regulatory pressures on organizations or legal protections for whistle-blowers may encourage whistle-blowing. Whistle-blowers may be more powerful when whistle-blowing is legally encouraged through the establishment of offices to serve as complaint recipients, or through regulatory agencies for reporting wrongdoing (step 4 of the decision process). The Civil Service Report Act of 1978 established "hot lines" and created agencies and subunits to protect federal employees against retaliation when they blow the whistle on wrongdoing in their agencies (MSPB, 1981). Similarly, more highly regulated industries, such as financial services and insurance, may experience more external whistle-blowing because of the existence of regulatory agencies to whom observers of wrongdoing might logically and more easily report. A report by the Panel on Government and the Regulation of Corporate and Individual Decisions (1980, pp. 60–62 and 67–70) supports this speculation by providing a discussion of some of the agencies responsible for regulation in the financial services and insurance industries and the uncertainty associated with regulatory changes. This uncertainty may increase external scrutiny of these organizations. The extent of this scrutiny and the reasons for it were documented in a recent *Wall Street Journal* article ("GAO says ...," 1989). Finally, the legal protection for whistle-blowing or media attention to the codes of ethics in certain industries may suggest to some employees that ethical behavior is expected and will be rewarded.

Second, the workforce attracted to certain industries may be different from that attracted to other industries. Individuals who join federal sector organizations may believe that such organizations are somehow shielded from the pressures for unethical resolution of competitive conflicts. This would reduce the expected costs of blowing the whistle (step 4). On the other hand, many of the best-known whistle-blowers have been federal employees who have suffered retaliation.

There is some empirical support for the idea that industry is related to whistle-blowing. In one study (Miceli, Near & Schwenk, 1991), external channels were more likely to be used by respondents from government agencies and from the financial industries. There are at least three possible explanations for this finding, although all must be viewed as highly speculative due to the exploratory nature of research on industry. First, it may be that the total amount of wrongdoing is greater in these organizations than in others and that wrongdoing is more accepted in these organizations. Tacit acceptance of such wrongdoing by the companies involved would discourage internal reporting and leave whistle-blowers with only one option—external reporting. This explanation seems more compelling in the case of financial services companies than government organizations. Frequent media reports of spectacular examples of wrongdoing by companies in this industry would seem to be consistent with this explanation. However, it seems less likely that the amount of wrongdoing is greater in government organizations than in most private organizations.

Second, these organizations may be more subject to external scrutiny than are companies in other industries (Swartz & Smith, 1988). In the case of financial services and insurance companies, regulatory agencies that have jurisdiction over companies may be more easily identified than in other industries. Further, there is more frequent contact between the agencies and the companies, which would also increase scrutiny of their operations by the regulatory agency. In the case of government organizations, high levels of external scrutiny would be expected because of the public service function of these organizations and the need for constituents to monitor their performance of this function.

Third, it is possible that whistle-blowers are more likely to use external channels in these organizations than in others simply because internal channels for blowing the whistle are relatively less available or are perceived as less effective or powerful. In other words, lack of feasible dissent mechanisms—or even lack of information about existing mechanisms—may encourage whistle-blowers to select external channels for reporting wrongdoing. This possibility is extremely speculative, however, and we lack data that would help us assess its validity.

In any case, it is clear that more research is needed to investigate the impact that industry may have on whistle-blowing. Other industry variables that might affect whistle-blowing include industry profitability, stage of industry evolution, level of industry rivalry, and threat of entry into the industry (see Porter, 1980, for a discussion of the effects of these variables) (Miceli, Near & Schwenk, 1991).

Finally, research on the incidence of wrongdoing in organizations may be useful in that organizations in which wrongdoing is more likely to occur may produce conditions that discourage whistle-blowing once wrongdoing has occurred. For example, Cochran and Nigh (1986) found that poor firm profitability, large firm size, high product diversification, and rapid growth were related to an increased likelihood that a major industrial firm engaged in illegal corporate behavior.

Organizational Environment. The environment encountered by organizations may result in more or less wrongdoing by them (Baucus & Near, 1991) (steps 1–2 of the decision model); it may also influence the degree to which organization members consider whistle-blowing legitimate (step 4 of the decision model). For example, it has been speculated that organizations faced with scarce resources in their environments are more likely to commit wrongdoing; in fact, the opposite seems to be true (Baucus & Near, 1991). Although we know of no empirical evidence on this matter, it would seem that the environment might influence the organization culture for or against whistle-blowing. Specifically, organization members may be less likely to blow the whistle when they believe that continuation of the wrongdoing is critical to the organization's continued survival.

Another environmental issue concerns the culture of the society in which the organization operates. Most whistle-blowing research has been completed in the United States, and it seems clear that many of the findings are not generalizable across cultures. The definition of "loyalty" is one point where organization members from different societies may hold varying views. Americans, for a variety of reasons, probably are more likely to engage in whistle-blowing than members of more authoritarian societies. One vignette-based study (Becker & Fritzsche, 1987) showed that French and U.S. managers were more likely than German managers to say that they would report an auto manufacturing defect. These managers gave rationales indicating potentially greater concern for the chances of injury or death to people, whereas the German managers emphasized loyalty and other considerations. However, it is not clear that these self-reports would necessarily translate into behavioral differences if the managers were faced with wrongdoing of varying types. Thus, there is a need for more research concerning characteristics of the organization's operational environment and whistle-blowing.

Variables Involving Both the Person and the Situation

In chapter 3, we discussed personal variables that may influence whistle-blowing directly, some of which might also interact with situational conditions. Earlier in this chapter, we discussed situational variables that may influence whistle-blowing directly. Now we turn our attention to those variables that are not necessarily expected to have a direct effect, but instead may interact with other variables to influence whistle-blowing. Figure 4–2 shows the combinations of situational and personal variables that may interact to influence whistle-blowing. Because these combinations are complex, we cannot always specify the direction of the expected relationship to whistle-blowing in the figure.

Variables Pertaining to Relationships with Work Group Members

NEED FOR APPROVAL AND OTHERS' EXPECTED REACTIONS.
Presumably, some organization members are dependent on others'

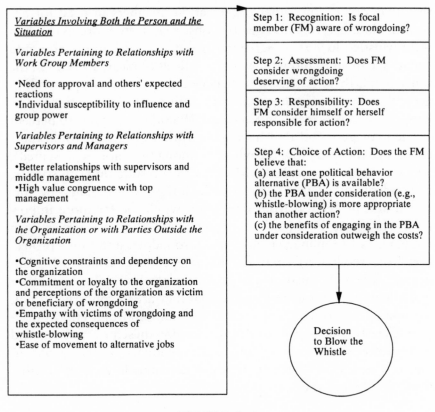

FIGURE 4–2

Variables Involving Both the Person and the Situation That Are Hypothesized to Affect the Decision to Blow the Whistle

approval—they have a high need for others to know about and respond favorably to their actions. If so, they will be heavily influenced by norms in the group and organization and by cues signaling whether others consider an observed activity to be wrongful and deserving of action, whether the focal member is responsible for action, and whether whistle-blowing is appropriate and likely to be reinforced by others. Consequently, we expect that need for approval and others' expected reactions will affect whistle-blowing, through their effect on all of the decision steps.

There is some very preliminary evidence that whistle-blowers are relatively unconcerned about how others might react, implying that they may differ from other organization members in need for approval. Nonobservers and inactive observers were more likely than were whistle-blowers to agree that having others' approval would encourage them to blow the whistle (Miceli & Near, 1984). On the other hand, there is reason to believe that co-worker approval, in general, is not a very important factor in most organization members' decision processes. In Keenan's (1988a) study, only 10 percent of the managers said that having co-worker approval would most encourage them to blow the whistle (among five choices presented), which is consistent with the MSPB (1981) results. In both studies, respondents noted that extent to which the problem could be corrected and protection from retaliation would be far more important. However, it should be remembered that co-workers can retaliate, as can management or the wrongdoer, and thus "protection from retaliation" may not be independent of co-worker approval. There is also a potential social desirability problem; individuals may not want to admit that they are so concerned about the opinions of others when faced with an important ethical decision. Clearly, research is needed to examine these propositions and to consider whether the factors that individuals *believe would* influence them to blow the whistle in fact coincide with the factors that *do* influence them.

INDIVIDUAL SUSCEPTIBILITY TO INFLUENCE AND GROUP POWER. Earlier, we described how groups can affect all steps in the decision process. But some organization members are likely to belong to several groups, including the immediate work group, the professional group, or friendship or neighborhood groups. Here, we propose that, where different groups maintain differing norms relevant to whistle-blowing, the susceptibility to influence is a function of the relative power of the groups and of the individual's characteristics. Latané's (1981) social impact theory suggests that social influence is a multiplicative function of the strength, immediacy, and number of members in the group. For example, where the majority is credible (Wolf & Latané, 1983) and unanimous (Allen & Wilder, 1980), pressures are increased, through strength. Groups that maintain more contact with the organization member are likely to be more influential; for example, professional group norms may be more salient when members have a "cosmopolitan" orientation

(Gouldner, 1957a, 1957b). And larger groups may be more influential as well.

On the other hand, certain focal members may be able to resist these influences more than others, as implied by our previous discussion. Members who believe they are competent (Stang, 1972), possess idiosyncrasy credits (Hollander, 1958, 1960), and do not depend on the group for friendship (French & Raven, 1959) or task-relevant assistance (Bavelas, 1968) can resist group pressure not to blow the whistle. As was the case with many of our previous propositions, inadequate research attention has been devoted to these issues.

Variables Pertaining to Relationships with Supervisors and Managers

RELATIONSHIPS WITH SUPERVISORS AND MIDDLE MANAGE-MENT. If whistle-blowing through the chain of command is a form of communication of problem matters, Gaines's (1980) findings are relevant (Near & Miceli, 1985). She found that ambitious subordinates who trust their superiors exhibit more upward communication on problem matters than do other organization members. Greater trust and confidence result when subordinates perceive the leader to be successful in upward interactions (Jones, James & Brunni, 1975). This suggests that greater supervisory trust would be associated with higher perceptions of efficacy and more use of the chain of command as an internal whistle-blowing channel (step 4).

Blackburn (1988) and Graham (1986) proposed that more supervisory support would lead to more whistle-blowing. Blackburn (1988) found that individuals with *unexpressed* "employee concerns" believed that their supervisors were less supportive of their concerns than did individuals who voiced concerns, and nonobservers; these latter two groups did not differ significantly. Further, inactive observers also believed that they had less positive relationships with their supervisors than did the other employees. Blackburn (1988) found that silence was associated with a negative perception of higher management. These results provide preliminary evidence that supervisory relationships are important in the whistle-blowing decision process. Blackburn (1988) suggested that further research is needed to identify whether actual behavior differences by supervisors or other members of management lead to or are associated with decisions to exercise the voice option.

VALUE CONGRUENCE WITH TOP MANAGEMENT. Enz (1986, 1988) provided evidence that the resource-dependency approach to power (as in Pfeffer & Salancik, 1978) should be supplemented by a value-based explanation of power. Defining organizational values as "the beliefs held by an individual or group regarding means and ends organizations 'ought to' or 'should' identify in the running of the enterprise" (Enz, 1988, p. 9), she contended that influence in organizations is shaped by the beliefs of the social players. More specifically, "value sharing between top management and a department increases the probability that the department has greater access to information, communicates more often with executives, is trusted by and attractive to top management and is thus in greater control and more secure in its organizational actions. All of these outcomes of value fit suggest heightened power. Whether the power is real or imagined is not important, since similarity in how the department and the executives see the organization will most likely lead to similarity in desired behaviors and levels of influence" (Enz, 1988, p. 11).

Consistent with these arguments, Enz (1988) found that greater perceived value congruity was associated with greater power. Although Enz's study was specifically concerned with subunit (department) power, her rationale could also be used to make predictions concerning individual power. When values are congruent, observers of wrongdoing have greater power (step 4), which would increase whistle-blowing. In an analysis that has not been included in a manuscript, we found that value congruence was positively correlated with whistle-blowing among Directors of Internal Auditing, but this result should be confirmed by other research.

Variables Pertaining to Relationships with the Organization or with Parties Outside the Organization

COGNITIVE CONSTRAINTS AND DEPENDENCY. Cognitive constraints may prevent organization members from "seeing" obvious wrongdoing, as when the focal member is selectively inattentive to critical pieces of information. This may occur because the focal member has committed resources (for example, his or her working life) to supporting the organization, or is dependent on the organization, and cannot accept that wrongdoing might occur there. An example of this might be the plant workers in the Silkwood case who minimized or ignored the potential danger of allegedly unsafe conditions at the plant.

In some cases the degree of selective inattention may change over time. The focal member may be vaguely aware that things are not right, but she or he refuses to recognize this until some dramatic event serves to integrate several pieces of information, making the pieces of the puzzle fit together as a coherent whole. Regular viewers of the television show "Murder She Wrote" will recognize this as the "Jessica Fletcher Light Bulb" phenomenon. Nearly every week, Mrs. Fletcher is unable to help police solve the murder until someone makes an offhand comment or spills the coffee. At that point (usually about five minutes before the end of the story), the mystery writer remembers or reinterprets a previously insignificant event. Mrs. Fletcher's face lights up at the discovery—like the light bulb's going on above a cartoon character's head signifies an idea—and she then pulls all the evidence together.

Sometimes the passage of time, repeated exposures to wrongdoing, and the accumulation of evidence may be necessary before the activity begins to offend the individual's sense of propriety. In the case of Robert Wityczak (Hanrahan, 1983), the disabled Rockwell employee allegedly was pressured by his supervisors and peers to charge his time spent on one government-contracted project to a different project that had less stringent budgetary limits. He complied but gradually, "it began to bother my conscience. There was all this cheating going on. I felt it was my duty to object to this" (Hanrahan, 1983, pp. 17–23). However, systematic research examining the issue of when constraints operate and when they do not remains to be initiated.

COMMITMENT OR LOYALTY TO THE ORGANIZATION AND PERCEPTIONS OF THE ORGANIZATION AS VICTIM OR BENEFICIARY OF WRONGDOING. Anecdotal evidence suggests that whistleblowers may be highly committed to their organizations (as in Powell, 1990). Commitment may affect whistle-blowing decision making in several ways. First, it may increase organization members' sense of responsibility for action (step 3). As suggested by equity theory (for example, Adams, 1963) and research on the "norm of reciprocity" (Gouldner, 1957a), highly committed employees may feel indebted to their employers. Indebtedness can arise from the employer's bestowing rewards on employees to a greater extent than they believed they deserved, or than they believed another employer would provide. Indebted employees may wish to reciprocate by helping their employers correct wrongdoing.

Second, commitment may affect one's judging of the appropriateness of whistle-blowing as a political behavior alternative (step 4). But the direction of influence is not entirely clear. Some researchers have proposed that observers who feel a great sense of loyalty or commitment to the organization may decide against whistle-blowing (Farrell & Petersen, 1982; Laver, 1976; Staw, 1984). In this "traditional" view of loyalty (Blackburn, 1988), organization members may view whistle-blowing as disloyal because it involves inappropriate criticism of the organization.

However, others have argued that loyalty would *increase* the likelihood of whistle-blowing (Graham, 1983; Kolarska & Aldrich, 1980), because loyal employees help the organization to correct its errors before they result in more serious allegations. In these cases, the organization member may believe that the dominant coalition does not know about the wrongdoing, so that informing them may reflect greater loyalty than not informing them; hence, whistle-blowing would be seen as highly appropriate. Consistent with this view, Farrell (1983) found that silence was viewed as passive and destructive. Westin's (1981) examination of case studies is also supportive (Baker, 1983). He found that the majority of corporate whistle-blowers consider themselves to be very loyal employees who tried to use "direct voice" (internal whistle-blowing), then were rebuffed and punished for this. Ultimately, many used "indirect voice" (external whistle-blowing). These organization members believed initially that they were behaving in a loyal manner, helping their employers by calling the attention of top management to practices that could eventually get the firm into trouble.

There are some additional research findings bearing on the relationship between commitment and whistle-blowing. As noted earlier, we (Miceli & Near, 1988a) found that positive job responses were associated with whistle-blowing, but Blackburn (1988) found that employees who voiced concerns did not differ from those who remained silent as to organizational commitment; both groups were less committed than nonobservers. Blackburn reconciled her findings with ours, maintaining that our measure of positive affect was more similar to her "positive attitudes toward general management measure" than her "commitment" measure.

Dozier (1988) found that team spirit affected wanting to help the team leader win. Those with higher levels of team spirit were *less* likely to blow the whistle, which might have prevented the team leader from winning. Finally, Graham (1989) found that individuals high in initiative were highly committed to the organization. Thus, the research is not entirely consistent with either theoretical position.

It may be that commitment interacts with other important variables to cause whistle-blowing. Hirschman (1970) argued that loyalty may interact with satisfaction to cause voice; specifically, he predicted that observers of wrongdoing who are more loyal and dissatisfied will be more likely to blow the whistle than other observers. This proposition remains untested.

A second variable that may interact with commitment concerns perceptions of victims of wrongdoing. Targets of prosocial behavior can be co-workers, the organization as a unit, or consumers (Brief & Motowidlo, 1986), but previous research generally has not examined the role of the observer's perceptions concerning the victims of wrongdoing. Specifically, as noted earlier, one rationale for linking commitment to whistle-blowing is that committed whistle-blowers want to help their organizations. But this may be true only when whistle-blowers perceived their organizations to be victimized by wrongdoing. To explore this possibility, we rely on a distinction between targets of wrongdoing described by Cochran and Nigh (1986). Following Clinard (1983), they differentiated *occupational* crime from *organizational* crime. Occupational crimes are committed primarily to increase *individual* wealth, whereas organizational crimes are committed on behalf of an organization by one or more of its employees, with the primary purpose of increasing *organizational* wealth. Presumably, an organization may be victimized by occupational crime, but it is likely to be enriched by organizational crime, at least over some period of time. It is also conceivable that the same crime may fall into both categories. For example, a financial manager may engage in fraudulent financial reporting, which may both enhance corporate stock prices and earn the manager a bonus.[1]

Organizations may be victimized by wrongdoing in several ways. For example, observers may believe that the organization's performance, climate, or culture is damaged when wrongdoing continues. But whether this belief leads to whistle-blowing may depend on how the observer views the organization. Brief and Motowidlo (1986, p. 720) proposed that "the commitment attitude" may predict prosocial behavior toward the organization. Thus, if observers perceive the wrongdoing to harm the organization in some way, and they are highly committed to the organization, they may be more likely to blow the whistle. In one investigation, however, there was support only for the direct positive effect of commitment on all types of whistle-blowing (Miceli, Near & Schwenk, 1991).

EMPATHY WITH VICTIMS OF WRONGDOING AND THE EXPECTED CONSEQUENCES OF ACTING. Where observers of wrongdoing can identify others harmed by the wrongdoing, such as co-workers, they may empathize to a greater extent than where the victims are unknown (Dozier, 1988). Empathy may predict prosocial behavior in organizations (Brief & Motowidlo, 1986). For example, Batson, Duncan, Ackerman, Buckley, and Birch (1981) found that subjects who felt they were similar to a victim receiving shocks were likely to help regardless of the difficulty of escape. Further, people become more emotionally involved when someone in their "we group" is in trouble, and consequently, they are more motivated to help them (Brief & Motowidlo, 1986, citing Hornstein, 1978). Therefore, whistle-blowing may be associated with the belief that co-workers are harmed by the wrongdoing, through its influence on steps 2, 3, and 4. External channels were used when observers felt that co-workers were harmed by the wrongdoing (Miceli, Near & Schwenk, 1991), though there was no measure of strength of empathy.

Where observers believe that the public is victimized by wrongdoing, they may view reporting to authorities outside the organization to be more appropriate than where they do not. On the other hand, whistle-blowing to external parties may be regarded as threat-

---

[1] We are indebted to the series editors for this suggestion.

ening to the organization (Brief & Motowidlo, 1986; Staw, 1984), implying that retaliation would be forthcoming and thereby discouraging external whistle-blowing. Therefore, we can make only a tentative prediction that external reporting will be associated with the belief that the perceived wrongdoing harmed the public; we found support for this hypothesis (Miceli, Near & Schwenk, 1991).

The observer of wrongdoing may identify the community as the potential beneficiary of his or her contemplated actions. Concerns about these parties' welfare may cause the focal member to view threats to their welfare to be deserving of action (step 2). For example, nuclear workers at the Comanche Peak plant in Glen Rose, Texas, complained to the Nuclear Regulatory Commission because they feared that the unsafe construction of the plant endangered the community (Glazer & Glazer, 1987). These observations suggest that the longer one resides in an area, the more similar one perceives himself or herself to be to the victim and more integrated the member is in the community. These conditions would facilitate empathy with the victim; consequently, whistle-blowing will be more likely to take place. We know of no field research testing this proposition. However, a laboratory investigation revealed no support for the hypothesis that empathy increases whistle-blowing; this was true whether empathy was operationalized as a score on a dispositional measure, or manipulated by the experimenter, through enabling observers of apparent wrongdoing to see "victims" (Dozier, 1988).

It is possible that empathy may interact with other variables, such as costs and benefits of acting. Batson et al. (1981) found that empathic subjects were willing to help the victim when the cost of helping (receiving mild shocks) was low. But when the cost of helping was high (receiving painful shocks), empathic subjects took the easy escape. On the other hand, Wagner and Wheeler (1969) and Shotland and Stebbins (1980) found that high cost reduced helping behavior, while need of the victim had no effect. Shotland and Stebbins (1980) explained the results by the use of the limited altruism model. This model contends that when a potential helper is deciding a course of action, the cost takes precedence over the victim's need. But this prediction seems to be at odds with the findings on whistle-blowing that the seriousness of the wrongdoing is associated with more whistle-blowing, whereas threatened retaliation generally is not (Miceli & Near, 1985). Clearly, more research is needed in this area.

EASE OF MOVEMENT TO ALTERNATIVE JOBS. According to March and Simon (1958), organization members who can easily locate and accept alternative jobs are more likely to leave their organizations than are members who have no alternatives. Such persons are less dependent on the resources the organization offers (Pfeffer & Salancik, 1978), suggesting that the potential costs of whistle-blowing might be lower (step 4). Similarly, these members who observe wrongdoing may be more likely to exit the organization and join another in which the objectionable practices do not occur (Graham, 1984). This suggests that where (a) unemployment is low, particularly in the field employing the focal member, or (b) individuals perceive that alternatives are readily available, or (c) individuals have lower investments in the organization that would be forfeited if they were to leave (such as nonvested pension benefits), then they would be more likely to blow the whistle than where these conditions weren't present. A high unemployment rate in the focal member's relevant labor market (determined by industry, geographical location, or occupation, such as certain professional groups) may discourage whistle-blowing, because it is an indicator that fewer employment alternatives are available (Near & Miceli, 1985). On the other hand, Hirschman (1970) argued that barriers to exit will increase the likelihood of whistle-blowing, because the individual will be more highly motivated to improve the current situation.

Research shows that organization members in the supervisory hierarchy with high levels of education, who presumably have good employment alternatives, have been shown to blow the whistle more frequently to persons inside the organization than do ostensibly less powerful members (Miceli & Near, 1984). Whether this is due primarily to their power in the organization or to a possibly enhanced opportunity to observe wrongdoing cannot be determined from this study; nonobservers, like inactive observers, also had lower levels of education and were less likely to be supervisors than the internal whistle-blowers.

Summary

As was the case with the literature reviewed in chapter 3, the current research literature has many limitations and should be viewed with caution, for the reasons described earlier. The MSPB's pioneering early research was conducted in the federal sector. Research since has been extended into the private sector, and upper-level executives as well as personnel executives, directors of internal auditing, and middle-level managers have been surveyed.

The preliminary results show that more whistle-blowing occurs where the evidence of the wrongdoing is clear or direct. There is some evidence, though it is not entirely consistent, that more serious wrongdoing is more likely to be reported—particularly to external channels and not anonymously. Illegal wrongdoing is no more likely to be reported than is wrongdoing that is objectionable on other grounds; however, external channels are more likely to be used when the wrongdoing involves theft. Observers of wrongdoing are somewhat more likely to report it (especially externally) when there are many other incidents of wrongdoing occurring in the organization.

Several hypotheses were offered concerning the focal member's immediate work or social environment. Although one might expect that being located at the home office might lead to greater whistle-blowing because of access to more information there, results show the opposite. There has been no research linking role overload and whistle-blowing, which are expected to be negatively related. There has been little research concerning group norms and power, though several studies have examined the "diffusion of responsibility" effect identified in the bystander intervention literature (Latané & Darley, 1968). The results show that this effect holds for external whistle-blowing, that is, the greater the number of other observers of wrongdoing, the less likely that external whistle-blowing will occur. The studies are consistent in showing that the number of other observers *is related to* internal whistle-blowing, but the direction of the relationship was not the same in every study. Thus, a search for intervening variables may be in order. External whistle-blowing is somewhat less likely when the wrongdoer is of higher rather than lower status. Finally, there is limited evidence that support from family and friends increases whistle-blowing.

Some research has been conducted concerning the signals the organization may provide about its likely response to whistle-blowing specifically. There is considerable evidence that organizational responsiveness may be associated with whistle-blowing. A general, shared perception that organizations would respond to complaints by correcting wrongdoing has been shown to be associated with greater whistle-blowing on the part of individual members who observe wrongdoing. It is encouraging that research is beginning to examine the effects of policies and the characteristics of these policies on internal and external whistle-blowing. For example, evidence suggests internal reporting will be enhanced in organizations that establish a complaint recipient office, direct employees to this office, and provide an effective appeal procedure. The role of complaint recipients has generally been neglected as a research topic. However, research suggests that whistle-blowers, particularly those who reported to recipients who would not reveal their identity, are influenced by perceptions of complaint recipients' responsiveness.

Providing cash incentives to whistle-blowers has not been evaluated fully, and results are contradictory. Organization members report that such incentives do not influence them, though there is some indication that incentives do increase whistle-blowing in some organizations. Further, administrative problems or insufficient funding may account for the limited known success of such programs. Some individuals do not believe such incentives will be effective, and perhaps they are inappropriate for inducing "moral" behavior. But further research is needed on these topics. Perhaps the most surprising finding, which has been replicated repeatedly in the empirical studies, is that threatened retaliation has no direct effect on whistle-blowing. We previously speculated that there may be several reasons for this finding, but all of our speculations await further controlled research.

Other organizational and environmental characteristics were examined. Whistle-blowing in response to wrongdoing is more likely in larger organizations and those perceived to be less bureaucratic than in other types of organizations. There is mounting evidence that climates and cultures of organizations affect whistle-blowing; we have reviewed several studies that conceptualize and measure climate in different ways. Climates that are less defensive and more participatory are associated with whistle-blowing, and they may also enhance employee satisfaction. There is no research on how codes of ethics may encourage or discourage whistle-blowing; Mathews's (1987) study suggests that the effects of these codes will depend at least partly on their content. Specifically, she found that many codes tend to deal more with wrongdoing directed against the organization than with the organization's actions, which would not necessarily encourage whistle-blowing.

There is preliminary evidence that more highly regulated industries may experience higher levels of external whistle-blowing, but the reasons why are unclear. Finally, the organizational environment may be important. Specifically, organization members may be less likely to blow the whistle when they believe that continuation of the wrongdoing is critical to the organization's continued survival and where the societal culture is less supportive of whistle-blowing.

We also examined a set of variables, both situational and personal, that may interact to produce whistle-blowing. There is some evidence that whistle-blowers have a lower need for approval from others than do other organization members. This tendency may interact with threatened retaliation or more subtle forms of disapproval. Members who believe they are competent, possess idiosyncrasy credits, or do not depend on the group for friendship or task-relevant assistance (Bavelas, 1968) can better resist group pressure not to blow the whistle. Although some research has examined these individual variables, the group norms and pressures were not measured in the studies. Preliminary results provide preliminary evidence that relationships between the focal member and his or her supervisor are important in the whistle-blowing decision process and that high levels of value congruence between the focal member and top management is associated with whistle-blowing.

We speculated that cognitive constraints may prevent individuals from recognizing wrongdoing immediately and that dependency on the organization may exacerbate the operation of these constraints. Organizational commitment may interact with satisfaction with specific facets of organizational operation to predict whistle-blowing; however, there is preliminary evidence that it does *not* interact with perceptions of the organization as victim of wrongdoing. Some research suggests that greater empathy with victims is related to external whistle-blowing, but other research casts doubt on this proposition; it may be that the expected costs and benefits of action interact with empathy. Finally, an argument can be made in either direction concerning the relationship between the focal member's ease of movement to another organization and whistle-blowing. Research shows that less dependent members are more likely to blow the whistle, but it is not clear that this is attributable to ease of movement.

Clearly, there are many variables that may predict the occurrence of whistle-blowing, and our list is by no means exhaustive. We would encourage researchers to undertake research investigating the role of situational and personal variables in the decision process of the focal member. In our next chapter, we move to the next stage of the whistle-blowing process, which focuses on the consequences of whistle-blowing for the individual and the organization.

5

After the Complaint Is Filed

Effectiveness, Retaliation, and Long-term Consequences

In this chapter, we describe the outcome of the initial whistle-blowing report. Whistle-blowing potentially has consequences for the complaint recipient, for the co-workers, for the organization, and sometimes for other parties, such as the general public. As a result, these parties may react to whistle-blowing in various ways. For example, they may ignore the complaint or they may retaliate against the whistle-blower. The whistle-blower then may react in a variety of ways. For instance, the whistle-blower may pursue the complaint with another complaint recipient or file a grievance or lawsuit against the organization. Our contention is that not every case of whistle-blowing plays out in the same fashion. Therefore, we are interested in identifying the variables that may predict the consequences in a given case. At this time, as noted earlier, there is little research on the consequences of whistle-blowing. Thus, our purpose is to build theory by examining related theoretical and empirical developments that suggest what factors may be involved. In this chapter, we first provide a model of the consequences of whistle-blowing, and then consider variables that may predict the steps in the model.

Consequences of Whistle-blowing

In figure 5–1 we note the possible effects of whistle-blowing. In the short term, the organization can decide either to terminate the alleged wrongdoing or to continue it. The response to the whistle-blower—independent of the decision concerning the termination or continuation of the wrongdoing—is to reward, to treat as before, or to retaliate. In the long term, the whistle-blower may respond to the organization's decision, perhaps by deciding to blow the whistle again or by deciding not to do so, under any circumstances; in addition, the whistle-blower's attitudes and behaviors in the organization may be affected. The long-term consequences for the organization are equally varied, and may be a mixture of good and bad results, ranging from increased costs of litigation with the whistle-blower to improved performance if the wrongdoing is terminated. Each of these steps is considered in turn. First, however, we discuss the key actors in this process and propose a classification schema for categorizing the basic types of independent variables that predict organizational response.

Who Responds to the Whistle-blower?

In much of our research concerning organizational response to whistle-blowers, we have referred to "organizational response" as though it were an integrated and coherent response by the entire organization. This, of course, is not true. Instead, most whistle-blowers encounter a variety of responses within their organizations. These include supportive co-workers who agree with the whistle-blower; negative co-workers who fear that termination of the wrongdoing may cost them their jobs or other benefits; a wrong-

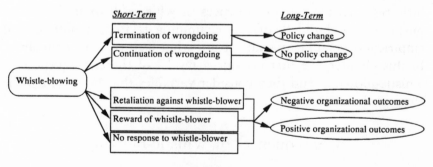

FIGURE 5–1

Short-term and Long-term Outcomes of Whistle-blowing

doer who may or may not know of being accused; supporters and detractors of the wrongdoer; a complaint recipient inside or outside the organization; the whistle-blower's immediate supervisor; and the dominant coalition (operationalized in most studies as the top management group). Add to this the fact that most whistle-blowers receive additional responses from outside the organization, from family and friends, and perhaps from outside complaint recipients, and the multiplicity of role demands on the whistle-blower is more obvious.

Even limiting ourselves to the responses of the organization members, it is clear that whistle-blowers probably receive a great deal of feedback, with the potential for much of it to be conflicting. In short, they represent a classical case of role conflict, with the obvious implications for stress inherent in this situation. Nonetheless, our focus here is on predictors of the responses of the organization members, and, in particular, those of the complaint recipient, the co-workers, and management, because they are the three sets of social actors that will be involved in most whistle-blowing cases. Because these three sets of social actors themselves hold different roles, their responses may be different in some cases, but similar in others. As a result, the predictors of their responses may vary somewhat, and we will discuss each of these sets of social actors separately.

A second complication is raised by the nature of the response. As noted before, the whistle-blowing itself and the whistle-blower may each warrant different responses: In the first case, the question is whether the alleged wrongdoing should be terminated, and in the second case, the question is whether the whistle-blower should suffer retaliation or reward, or something in between. However, the two responses may be difficult to separate. While preliminary empirical evidence suggests that effectiveness and retaliation are not strongly correlated, it is clear that in some cases the whistle-blower is both effective and not retaliated against because that individual is viewed as credible and perhaps powerful within the organization; conversely, whistle-blowers seen as unimportant or wrong may suffer retaliation as well as the indignity of being ignored, in terms of the organization terminating the alleged wrongdoing. Again, then, we would expect overlap among the predictors of effectiveness and retaliation; where we think there may be separate or different effects for a given predictor variable, we will note these.

Classification of Predictor Variables

Following our earlier classification of variables in chapter 2, and modifying it slightly, we propose that there are four overall types of predictors or organizational response to whistle-blowing: (1) personal or individual difference variables, relating to characteristics of the whistle-blower; (2) situational variables, focusing on the content of the wrongdoing and the process of the wrongdoing; (3) organizational variables, focusing on characteristics of the work group or organization; and (4) power or dependency relations, focusing on the dependence of the organization on the wrongdoing, the wrongdoer, the whistle-blower, and the complaint recipient.

Combining these four categories of predictor variables with the three types of social actors who make the organizational response and the two types of short-term organizational response produces a matrix of possible outcomes, as portrayed in figure 5–2. Ideally, we would be able to identify likely organizational responses for each cell in the matrix, based on the type of predictor variable, the social actor involved, and the type of response. In reality, two factors prevent us from hazarding these predictions: (1) We believe that the responses are more similar than would be suggested by such an exercise, that is, many of the cells would be the same; and (2) nonetheless, we have no empirical evidence for making such fine distinctions at this point. Figure 5–2 is intended only to suggest the possible range of responses that might be possible, although we think it unlikely that the full range would be used by any particular organization for any given whistle-blowing incident. With this caveat in mind, we propose to first discuss the perspectives of the three social actors, to next describe each of the four broad categories of predictor variables, and finally, to discuss their possible effects on the short-term and long-term consequences of whistle-blowing.

Characteristics of the Social Actors

Individual characteristics of the social actors, to the extent that these can be systematically described, may influence the organization's response to the whistle-blower; some individual difference factors will, of course, be too idiosyncratic to predict ahead of time and will simply contribute to "error variance" in the prediction of organizational response. At the most basic level, however, the three sets of social actors vary depending on their role in the organization, and it is really this type of characteristic that is most interesting.

Complaint Recipient as Social Actor

Of the three types of social actors, the complaint recipient is perhaps the most problematic, because this individual's role can vary so dramatically. According to our basic definition of whistle-blowing, the complaint recipient must be someone who has the power to change the situation, whether internal or external to the

| | Social Actors | | | | | |
| | Complaint Recipient | | Co-workers | | Management | |
Predictor Variables	Effec-tiveness	Retaliation	Effec-tiveness	Retaliation	Effec-tiveness	Retaliation
Individual						
Situational						
Organi-zational						
Dependence						

FIGURE 5–2

Matrix of Whistle-blowing Outcomes, Predictor Variables, and Social Actors

organization. Thus, the complaint recipient could be one's immediate supervisor, a co-worker, a member of top management, or an individual external to the organization; in short, this category or social actor is not independent necessarily of our others, except to the extent that the individual is being asked to play a different role temporarily than that normally played.

For example, if the whistle-blower approaches the immediate supervisor to report the alleged wrongdoing, she or he may react as the complaint recipient—someone who has the responsibility to report and or change alleged wrongdoings—or as the supervisor—someone who has the responsibility for supervising the activities of the whistle-blower who is really her or his subordinate. These may be conflicting roles, because the supervisor, when acting in the complaint recipient mode, may agree that the wrongdoing has occurred and feel compelled to act to terminate it, yet feel defensive that the subordinate has implicitly criticized her or his behavior in somehow allowing the wrongdoing to occur, even if she or he is not directly responsible for committing the wrongdoing. With regard to the latter point, we must remember that an implicit managerial norm in our society is that managers who claim ignorance of subordinates' misdeeds (for example, Nixon in Watergate or Reagan in the Iran–Contra affair) are often blamed anyway for allowing their subordinates to run out of control. Thus, implicitly, if not explicitly, any allegation of wrongdoing in a subunit suggests that the supervisor is somehow at fault. The supervisor must then respond from two roles, that of supervisor and that of complaint recipient. Similarly, a member of top management may also feel defensive toward alleged misdeeds, as may certain co-workers (for example, if both the whistle-blower and the co-worker are high-level managers in the organization and the wrongdoing occurs in the co-worker's subunit).

In contrast, the complaint recipient might fill some official capacity as a complaint recipient, such as an internal auditor or ombudsperson within the organization, or as a member of the external audit term, as a regulator, or as a media representative outside the organization. Because we consider whistle-blowing to include cases of reporting wrongdoing through either internal channels or channels external to the organization, the complaint recipient could likewise be inside or outside the organization. Preliminary evidence suggests that whistle-blowers who report wrongdoing to external channels are no more likely to be effective than those who do not (Near & Miceli, 1990); unfortunately, they may also be more likely to suffer retaliation (Miceli & Near, 1989).

Co-worker as Social Actor

The role of the co-worker is also somewhat problematic, even when this person does not serve as the complaint recipient. This person also fills two roles: that of "co-worker," which implies some task interdependence and sense of norms for appropriate or even ethical behavior with regard to one's peers (Moberg & Meyer, 1989), and that of organization member, which implies some sense of loyalty to the organization as a whole. Needless to say, these may conflict. In the most extreme cases, co-workers may even agree that wrongdoing has occurred but not be prepared to complain about it, because they feel that doing so may jeopardize the organization's performance and therefore their own job stability. In the latter case, the co-workers' extra-role obligations (such as breadwinner for family members) may further complicate their reaction to the whistle-blower.

Management as Social Actors

As with complaint recipients and co-workers, management members also fill different roles, depending on their own level in the hierarchy and that of the whistle-blower. Research has indicated that top management and middle management support for the whistle-blower, while correlated, is not synonymous by any means, and may have differential effects on the likelihood of retaliation against the whistle-blower (Miceli & Near, 1989; Near & Jensen, 1983; Near & Miceli, 1986).

Individual Predictors of Organizational Response

We are interested here in characteristics of the whistle-blower that would influence the organization's response to him or her as a credible source for reporting wrongdoing. Unfortunately, credibility is often confounded with power, because many of the status or position variables that confer power on an organization member also make that person a respected or credible source of information. Those characteristics that we think relate directly to power are discussed later in this chapter in the section on dependence; despite this, we recognize that these distinctions may be too fine, and they are used only for purposes of analysis, as would be necessary in cases where the whistle-blower had one of these characteristics but not the other, for instance, a low-level whistle-blower who was nonetheless respected as a fair and objective observer with no ulterior motive for making accusations of wrongdoing.

In chapters 3 and 4 we have described the types of individual difference characteristics that motivate organization members to blow the whistle. Here we are concerned with individual difference variables only to the extent that they predict the organization's response to the whistle-blower. As such, these must be characteristics that other organization members use to describe the whistle-blower, even though they may be unrelated to the whistle-blower's perception of herself or himself. Key among these, probably, is loyalty to the organization. To the extent that the whistle-blower is viewed as a loyal team player, she or he is probably more likely to protest effectively and to avoid retaliation. Issues pertaining to this variable are discussed later in more detail, when we consider specific predictors of effectiveness and retaliation.

Situational Predictors of Organizational Response

Situational predictors or organizational response themselves fall into two broad categories: characteristics of the wrongdoing relating to its content, and characteristics of the wrongdoing relating to the process by which it occurs and is interpreted. Characteristics of the wrongdoing itself will affect how the organization responds. Another critical aspect of the wrongdoing concerns the organization's dependence on its continuation, but this issue is discussed in our section on the organization's dependence on various actors and their effects on the organization's response to the whistle-blowing. Situational variables relating to the process of whistle-blowing have to do with the process followed in reporting the wrongdoing. Process variables also concern the process of response of the organization. In short, we place in the category of situational variables any factor relating to the situation of the particular whistle-blowing case at hand, as opposed to characteristics of the whistle-blower, the organization itself, or the power relations among key actors.

Organizational Predictors of Organizational Response

In this category, we actually include both characteristics of the sub-unit and characteristics of the organization that may predict the organization's response to the whistle-blower. The key distinction between these and situational characteristics is that we regard these to be fairly long-term and stable, whereas the situational variables refer only to the particular case of whistle-blowing at hand.

Characteristics of the subunit concern its overall "culture" for whistle-blowing. True organizational variables focus more directly on the organization as a whole, although it is possible that variations might be found in these variables at the subunit level of analysis. Nonetheless, for the time being, we assume some homogeneity across subunits of the organization in these characteristics, although clearly this might not be the case in certain organizations (such as multidivisionalized firms with unique cultures in each division). At the most basic level are variables concerned with the organization itself, including its size, structure, and ethical culture, by which we mean its approach to wrongdoing and whistle-blowing, generally. The organization's environment may also play a role, including norms associated with its task domain, and societal norms that may affect the organization's ethical culture. Environmental variables influencing the organization's level of dependence on the particular incident of wrongdoing are considered next, in our discussion of power.

Power Relations Predictors of Organizational Response

This may be our most complicated category of variables because it rests on a theoretical assumption about the basic power relationships in organizations and how they affect the whistle-blowing process. Our primary question here concerns the extent to which the organization depends on each of several key elements in the whistle-blowing process: (1) the wrongdoing, (2) the wrongdoer, (3) the complaint recipient, and (4) the whistle-blower. To the extent that dependencies on these elements are not in balance but are asymmetrical, we would expect different configurations of organizational response. Other theories of power have been used as well to predict the whistle-blower's power in the organization, and these are considered too.

Dependence on the Wrongdoing

Perhaps key to all of the dependence relationships is the nature of the organization's dependence on the wrongdoing. If the organization cannot survive without continuing this wrongdoing, due to competitive pressures, then it seems likely that its response to the whistle-blower will be more negative than would otherwise be the case. Related to the question of dependence may be characteristics previously classified as relevant to the situation, particularly the seriousness of the wrongdoing; in our earlier research, we have viewed the seriousness of the wrongdoing as a possible indication of an organization's dependence on the wrongdoing, under the assumption that the organization would not knowingly continue serious wrongdoing for long unless it were highly dependent on this wrongdoing.

Dependence on the Wrongdoer

Many of the most dramatic case studies of whistle-blowing have focused on serious wrongdoing by high-level managers, yet wrongdoing can also be committed by low-status individuals working alone for personal gain, as opposed to the supposed benefit of the organization. Under our definition of whistle-blowing, wrongdoing of any type may qualify—whether embezzlement of minor funds by individual and low-status organization members, or massive harm to society by colluding teams of top managers. Clearly, the power of the wrongdoer(s) will influence whether the organization protects them or sanctions them; this variable may also be correlated with the dependence of the organization on the wrongdoing.

Dependence on the Complaint Recipient

Whistle-blowers who report wrongdoing to powerful complaint recipients may receive differential organizational treatment. The position of the complaint recipient—whether internal or external to the organization, serving in an official capacity (that is, complaint recipient role), or at different levels of the organization—provides one indicant of the individual's power. If, in addition, the whistle-blower contacts multiple complaint recipients, greater support may be forthcoming.

Dependence on the Whistle-blower

Many personal characteristics of the whistle-blower will be important primarily because they influence his or her power within the organization. For example, organizations may depend more on whistle-blowers who: (a) have support from others; (b) have credibility within the organization because of position or idiosyncrasy credits or how they have handled the whistle-blowing; (c) have competent legal advice; (d) have shown that their case will benefit other members of the organization or at least not harm them; and (e) are considered high performers or powerful individuals for other reasons. Because the organization's dependence on the whistle-blower is influenced by its relative dependence on the wrongdoing, the wrongdoer, and the complaint recipient, all of the variables discussed in this section should be considered together rather than independently.

Effectiveness as an Outcome Variable

Finally, having defined the categories of variables that may influence the organization's response to whistle-blowing, we will now consider specific predictions of the two short-term outcomes—effectiveness and retaliation—and empirical evidence (which is admittedly sparse) that supports or does not support these predictions. Finally, we will discuss the long-term implications for the whistle-blower and the organization.

Having described in detail our basic model of the outcomes of the whistle-blowing process and the predictor variables we believe to influence the process, we now turn our attention to the outcomes, themselves, and a discussion of the particular predictor variables that we think affect each outcome. We begin with the effectiveness of the whistle-blowing process.

Defining Effectiveness

A review of various case studies of whistle-blowers suggests that their "success rates" vary widely (as in Glazer & Glazer, 1989); in some cases, whistle-blowers have succeeded in getting the organization to terminate its wrongdoing or perhaps to change altogether faulty policies and procedures that led to the wrongdoing. Effectiveness may be defined in a variety of ways, resulting in further difficulty in comparing outcomes of whistle-blowing incidents. Legal scholars tend to define the effectiveness of the outcome in terms of win or loss ratio of lawsuits placed by whistle-blowers, a figure which seems to be fairly low in sexual harassment cases (Terpstra & Baker, 1988), but may be somewhat higher in other types of cases, depending on whether tort law or one of the new state statutes protecting whistle-blowers is used as the basis of the case (Dworkin & Near, 1987; Near, Dworkin & Miceli, in press). Apart from the outcome of legal suits, which usually are filed only when the whistle-blower suffers retaliation (Near, Dworkin & Miceli, in press), we should consider the impact of the whistle-blowing on the organization, in particular whether the dominant coalition takes steps to terminate the wrongdoing, or makes other organizational changes consistent with the whistle-blower's recommendations. This definition appears more in line with the whistle-blower's initial goal of changing the system (Near & Miceli, 1987).

Having thus defined effectiveness as the short-term decision by the organization to terminate the alleged wrongdoing (note that this does not require that the organization admit that wrongdoing has occurred, but only agree that any further activity of the same sort is discontinued), we may now consider possible predictors of effectiveness. We begin with individual variables predicting effectiveness and then consider, in turn, situational variables, organizational variables, and power variables. At this point, we know of only two studies examining predictors of whistle-blowing effectiveness, both of which are described in Near and Miceli (1991). Results of these studies are summarized and described in table 5–1, which follows.

Individual Variables

There is some debate as to whether whistle-blowers are prosocial in orientation or interested in selfish benefits (Brief & Motowidlo,

TABLE 5–1

Direction of Relationships Between Predictor Variables and Effectiveness[a]

	Studies	
	A	B
Individual Variables		
Organization commitment		0
Job satisfaction		0
Situational Variables		
Unsafe/illegal behavior	+	0
Employee theft	0	+
Direct evidence	−	0
Co-workers thought wrongdoing occurred		−
External channels for reporting	0	0
Multiple complaints	0	0
Time since wrongdoing began		+
Organizational Variables		
Culture	+	0
Bureaucratic structure		0
Power Variables		
Whistle-blower's pay	+	0
Whistle-blower's hierarchical level	0	0
Whistle-blower's job performance		0
Whistle-blowing role-prescribed	−	−
Retaliation against whistle-blower	+	0
Value congruence		0
Complaint recipient's status		0
Wrongdoer's status		0
Org. performance harmed by termination		0
Seriousness of wrongdoing		0
Personally harmed by wrongdoing	0	−
Public harmed by wrongdoing		0
Time since wrongdoing began		0

[a] This table presents a summary of results from Near and Miceli's (1991) studies of effectiveness. Figures listed in column A refer to results from the 1980 MSPB sample of federal employees; figures listed in column B refer to results from our study of directors of internal auditing.

1986; Graham, 1983, 1986), loyal employees or disloyal hecklers (Kolarska & Aldrich, 1980), dedicated to truth and honesty or simply snitches (Bok, 1982; Elliston, 1982b; Polman, 1989). In fact, of course, different whistle-blowers act for different reasons. More importantly, observers of whistle-blowers may challenge their credibility if their motives seem questionable; thus, whistle-blowers who appear to be satisfied and committed members of the group are likely to be taken more seriously than whistle-blowers who are viewed as alienated miscreants (Greenberger et al., 1987; Near & Miceli, 1987).

ORGANIZATION COMMITMENT AND JOB SATISFACTION. Prior research using ad hoc measures of job effect has suggested that whistle-blowers tend to be more satisfied and committed than other organization members (Miceli & Near, 1988a), but only one study has investigated whether these attributes are associated with whistle-blowing *success*. As a result, we predict that whistle-blowers who are satisfied and committed organizational members will be more likely to be effective than whistle-blowers who are dissatisfied and uncommitted—who will be seen as organizational miscreants and not worth listening to. Unfortunately, preliminary empirical evidence does not support this proposition (Near & Miceli, 1990, 1991).

Situational Characteristics

The facts of the case should presumably influence the organization's response to the whistle-blowing, at least to the extent that organizational rationality can be assumed (Thompson, 1967). Two subtypes of situational characteristics would seem most pertinent here: characteristics of the content of the case (for example, type of wrongdoing or credibility of evidence) and characteristics of the process of the case (for instance, whistle-blowing channel or number of whistle-blowers).

TYPE OF WRONGDOING. The type of wrongdoing may range from employee stealing or embezzlement, on an individual or small group basis, to wrongdoing by corporate executives on behalf of the organization, for example, reporting of misleading financial statements or involvement in unsafe production processes because they are more profitable than safe production processes. Employee wrongdoing would probably be easier to terminate (depending on the power of the employee, as discussed later) than organizational wrongdoing. Employee wrongdoing benefits a small group of people only, while the organizational wrongdoing is more pervasive, involving wrongdoing of greater import to the organization. Moreover, cessation of employee theft may be viewed by powerful complaint recipients or others in the organization to be beneficial, rather than threatening, to the organization, whereas the organization may resist correcting other activities that may seem to enhance profits. Such a view would be in keeping with reported insurance industry estimates that 30 percent of annual business failures are the result of internal theft (Reid, 1989).

Empirical data reported thus far do not support this notion. In one study of federal employees, unsafe or illegal behavior by the organization was found to be associated with effective whistle-blowing (Near & Miceli, 1991); among directors of internal auditing who reported wrongdoing, however, the only type of wrongdoing found to be significantly associated with whistle-blowing effectiveness was employee theft (Near & Miceli, 1990).

It might be speculated that the reason a particular type of wrongdoing may be related to effectiveness is that it represents a particularly egregious case of wrongdoing. In the instance of employee theft and unsafe behaviors, the variance explained by those variables was in addition to the variance explained by the seriousness of the wrongdoing (another variable measured by the dollar amount of damage or frequency of wrongdoing).

CREDIBILITY OF EVIDENCE. The credibility of the evidence also is an element of case content. Whistle-blowers in media accounts are often asked their advice to would-be complainants. Frequently, this advice includes an exhortation to obtain written documentation in order to strengthen one's case (for example, Shepherd, 1987a). But there are few empirical tests of this proposition. Tangible evidence, that is, written documentation of questionable activity, would also be more difficult to refute than would oral testimony of only one person, who may have been mistaken or who may lack credibility.

Obviously, whistle-blowers may possess several types of evidence concerning wrongdoing. It appears reasonable to suggest that (a) whistle-blowers who have at least some written documentation will be more credible, and hence more effective, than those who have none; (b) those who have several types of unwritten evidence will be more credible than those who have less evidence; and (c) those with more direct evidence of wrongdoing based on personal observation or actual data will be more credible that those who rely on hearsay. In addition, clear evidence that wrongdoing had occurred, in the form of consensual validation by co-workers, would bolster the case. Again, preliminary findings do not support our argument. Among federal employees, having direct evidence of wrongdoing was negatively related to whistle-blowing effectiveness; further, whistle-blowing effectiveness reported by directors of internal auditing was lower when co-workers agreed that wrongdoing had occurred (Near & Miceli,1991). These results are counter-intuitive and certainly require validation, but they do raise questions about the utility of direct evidence.

WHISTLE-BLOWING CHANNEL. Previous research has indicated that the vast majority of whistle-blowers use internal channels before using external channels, thus suggesting that they blow the whistle publicly, that is, outside the organization, only as a last resort (Miceli & Near, 1984; Rowe & Baker, 1984). In addition, selecting external channels seems to offer whistle-blowers little protection from retaliation (Miceli & Near, 1989). Nonetheless, whistle-blowers may believe that the case will be seen as more credible if they use external channels rather than internal channels alone for reporting the wrongdoing; certainly, the case if likely to attract more attention from the organization (Ewing, 1983), and powerful outsiders may exert pressure on the organization to take corrective action. In fact, in neither study were those who reported wrongdoing through external channels more or less effective in whistle-blowing than those using internal channels only (Near & Miceli, 1991). These counter-intuitive results may reflect the unique characteristics of these samples and resulting restriction of range in the variable. Internal auditors in this study used external channels rarely; in fact, their role normally encourages them to report wrongdoing to the audit committee (a subset of board of directors) rather than to the chief executive officer (CEO) or chief financial officer (CFO), who may respond in a more adversarial role. Federal employees may feel that a sufficient number of internal channels is provided to them, as their use of external channels also was less frequent than we expected.

MULTIPLE WHISTLE-BLOWERS. In a similar vein, there may be "power in numbers," that is, the organization may assign greater credibility to a report of wrongdoing coming from multiple whistle-blowers (Weinstein, 1979). The tactic of registering multiple complaints, then, may gain greater attention for the allegation of wrongdoing (Weinstein, 1979). Based on existing empirical evidence, however, there is little support for this view (Near & Miceli, 1991).

Characteristics of the Organization

Organizations vary in their response to change (as in Kanter, 1983); in particular, some resist change while others seem to embrace it. This partially reflects the perspective of the dominant coalition toward change, and its sense of comfort or discomfort with change. Beyond this, the climate or culture, as well as the structure, both reflect and influence the dominant coalition's response to change.

CULTURE. Organizational cultures may be described in various ways, but, in regard to whistle-blowing, the most pertinent aspect of culture is probably the organization members' shared values regarding wrongdoing (Baucus, Near & Miceli, 1985). In short, we can characterize an organization by its culture or climate encouraging or discouraging both wrongdoing and whistle-blowing (Blackburn, 1988; Keenan, 1988a; Zalkind, 1987). In so doing, we can compare the espoused culture of the organization's members (that is, their shared beliefs about wrongdoing, whistle-blowing, and retaliation) to the actual behavior of the organization, or its culture-in-use, with regard to the way in which it responds to wrongdoing and whistle-blowing (Near, Baucus & Miceli, 1989). Generally, we would expect whistle-blowers to be more effective in organizations where both the espoused culture and the culture-in-use seem to discourage wrongdoing and to encourage whistle-blowing, although it should be noted that the two aspects of culture will not always be closely related (Near et al., 1989). In previous research, climate or culture was related to effectiveness as predicted for one sample of whistle-blowers (federal employees) (Near & Miceli, 1991), but not for a second sample of whistle-blowers (internal auditors) (Near & Miceli, 1990).

STRUCTURE. Organizations also vary in their response to change in general, apart from the content of the change. Bureaucratic organizations, in particular, are known to be less responsive to change than others (for instance, Daft, 1978), and thus might be expected to resist whistle-blowing for that reason. Bureaucracies may also respond more negatively to whistle-blowing than other organizations do, because it represents a challenge to the authority structure of the organization, which is the basis of the bureaucracy and, in some sense, its dominant feature (Weinstein, 1979). When the authority structure of a bureaucracy is challenged, the supporting structure of the entire organization may be eroded; from the traditional Weberian perspective, an effective authority structure is critical to the success of the bureaucracy (Weber, 1947). Because the bureaucracy is more threatened by whistle-blowing incidents than other forms of organization would be, its response is likely to be more retaliatory against the whistle-blower (Weinstein, 1979). For all of these reasons, then, we would also expect the bureaucratic organization to be less likely than others to change its operations or terminate the wrongdoing reported by the whistle-blower. Whistle-blowers' perceptions of their organizations as relatively bureaucratic or unbureaucratic were unrelated to whistle-blowing effectiveness, but their objectivity in making these assessments is obviously open to question (Near & Miceli, 1990).

Power of the Players

Consistent with the process view of whistle-blowing, we believe that one of the key elements in determining whether whistle-blowing is effective lies in the power plays among the individuals involved: (a) the whistle-blower, (b) the dominant coalition of the organization, (c) the recipient of the whistle-blowing information, and (d) the perpetrator of the wrongdoing alleged to have occurred. Following a resource dependence perspective (Pfeffer & Salancik, 1978) and its consolidation of the earlier strategic contingencies theory of intraorganizational power (Hickson, Hinings, Lee, Schneck & Pennings, 1971), we argue that the dependence of the whistle-blower on the organization reflects the relative power of the organization over that individual (Near & Miceli, 1985, 1987). Likewise, the dominant coalition's dependence on either the perpetrator of the wrongdoing or on the wrongdoing itself (because it benefits the organization) will reduce the relative power of the whistle-blower to influence the organization to change its operations. Finally, the dominant coalition's dependence on the recipient of the whistle-blowing information may affect its response to the whistle-blower's allegations; a powerful recipient who also appears to support the whistle-blower will provide credibility and power to that individual. In short, we expect whistle-blowing to be more effective when the whistle-blower is powerful for whatever reason: because the organization depends on him or her, or is not dependent (relatively) on either the wrongdoer or the wrongdoing, or because the organization is dependent on the complaint recipient.

A second view of power, or more properly influence, comes from the minority influence literature (Greenberger et al., 1987). From this perspective, whistle-blowers who have credibility—because of their status in the organization—will have greater influence and be more likely to persuade powerful others to terminate the wrongdoing. This credibility may come from factors that give them power in the organization, for example, education, pay, or tenure. Credibility may derive from the attribution about why the individual acts. For instance, if it is role-prescribed for the individual to blow the whistle, as in the case of an auditor's reporting financial misconduct to top management, this person may have less credibility than an individual who goes out of his or her way to report wrongdoing, that is, someone for whom whistle-blowing is not part of the job but can be attributed instead to personal moral beliefs or extra concern toward the job.

A third view of power may apply here also. In her value congruence theory of power, Enz (1986, 1988) argues that individuals whose values are congruent with those of their organization's dominant coalition gain power in their organizations. From this view of power, it can be argued that whistle-blowers who are similar to their top managers (Kanter, 1977) and believe themselves to hold the same values (Enz, 1986, 1988; Enz & Fryxell, 1987; Enz & Schwenk, 1989) will be more likely to be relatively powerful and therefore be more likely to influence top management to terminate the wrongdoing.

Each of these views of power is considered here, with the whistle-blower as the primary focus, but with the relative power of other key players and elements also taken into account.

THE WHISTLE-BLOWER'S POWER. Whistle-blowers' power in the organization, then, may derive from three possible sources: the organization's dependence on them, their credibility in the organization, and their value congruence with top managers. Hypotheses concerning each of these sources are discussed in turn.

Status. The organization's dependence on the whistle-blower may be partly reflected by the whistle-blower's status. Whistle-blowers who are low in status are generally more vulnerable to job loss, as are whistle-blowers who, for personal reasons, consider themselves vulnerable; these might include individuals with a large number of dependents, or people who believe that their job mobility is limited. On the other hand, organizations may depend more highly on individuals with high status, because of their technical or executive value to the organization. Among a sample of federal employees, pay grade was positively associated with whistle-blowing effectiveness (Near & Miceli, 1991); among directors of internal auditing, no status variable was associated with whistle-blowing effectiveness (Near & Miceli, 1991). Beyond this, we may assume that whistle-blowers who suffer reprisal are less powerful; in fact, in the federal sample, retaliation was negatively associated with effectiveness (Near & Miceli, 1991).

Credibility. The same variables that convey status and power may also reflect the whistle-blower's credibility in the organization. Other variables may enhance whistle-blowers' credibility, including high performance and high aspirations, to the extent that they indicate future upward mobility, or being a non-role-prescribed whistle-blower who acts from extra effort and presumed dedication. In fact, non-role-prescribed whistle-blowers were found to be more effective in whistle-blowing in both samples (among federal employees); other "credibility" measures were found to be unrelated to whistle-blowing effectiveness (Near & Miceli, 1991), with the exception of personal harm to the whistle-blower, which was negatively associated with effectiveness for the auditors.

Value Congruence. Third, the power of the whistle-blower could be assessed through means of the value congruence theory (Enz, 1986, 1988). Whistle-blowers who believe they hold organizational values similar to those of top management will be in a better position to influence management to terminate the wrongdoing. This argument was unsupported in preliminary research (Near & Miceli, 1991).

Recipient's Power. The power of the complaint recipient may also affect how top management responds to the allegation of wrongdoing. In essence, a powerful or high-status complaint recipient who is seen as supportive of the whistle-blowing effort may enhance the whistle-blower's credibility. We predict, then, that high-status complaint recipients will be found to be linked to successful change efforts, but this prediction was not upheld in exploratory research (Near & Miceli, 1991).

Wrongdoer's Power. Top managers may be loath to terminate wrongdoing committed by one of "their own." We would expect, then, that wrongdoers who are members of the organization, and particularly those of high status, will be in a better position to persuade top management not to terminate the wrongdoing. Preliminary evidence does not support this contention, however (Near & Miceli, 1991).

Dependence on Wrongdoing. Finally, if the organization is highly dependent on the wrongdoing for its survival, the dominant coalition may be unable to terminate the wrongdoing. For example, if the organization relies on unsafe production processes because the installation of safety equipment would be prohibitively expensive, then the dominant coalition will probably resist termination of the wrongdoing. The organization's dependence on the wrongdoing renders it relatively powerless to terminate the activity.

Various ways may be used to assess dependence on the wrong-doing. One approach is simply to ask the respondent whether termination of the wrongdoing would reduce the organization's performance. A second method involves using proxy variables to assess dependence: If the wrongdoing has been costly, frequent, long-lived, or harmful to large groups of people (as society at large), this would suggest that it is important to the organization. Our assumption is that the dominant coalition would not engage in serious wrongdoing (meaning costly, frequent, harmful to important stakeholders) or continue it for a long period of time, unless the organization's performance depended on it. Only one of these measures of dependence, time since wrongdoing began, produced significant effects, however, in a study of whistle-blowing by directors of internal auditing (Near & Miceli, 1991); in a study of federal employees, seriousness of wrongdoing was positively associated with effective whistle-blowing (Near & Miceli, 1990).

Retaliation as an Outcome Variable

Are the factors that cause whistle-blowers to experience retaliation the same as those that will cause effectiveness? We expect not entirely—although little research has been completed—for the following reasons. Both represent resistance strategies when directed by management, so in that sense they could occur together and be triggered by the same forces. However, multiple parties observe the whistle-blowing and could have different reactions, positive or negative. It may be that the whistle-blower's action is not witnessed by other observers. We do expect that some of the same factors that predict whether whistle-blowing is undertaken will predict effectiveness, because whistle-blowers are primarily motivated by expected effectiveness.

While effectiveness and retaliation may occur together—what we have labeled a "consistent organizational response" in figure 5–3—it is conceivable that some parties in the organization (such as the co-worker group) may retaliate, while others (such as those responsible for the wrongdoing) terminate the wrongdoing. Near and Jensen (1983) and Miceli, Near, and Jensen (1983) found no significant relationship between perceived effectiveness and perceived retaliation, in a sample of whistle-blowers who filed sex

	Effectiveness of Whistle-blowing	
Occurrence of Retaliation	Terminate Wrongdoing	Continue Wrongdoing
Retaliation	Inconsistent Organizational Response *Cell 1*	Consistent Organizational Response *Cell 2*
No Retaliation	Consistent Organizational Response *Cell 3*	Inconsistent Organizational Response *Cell 4*

FIGURE 5–3

Organization Responses to Initial Whistle-blowing

discrimination complaints. In one sample of federal employees, however, retaliation was negatively associated with effectiveness (Near & Miceli, 1991), as noted previously. No relationship was found in the auditors' study, however.

Attribution theory (for example, Fiske & Taylor, 1984) provides one explanation as to why it would be difficult to separate reactions to the complaint from reactions to the complainant. Specifically, reactions to the complaint may depend on attributions made by managers about whistle-blowers. For example, as noted earlier, observers may judge the validity of the complaint by examining the characteristics of the complainant; if the individual is a "chronic complainer" or a newcomer who has yet to "learn the ropes," others may be less inclined to attend to the present complaint. The complaint will be attributed to personal limitations of the complainant rather than to an environment in need of change.

Defining Retaliation

Just as it can be difficult to separate clearly the response of the organization to the complaint from its response to the whistle-blower, so defining retaliation in specific terms is probably impossible. For one thing, retaliation—as with wrongdoing—resides in the eye of the beholder. As a concrete example, in a study of whistle-blowing among directors of internal auditing, one of the respondents reported on his questionnaire that he suffered no retaliation, yet described in a follow-up interview how the wrongdoer in the case had hired a "hit man" who followed him down dark streets and otherwise harassed him (although apparently without intent of doing serious harm). According to him, however, this was not retaliation (Near & Miceli, 1988)!

In light of this basic difficulty in providing a conceptual definition of retaliation, operational definitions of retaliation used in research have taken a fairly arbitrary form. The standard approach is to provide a checklist of possible forms of retaliation and to ask respondents to check those which they've experienced and those with which they've been threatened. Elsewhere, we have argued that a sum of these experienced and threatened reprisals represents a measure of the extent to which retaliation is not an isolated event but is rather a concerted effort by the organization to systematically harass the whistle-blower. We have termed this the "comprehensiveness" of retaliation (Miceli & Near, 1988b, 1989; Near & Miceli, 1985; Parmerlee et al., 1982), and it represents merely an attempt to gauge the degree to which the organizational response to the whistle-blower is part of some integrated strategy.

A second critical dimension, of course, is the severity of the retaliation. Among the possible forms of retaliation, some are clearly more serious than others: for instance, termination is clearly more serious than reprimand. Other forms of retaliation are less easily rated, however; is exclusion from meetings more serious than exclusion from training programs, as a case in point? Thus, deriving a valid measure of severity of retaliation seems to us a futile exercise, because different forms of retaliation will be experienced differentially by specific whistle-blowers, depending on their personal situation.

A related problem, however, lies in trying to assess whether retaliation from different sources should be treated as equivalent. To illustrate, many whistle-blowers experience harassment by their co-workers who, perhaps, refuse to socialize with them any longer. Does this represent the same process of retaliation as one initiated by top or middle management? In trying to address this question, we have studied different forms of retaliation from different sources and the sometimes conflicting results are presented in the following section.

Incidence of Retaliation

A point related to the problem of defining retaliation is that estimates of the overall incidence of retaliation vary dramatically. While case studies of whistle-blowers popularized in the media present the impression that all whistle-blowers suffer extensively, survey research from somewhat larger and more diverse samples suggest that the rate of retaliation is much lower, probably less than 20 percent (Near, Dworkin & Miceli, in press); of course, the rate of retaliation probably varies widely across cases of whistle-blowing, so that even attempts to produce generalizable results from reasonable samples of whistle-blowers may be flawed. One of the methodological problems here makes the question particularly agonizing; while we would certainly hope that the incidence of retaliation remains small, this creates difficulties, too, because only in the largest samples can enough whistle-blowers who have suffered retaliation be identified so that we can begin to characterize their experiences reliably. Nonetheless, with all these caveats in mind, we now turn our attention to describing the predictor variables that seem to be related to retaliation. Yet one further warning is necessary however: Because many of the studies discussed here were based on secondary analyses of existing data, some of the most interesting potential predictors could not be included. That being the case, our discussion is limited primarily to variables that have actually been investigated, as listed in table 5–2, although, in passing, we also note interesting propositions that warrant testing in future research.

TABLE 5-2

Direction of Relationships Between Predictor Variables and Retaliation[a]

	Studies				
	A	B	C	D	E
Individual Variables					
Pay/Occupational Prestige	0		0	0	
Age	+		0	0	
Education	+		0	0	
Tenure				0	
Gender				0	
Race				0	
Performance awards				0	
Role			+	−	0
Whistle-blower harmed by wrongdoing					−
Situational Variables					
Merit of the allegation	−	−			
Co-worker support	0			0	
Top-management support	−	−	−	−	
Middle-management support		0	−	−	
Opportunities for retaliation	0				0
External channels for whistle-blowing			+		
Evidence of wrongdoing					−/0
Organizational Variables					
Size of work group				+	
Incidence of wrongdoing			0		
Military mission				0	
Fairness of reward system				0	
Power Variables					
Seriousness	+	0	0		
Org. performance harmed by wrongdoing					0/+
Org. culture harmed by wrongdoing				+/0	
Org. performance harmed by termination				0	
Multiple sources of wrongdoing	0				
Multiple incidents of wrongdoing		0			
Multiple groups involved		0			
Attempted anonymous whistle-blowing			+		
Resolved after first report					−/0
Co-workers harmed by wrongdoing		0/+			
Public harmed by wrongdoing		+			
Value congruence					−

[a] This table presents a summary of results from studies of retaliation. The studies are: (a) Parmerlee et al., 1982; (b) Near & Jensen, 1983; (c) Near & Miceli, 1986; (d) Miceli & Near, 1989 (second data set only because results of the first data set are reported in Near & Miceli, 1986); (e) Miceli & Near, 1988b. When results for different samples within a study are conflicting, both outcomes are shown.

Individual Variables

As noted earlier, the attributions others make about whistle-blowers may influence their reactions to whistle-blowers (Graham, 1986; Greenberger et al., 1987; Near & Miceli, 1987). For example, if a whistle-blower is perceived to be motivated by selfish concerns, others may view the complaint as less credible, legitimate, or important. The cognitive response analysis model states that attitude change will occur to the extent that several conditions are present: (1) The communicators are credible; (2) The message is initially repeated; (3) The message is comprehensible and supported by cogent arguments; and (4) The audience feels involved (Fiske & Taylor, 1984).

As shown in figure 5–4 the group's reactions to whistle-blowing may depend on *resistance variables* and *accommodation variables*. Resistance variables refer to processes that help the group to resist

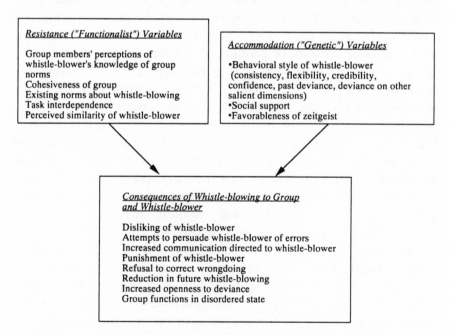

FIGURE 5–4

Factors Hypothesized to Affect the Group's Reaction to Whistle-blowing

Taken from Greenberger, Miceli & Cohen, 1987, p. 535. Reprinted by permission of Kluwer Academic Publishers.

change and maintain stability. In contrast, accommodation variables represent processes that allow the group to alter its norms and adapt to the deviant behavior of the whistle-blower.

Research has been conducted in laboratory contexts for the most part (Greenberger et al., 1987). As the reader will see, it is difficult to generalize from the laboratory studies—even to form hypotheses, because the laboratory tasks and settings were not designed to examine whistle-blowing. Not surprisingly, they do not perfectly resemble whistle-blowing contexts. For example, the studies of consistent versus inconsistent conformity-manipulated perceptual stimuli that were somewhat similar (as colored blocks) may not generalize to an organizational setting where group members may distinguish different instances of wrongdoing (as, for example, making personal copies on the company photocopier versus submitting false time cards).

As in earlier discussions, we draw heavily from the work of Greenberger et al. (1987). In developing the following ideas, there is a presumption that group norms oppose whistle-blowing. As noted by Jensen (1987), co-workers' lives may be made miserable with increased tension, or probing by authorities or reporters. Co-workers may feel betrayed, or they may feel guilty for not having come forward themselves (Jensen, 1987). Consequently, they may reject whistle-blowers, though they may not always be free to do so. Members of work groups are freer to retaliate against whistle-blowers on whom they are less dependent. In larger groups (all else being equal), there is less dependence on each member because withdrawal may be less disruptive than in smaller groups. Further, in small groups, the size and resulting power of the majority is reduced, and the whistle-blowing "deviant" may be able to persuade other group members that wrongdoing should be stopped, thereby avoiding rejection (Greenberger et al., 1987). We therefore predict that the larger the work group, the more comprehensive the retaliation. Even where organizations may appear to support whistle-blowing, co-workers may sometimes oppose it, and this opposition may take the form of harassment or retaliation (Jensen, 1987; Mathews, 1988). There are many reasons why co-workers may take steps to oppose whistle-blowing (Greenberger et al., 1987). As evidenced in the research on sexual harassment (e.g., Gutek, Morasch & Cohen, 1983), some individuals may judge ambiguous activities to be wrongful, while others do not. Those who do not may resist alternative interpretations. Expression of opposition may sometimes involve emotional differences about questionable activity where the whistle-blower feels that an activity is wrongful, and co-workers do not share that feeling. Organization members who express inner feelings that are at odds with the prevailing norms or rules may be punished (Rafaeli & Sutton, 1987). Consequently, the level of co-worker retaliation may differ in different settings.

Co-worker retaliation also may be a function of resource dependency relationships, but these relationships may be different between whistle-blowers and their co-workers versus whistle-blowers and their organizations. For example, co-workers' reactions to whistle-blowing may be unrelated to measures reflecting organizational dependency on the wrongdoing, because co-workers may not have a sense of what alternatives may exist and the likely consequences of alternative implementation for themselves. This suggests that separate measures of retaliation are needed: one representing actions of retaliation under the control of management, and the other representing retaliation carried out by co-workers (Miceli & Near, 1988b). Further, previous authors did not explicitly include co-worker retaliation within the operational definition of retaliation. Therefore, when making comparisons between the present findings and those of previous studies, it would be helpful to know whether differences in findings concerning the predictors of retaliation are attributable to definitional differences as opposed to other causes. Most of the prior research on retaliation (as in Parmerlee et al., 1982; Near & Miceli, 1986) used measures that probably represent retaliation directed by managers rather than other parties.

KNOWLEDGE OF GROUP NORMS. While knowledge of group norms may actually represent a group variable because group perceptions and attributions are important, the primary factor that will affect these perceptions and attributions is personal. Group members may direct more communication toward the whistle-blower who they believe isn't aware of prevailing norms than toward one who knows the norms. Newcomers may be "given some slack" by the group; rejection may be deferred, and communication attempts may be stronger (Greenberger et al., 1987). Similarly, experienced whistle-blowers may convey through their actions that they were unaware of the norms for a given situation. For example, a long-term member who has never previously faced a given problem may file a formal complaint with an ombudsperson; group members may interpret this as confrontational, or they may attribute the action to a lack of experience with a specific problem. If the interpretation is that the whistle-blower knew the norms, group members may make fewer communication attempts and may reject or punish the individual more rapidly.

CREDIBILITY OF THE WHISTLE-BLOWER. The accommodation perspective suggests that the degree to which the norms are changed will depend in part on the group's perception of why the source of the new norms (the whistle-blower) deviated (Greenberger et al., 1987). If the whistle-blower is believed to have a sound basis for complaining—that is, if the whistle-blower is credible—the attitude change literature (Kiesler et al., 1969) suggests that norms will change to a greater extent. One variable that may influence others' attributions would be their perceptions of whether the correction of the wrongdoing might be advantageous to the whistle-blower. For example, if the whistle-blower filed an age discrimination charge, he or she might be viewed as the primary beneficiary of a favorable outcome. This suggests that whistle-blowers who are harmed by the wrongdoing would be more likely to experience retaliation, but surprisingly, empirical research suggests that managerial retaliation tends to be greater when the whistle-blower is not harmed by the wrongdoing (Miceli & Near, 1988b). In this study, none of the persons who experienced co-worker retaliation believed they were harmed by the wrongdoing, indicating that there was no support for the hypothesized relationship between harm to the whistle-blower and more retaliation by co-workers.

Similarly, whistle-blowers who act in a more official capacity or are seen to be role-prescribed whistle-blowers (such as internal auditors or inspectors) may be held less responsible for their actions (as in Near et al., 1989); when they blow the whistle they are only "doing their job." Although the degree to which whistle-blowing is truly role-prescribed in any job is questionable (Miceli & Near, 1988b), it is clear that there is some variance on this measure, related to the requirements of the job; thus, some whistle-blowers may be seen as more credible than others simply because their actions are viewed as role-prescribed and therefore less self-serving. Thus far, empirical data on this point have proved conflicting; in one study of federal employees, holding the role of inspector or internal auditor was positively associated with retaliation (Near & Miceli, 1986), but in a second sample from a similar population, the association was negative (Miceli & Near, 1989). In yet a third sample, no association was found between internal auditors' perceptions that their actions were role-prescribed and retaliation (Miceli & Near, 1988b).

Further, a whistle-blower could conceivably be more credible when the situation that is the complaint's focus suggests that wrongdoing has occurred; because we view this instance as involving situational variables, it is discussed in a following section. However, two streams of research on social influence suggest that personal variables may predict credibility and hence the degree of influence on group norms.

Extending the literature on social influence to whistle-blowing contexts is not easy, because the laboratory tasks used in most of the studies do not have a direct parallel in organizational contexts. To illustrate, when a laboratory group reacts to a series of controversial issues and the confederate "minority" deviates only on certain issues, it is not clear whether the group views "the task" to be the discussion of controversial issues, or whether the group views each issue as a separate task. This point may be clearer as we discuss the findings from this research.

The first stream of research on minority influence proposes that a consistent behavioral style of nonconformity will cause group members to make attributions of certainty, competence, and commitment, which presumably affect credibility (Moscovici & Faucheux, 1972; Mosocovici et al., 1969; Moscovici & Nemeth, 1974). This suggests that the whistle-blower would not appear credible if she or he first seemed to accept the wrongdoing but later objected to it, because such a change would be inconsistent with respect to the same incident. But it is not clear whether this research suggests that where multiple incidents involving different types of wrongdoing were observed over a long period of time, then the whistle-blower must object to every incident.

A second stream of research suggests that whistle-blowers who conform to group norms on most issues (that is, including issues unrelated to wrongdoing) but deviate when confronting obvious wrongdoing will be more influential than where whistle-blowers deviate on many issues. This stream provides evidence that when group members demonstrate competence and accumulate "idiosyncrasy credits" (Hollander, 1958, 1960), they are less likely to be rejected by the group. Idiosyncrasy credits are earned by demonstrating that one is a "good team player" (conforming) and forfeited when the groups' norms are violated. Group members who have greater seniority or higher performance may possess higher stocks of idiosyncrasy credits (Miceli & Near, 1988a) unless they repeatedly have fought battles with the group. Levine (1980) suggested that if the stimulus is ambiguous, one should be consistent in judgment; however, whenever a clearly different situation is presented, deviance may be essential to maintain credibility for a minority. Thus, whistle-blowers may need to report every clear-cut case of wrongdoing until it is corrected.

This stream of research suggests that one must choose battles carefully. Similarly, individuals who are viewed as deviants when they first join the group are at a disadvantage. For example, if the whistle-blower appears very different from the others—because of race, sex, or national origin; because of dress customs; because of language patterns, or similar factors—a greater amount of conforming behavior may be required before any deviance over issues will be accepted. Research reviewed by Maass and Clark (1984) suggests that whistle-blowers who deviate in terms of beliefs and one other category, such as ethnic membership, will have less influence than do "single" minorities.

There is very little research concerning the effects of consistency and credibility on the outcomes of whistle-blowing, and the existing research did not include ideal measures of the constructs suggested by the psychological research on minority influence, nor did it show cause-effect relations. We know only of one study that used archival survey data (Miceli & Near, 1989) to examine the relationship between variables that may have represented stocks of idiosyncrasy credits and the comprehensiveness of retaliation experienced by whistle-blowers. These idiosyncrasy credit variables were self-reported performance awards, years of service (tenure), and being white and male. We found that none of the variables were significantly related to comprehensiveness of retaliation (Miceli & Near, 1989). Other demographic variables that might be associated with credibility have not been fully examined. While pay or occupational prestige appear unrelated to retaliation, age and education were each positively associated with retaliation in one study (Parmerlee et al., 1982) but were unrelated to retaliation in two other studies (Miceli & Near, 1989; Near & Miceli, 1986).

While this is not a strong test, and speculation should consequently be limited, in one sense the results may be encouraging. If the degree of truthfulness or validity in the complaint (that is, the extent to which objectionable wrongdoing actually occurred) is not a function of the individual's own credibility or image, individuals' characteristics should not affect retaliation or other outcomes, such as the extent to which the triggering event is changed by the organization. Others should respond to the validity of the complaint rather than to the individual's characteristics. Thus, there would be no relationship between outcomes or whistle-blowing and the whistle-blower's image. However, more rigorous empirical research must be conducted before this conclusion can be accepted. For example, the results reported here might have been a function of measurement weaknesses in the reliance on archival data rather than more direct measures of idiosyncrasy credits. It may be necessary to measure and control for the norms that have developed in the group and organization before the effects of idiosyncrasy credits and co-worker support can be observed.

Situational Variables

In this section, we would first like to discuss predictor variables for which we have empirical results and, next, to discuss more speculative propositions about potential predictor variables, whose effects have not yet been tested. A summary of empirical results is provided in table 5–1, and specific findings follow in this section.

MERIT OF THE ALLEGATION. One of the most obvious difficulties in studying whistle-blowing is determining whether the allegation of wrongdoing was in fact valid. Since the data used in all of the research thus far have come solely from the whistle-blower, with no attempted validation of findings from other parties involved, we must usually take that person's word about the allegation. For one sample of respondents, some additional corroboration was provided when respondents were asked whether their sex discrimination suits, filed with the appropriate state or federal agency, had been judged to be meritorious. While these data were still self-report in nature, and therefore subject to some error based on respondents' recall, the nature of the question was somewhat more objective than would have been possible with subsequently analyzed data. The results suggested that meritorious cases were indeed less likely to result in retaliation for the whistle-blowers involved (Near & Jensen, 1983; Parmerlee et al., 1982).

CO-WORKER SUPPORT. When co-workers, supervisors, or top managers side with whistle-blowers, whistle-blowers gain more power relative to their organizations; as s result, organizations may be less willing to challenge them (Weinstein, 1979). In a prescriptive article, Shepherd (1987a) recommended that whistle-blowers try to find potential support among co-workers to establish their credibility. Similarly, researchers have proposed that with greater co-worker support, the whistle-blower will experience less retaliation. However, they have found no relationship between the comprehensiveness of retaliation and (a) the extent to which the whistle-blower perceived co-workers were generally supportive (Near & Miceli, 1986); (b) the number of co-workers who were supportive (Parmerlee et al., 1982); or (c) the diversity of types of co-workers who were supportive of the whistle-blower (Parmerlee et al., 1982).

SUPERVISOR AND TOP MANAGEMENT KNOWLEDGE AND SUPPORT. Where top management is unaware of the wrongdoing and is happy to discontinue the questionable practice once they are made aware of it, less retaliation and resistance is expected. A key issue for whistle-blowers is determining what signals indicate that management would welcome information. Parmerlee et al. (1982) and Near and Miceli (1986) found that the lack of support from managers or supervisors was positively associated with retaliation. Miceli and Near (1989) compared results from the 1980 MSPB data analyzed by Near and Miceli (1986) and those collected by the MSPB in 1983. They performed several analyses designed to enhance comparability between the two samples. In this way, differences in results could more easily be attributed to real differences occurring because of legal change intervening between the two years than to sample differences (such as somewhat different organizations and hierarchical levels of employees surveyed). For the "matched" subsets of data, the hierarchical regression results were very similar for 1980 and 1983. The best predictors of comprehensiveness of retaliation were supervisor lack of support and management lack of support. Lack of co-worker support did not play a role. The results suggest that basically the same variables predicted retaliation in 1983 as did so in 1980, before the new law took effect.

It should be noted that, while management support variables have been correlated with retaliation, they seem to be tapping different dimensions; thus, the correlations themselves are not sufficiently strong that lack of discriminant validity seems to be a problem. A more serious problem is method variance inherent in these measures. It is hard to believe that a whistle-blower who had suffered retaliation would not report that his or her managers were unsupportive (unless the retaliation came from some other source). This potential measurement problem is difficult to solve.

It should also be obvious that one of the reasons management support is so critical to a whistle-blower is that it bolsters his or her overall power in relationship to the organization. Therefore, we might as easily have classified this predictor variable as a power variable. That we did not do so reflects only our sense that reasons other than power might explain the benefit of management support to whistle-blowers, although it is not clear to us at this point, based on the empirical results available to date, what those might be (certainly we could speculate on a variety of potential reasons).

EVIDENCE OF WRONGDOING. Similarly, if co-workers do not view the activity that triggered whistle-blowing to be clearly wrongful or deserving of action, they may be less supportive, and the whistle-blower will be less powerful. Further, such co-worker views may suggest the complaint really is frivolous, and retaliation may be used as a control mechanism directed against frivolous complaints, not against valid whistle-blowing. Under this rationale, co-worker agreement that wrongdoing has occurred may be taken as a measure of evidence of wrongdoing. Despite this argument, in one empirical examination of the issue, co-worker agreement on wrongdoing was positively associated with managerial retaliation, and was unrelated to co-worker retaliation (Miceli & Near, 1988b).

OPPORTUNITIES FOR RETALIATION. Parmerlee et al. (1982) suggested that greater opportunity for retaliation will make it more likely, for example, when a longer period of time has elapsed since the complaint was filed. Similarly, greater opportunity for retaliation may occur when the whistle-blower has more frequent workplace interactions with the person(s) responsible for the questionable activity. Despite this reasoning, Miceli and Near (1988b) found that co-worker retaliation was unrelated to length of time since the complaint was filed. However, more opportunity for workplace interactions with wrongdoers was associated with co-worker retaliation. Thus, organizations may wish to develop policies to protect whistle-blowers who must deal frequently with whistle-blowing targets. In such instances, perhaps, anonymous whistle-blowing is more ethically justifiable (Elliston, 1982a), and whistle-blowers should be encouraged to report anonymously.

Similarly, managerial retaliation may be more likely when there is greater opportunity for retaliation, as when a longer period of time has elapsed since the complaint was filed, or when the whistle-blower has more frequent workplace interactions with the person(s) against whom the complaint was filed. Yet Miceli and Near (1988b) found no relationship between opportunity for retaliation and managerial retaliation. This suggests that quick resolution is not needed to avoid retaliation. On the other hand, measurement might have been incomplete, obscuring the relationship. We did not ask on what date the complaint ultimately was resolved, if at all. So, it is possible that expeditiously resolved complaints filed long ago (with no retaliation) have offset recently filed complaints that will take time to resolve and will result in retaliation. This is unlikely, however, because an earlier study that included both measures (Parmerlee et al., 1982) obtained the same results.

Number of Whistle-blowers. A review of the literature on social influence (Tanford & Penrod, 1984) indicates that the impact of the minority is greatest when the minority includes at least two members. This is consistent with Latané's (1981) social impact theory, which views minority as well as majority influence to be a multiplicative function of the strength, immediacy, and number of its members (Wolf, 1985). Thus, we would expect that the number of whistle-blowers would be negatively related to retaliation. From another perspective, there is greater power in numbers—the organization would be too dependent on a group of whistle-blowers to risk reprisal against all of them. Further, the increased risk of negative attention associated with retaliation against a larger group of whistle-blowers might also dissuade managers from retaliating against multiple whistle-blowers. To date, this proposition has not been tested empirically.

ORGANIZATIONAL VARIABLES. In this section, we include variables related to either the work subunit or the larger organization; we begin with the subunit variables.

Subunit Culture. As Greenberger et al. (1987) noted, Paicheler (1976) suggested that the impact of the minority must be examined in the context of the "zeitgeist" (the other prevailing norms), and Maass and Clark (1984) suggested that a minority will be more influential where originality and innovation are desirable and favorable to the minority's position. If the social influence literature is generalizable to whistle-blowing, this suggests that the more open the culture in the subunit, the less likely that group members will retaliate against whistle-blowers.

Number of Co-workers. The review cited earlier (Tanford & Penrod, 1984) also indicated that the minority is more likely to be influential in small groups (six or fewer members) than in larger groups. Thus, we might expect that smaller groups would be less likely to retaliate against whistle-blowers, particularly if more than one group member is involved in the whistle-blowing. This prediction was not, however, borne out by the one study in which it was tested; instead, Miceli and Near (1989) found that size of the work group was positively related to retaliation.

Group Cohesiveness. The greater the cohesiveness, the more likely that the group will punish or reject the deviant after unsuccessful communication attempts (Emerson, 1954; Schachter, 1951). This finding, along with the findings concerning the size of the majority, suggests that where the whistle-blower's group is smaller and less cohesive, the more likely he or she will be to change the opinions of other group members. Following this reasoning, we would also expect the whistle-blower to be less likely to suffer retaliation in such a group.

Task Interdependence. The greater the task interdependence among members, the more likely that whistle-blowing will be viewed as a threat to group functioning, and so the more likely that resistance in the form of pressures to conform will be directed toward the whistle-blower (Greenberger et al., 1987). To the extent that reprisal represents a strategy for forcing the whistle-blower to conform, then, we would expect that more interdependent groups would engage in reprisal more frequently than groups where task interdependence is low.

Organization Size, Structure, and Culture. We noted earlier that the characteristics of the organization, such as its size, structure, and culture, may affect the responses of its members to wrongdoing. These characteristics may also affect response to whistle-blowing (Graham, 1986; Near & Miceli, 1985). Glauser (1982) pointed out that large or tall organizations may have impeded communication channels. Further, more innovative organizations—those that encourage innovation through empowerment—may be capable of responding flexibly to change (Kanter, 1983). Consequently, they may be more open to internal dissent simply because they are accustomed to the change process and have available the necessary mechanisms for change (Near & Miceli, 1987). They may also lack the norms proscribing whistle-blowing. On the other hand, without clear rules or definitions of wrongdoing, more flexible organizations may be less responsive because they may be more tolerant of a wider range of activities. In short, norms concerning what constitutes wrongdoing may be more ambiguous in flexible organizations. The overall incidence of wrongdoing is one variable that may reflect the ethical culture of the organization as a system; it was unrelated to retaliation against individuals in one study, however (Near & Miceli, 1986). Using the organization as the unit of analysis, Near et al. (1989) found that the overall incidence of retaliation in the organization was related to one of three measures of organizational culture.

Competitive Pressures. Preliminary evidence suggests that organizations engage in wrongdoing in situations where their survival is threatened by inhospitable environments (Finney & Lesieur, 1982; Staw & Szwajkowski, 1975). But later evidence suggests (Baucus & Near, 1991) that the opposite situation holds true. If organizations are facing a threat to their survival, then they may be more resistant to change and more retaliatory as their dependence on the wrongdoing increases. Intense competitive pressures may suggest to organizations that engaging in wrongdoing and resisting change is necessary. Thus, perceptions that competition is intense or increasing and that the wrongdoing provides a competitive edge will be associated with more comprehensive retaliation and continuation of wrongdoing. Societal norms may support or discourage this ethical stance.

Procedural Justice. To the extent that a top-management team's approach to retaliation against whistle-blowers reflects its other procedures for dealing with employees, we might expect that the sense of procedural justice ascribed to the organization by its members might generalize to its actions with regard to reprisal. In other words, an organization that does not treat its employees fairly under other circumstances would seem more likely to retaliate against whistle-blowers than would an organization that is seen as fair. Supporting this contention, Miceli and Near (1989) found that comprehensiveness of retaliation was negatively associated with whistle-blowers' perceptions that the reward distribution system in their organization was fair.

POWER VARIABLES. Previous researchers (such as Near & Miceli, 1986) have shown that theories of power may be useful in examining retaliation toward whistle-blowers. One such theory has been proposed by Pfeffer and Salancik (1978), following Emerson (1962), who argue that where one party controls important resources on which another party depends, the first party maintains power, while the second is dependent on the first. This resource dependency perspective suggests that in the case of whistle-blowing, organizational wrongdoing may depend on the wrongful activity in that leaders don't perceive the availability of alternative activities. This perspective also suggests that where whistle-blowers lack support or potential support from other organization members or outsiders, they may be relatively powerless. To the extent that either of these conditions holds, we expect that the organization would resist attempts to stop the wrongdoing. One way to resist such change attempts may be to retaliate against the whistle-blower who reports wrongdoing on which the organization depends. Thus, factors that suggest dependency on the wrongdoing or the power of the whistle-blower may also predict organizational retaliation.

Weinstein (1979) argued that the most severe retaliation would be directed toward those whistle-blowers who raise the greatest potential threat to the organization. Consistent with this perspective and based on a resource-dependence approach (Emerson, 1962; Pfeffer & Salancik, 1978), it is possible to identify potential predictors or resistance to change and retaliation against whistle-blowers (Near & Miceli, 1985). Presumably, managers who perceive that a whistle-blower poses a greater threat are more likely to retaliate and to resist changing the organization by correcting the wrongful practice.

This point is illustrated anecdotally by the case of Marie Ragghianti (Donahue, 1983). Within three days of assuming the position of chairperson of the Tennessee Parole Board, Ragghianti discovered evidence that substantial kickbacks were being given to state officials in exchange for the prison release of convicted felons. Such activity would generally be viewed as unquestionably and seriously wrong. After informing higher officials who continued the practice, Ragghianti blew the whistle to the media. Unfortunately, perhaps because this whistle-blowing posed a substantial threat, Ragghianti experienced death threats and was subjected to defamatory remarks by individuals in the media as well as in her organization.

Although the resource dependency perspective concerning power relations has empirical support, Enz (1986, 1988) provides evidence that this approach should be supplemented by a value-based explanation of power. Defining organizational values as "the beliefs held by an individual or group regarding means and ends organizations 'ought to' or 'should' identify in the running of the enterprise" (Enz, 1988, p. 9), she contends that influence in organizations is shaped by the beliefs of the social players. More specifically, "value sharing between top management and a department increases the probability that the department has greater access to information, communicates more often with executives, is trusted by and attractive to top management and is thus in greater control and more secure in its organizational actions. All of these outcomes of value fit suggest heightened power. Whether the power is real or imagined it not important, since similarity in how the department and the executives see the organization will most likely lead to similarity in desired behaviors and levels of influence." This feeling of power may "drive the department to believe it deserves influence over other departments. Over time this belief becomes institutionalized and other departments accept it as a given" (Enz, 1988, p. 11). Consistent with these arguments, Enz (1988) found that greater perceived value congruity was associated with greater power. Although Enz's study was specifically concerned with subunit (department) power, her rationale could also be used to predict that whistle-blowers have greater power when their values are more congruent with those of top management. As a result, we expect that lower congruity would be associated with more retaliation.

Thus, alternative theories of power relations could be used to examine the relationship of the whistle-blower to the organization, in the context of the organization's dependence on the wrongdoing, the wrongdoer, and the complaint recipient. Next, we consider predictors of the relative dependence of the organization on each of these elements.

Dependence on the Wrongdoing. Organizations may be more likely to retaliate against the whistle-blower where the act of wrongdoing represents a critical and nonsubstitutable resource, that is, if the organization is dependent on the continued wrongdoing (Near & Miceli, 1985). The seriousness of perceived wrongdoing, which may be reflected in its frequency of occurrence or in the amount of financial resources it involves, may indicate its criticality to organizational survival (Near & Miceli, 1986). One survey-based study showed that federal employees were more likely to suffer retaliation when the wrongdoing in question was particularly serious (Near &

Miceli, 1986), but later investigations did not support this hypothesis (Miceli & Near, 1988b, 1989).

Similarly, questionable activities that directly help maintain organization survival, profitability, or performance may be more critical to the organization than activities that are seen as more peripheral. Terminating such activities would have a negative impact on organization performance. Thus, we would expect that criticality would be associated with greater retaliation, because the organization is more dependent on the activity and therefore has greater motivation to resist change when the activity enhances its performance.

Criticality may be assessed through various means. If the wrongdoing harms the organization's performance, the organization is likely to be less dependent on it than if the wrongdoing enhances (or does not affect) performance; therefore, conceivably, the organization would refrain from retaliating. Similarly, if the organization's climate or culture is unaffected by the wrongdoing, retaliation may be more likely. Whistle-blowing may be viewed less as an attempt to help the organization stop an activity that harms it (Near & Miceli, 1987) and more as a threat to the authority structure that should be discouraged (Weinstein, 1979). Moreover, a climate or culture that is not harmed by the continuation of wrongdoing may be a climate that encourages or does nothing to prevent additional wrongful activity that takes the form of retaliation.

Miceli and Near (1988b) found that, contrary to prediction, management retaliation was more likely when the organization's culture or climate was thought to be harmed by the wrongdoing. Managerial retaliation was not related to perceptions of harm to co-workers or to the public. Nor was retaliation related to perceptions that the organization's performance was harmed by the wrongdoing, or, conversely, that the organization would be (or was) harmed by termination of the wrongdoing.

DEPENDENCE ON THE WRONGDOER AND COMPLAINT RECIPIENT. For the same reasons we expected that dependence on the wrongdoer might lead the organization to ignore the whistle-blower's allegations (as discussed before under the question of effectiveness), so we would expect that dependence on the wrongdoer might increase the likelihood or retaliation against the whistle-blower—both as a way to silence the current whistle-blower and as a deterrent to future attempts at whistle-blowing against that wrongdoer. Conversely, dependence on a complaint recipient perceived to be supportive of the whistle-blower might serve to protect the whistle-blower from reprisal. Unfortunately, no study has examined these predictions to date.

POWER OF THE WHISTLE-BLOWER. As previously discussed, whistle-blowers might gain power from two sources: the organization's dependence on them, or the organization's perceived value congruence with them. A third source of power might be credibility in making the allegation of wrongdoing; we have discussed this topic at length, however, under the category of individual variables, and we simply wish to note here that credibility may also influence the organization's response to the extent that it enhances the whistle-blower's power. Finally, a fourth source of power might be support from outside sources, as for example, legal support. Each of these sources of power is considered in turn.

Organizations may depend on whistle-blowers who are also valued organization members; conversely, whistle-blowers who depend on the organization because of low status or vulnerable position are less powerful in their relationship with the organization—and therefore in their whistle-blowing actions. Observers of wrongdoing who lack power may attempt to remain anonymous in order to bring about change in the organization without risking career harm. But they may not succeed; their identities eventually may become known to others, either because they choose to be identified, or because a complaint recipient releases the information. This can occur because whistle-blowers may make multiple reports; for example, they may first contact the head of the department where they think wrongdoing is occurring, and later may notify the chief executive officer or the audit committee. Even when only one report is made, the process of resolving the complaint may take months.

Where whistle-blowers' identities are later revealed, we expect that greater retaliation would be directed toward them than against whistle-blowers who reveal their identies from the outset, for two reasons. First, if certain conditions—such as a climate that permits wrongdoing or relative weakness of the whistle-blower—serve to signal potential retaliation, then identified whistle-blowers will experience greater retaliation than if they were identified under more supportive conditions. If whistle-blowers perceiving unfavorable conditions remain anonymous, they can escape retaliation, like the whistle-blowers in the more supportive organizations. But if the anonymous whistle-blower whose identity is discovered later has accurately assessed the situation, he or she is powerless and vulnerable to retaliation. In other words, anonymous whistle-blowers may tend to work in a subgroup of the organization more hostile to whistle-blowers, or be in a subgroup of positions that connote less power, while identified whistle-blowers may tend to work in more supportive climates or may be more powerful. When anonymous whistle-blowers' "cover is blown," hostile forces can be unleashed. A second reason why discovered anonymous whistle-blowers may experience greater retaliation is that the attempt to remain anonymous itself may be viewed as behavior needing the organization's control or punishment. One study produced findings consistent with this view, that is, attempting unsuccessfully to remain anonymous was positively associated with retaliation (Miceli & Near, 1988b).

Earlier, we considered the argument that role-prescribed whistle-blowing may not violate group or organizational norms, which empowers the whistle-blower. But we also argued earlier that whistle-blowing is not always role-prescribed, even for such jobs as internal auditor. The nature of the incident may determine the appropriateness of reporting. For example, reporting an activity that the whistle-blower views as immoral but not illegal, or an activity that does not involve accounting and control, may be less clearly role-prescribed. Thus, role prescription could be incident-specific. Where whistle-blowing with respect to that incident is not viewed as part of the job, we might expect that the whistle-blower will have less power and consequently will experience greater retaliation. In fact, as noted in the section on individual variables, results on this point were inconsistent.

As already noted, a second source of power may be the whistle-blower's perceived value congruence with management. In fact, whistle-blowers who described their organizational values as similar to management's were less likely to suffer retaliation from both management and co-workers.

If other members of the organization, such as the management hierarchy or co-workers think the whistle-blower's complaint is valid, the whistle-blower may be seen as more credible and therefore more powerful. As noted earlier, whistle-blowers may make multiple reports, sometimes because insufficient action is taken in response to the first report. Unresponsiveness may occur because management does not view the complaint as valid or appropriate—thus, the whistle-blower is relatively powerless. Also, as suggested earlier, an unwillingness to change may stem from the organization's dependency on wrongful activities; the organization has no feasible alternative to the wrongful activity, so it allows the wrongdoing to continue. In either case, resistance to change can be manifested in a lack of action in response to the initial report as well as in retaliation directed toward the whistle-blower; thus, we expect these responses to occur together. Consistent with this view, Miceli and Near (1988b) found that allegations of wrongdoing that were resolved after the first report were less likely to be associated with retaliation; whistle-blowers who were required to make their allegations in successive reports (usually to higher levels of authority) were more likely to experience retaliation.

Whistle-blowers may also be more powerful when whistle-blowing is legally encouraged through the establishment of official channels for reporting wrongdoing and protection from retaliation. The Civil Service Reform Act of 1978 (CSRA) encourages federal employees to report fraud, waste, and mismanagement (MSPB, 1981). It established "hot lines" and created agencies and subunits to protect federal employees against retaliation when they blow the whistle on wrongdoing in their agencies (MSPB, 1981). Members of private sector firms, non-profit organizations, and state and local governments are not covered by the CSRA protections, and more than half of the states have no state statues protecting these individuals (Hoerr et al., 1985). Further, research suggests that state laws have not had the desired effect of encouraging whistle-blowing (Dworkin & Near, 1987). These circumstances suggest that federal employees will be more likely than other employees to escape retaliation because of more specific protections provided by the CSRA.

In the same vein, Shepherd (1987a) suggested "spending money for solid legal advice." In general, lawsuits filed by whistle-blowers, under tort law, have been more successful when the wrongdoing involved a violation of law or norms supporting public policy, that is, the public at large was harmed (see chapter 6). This is not surprising, because it has been a widely held tenet of the courts that the "employment at will" doctrine should be supported, except in cases violating the law or detrimental to the public at large. In essence, then, examination of recent cases suggests that the courts should follow this tenet fairly consistently.

Long-term Consequences for the Whistle-blower

Case studies of whistle-blowers suggest that the experience of retaliation can be traumatic, to say the least (as in Glazer & Glazer, 1989). Survey-based studies have suggested that even the observation of wrongdoing by an organization to which one has committed part of one's life is also disconcerting, apart from the fact of whether the whistle-blower suffers reprisal (Near & Miceli, 1986). The question arises then: What happens to whistle-blowers after the fact?

Near & Miceli (1986) examined several dependent variables thought to be influenced by retaliation, as well as other predictor variables. The dependent variables were involuntary exit from the organization, voluntary exit, performance, future whistle-blowing activities, and complaint filed about the retaliation. In some sense, both voluntary exit and involuntary exit represent forms of retaliation. For analytic purposes, however, they were treated as separate variables because they occurred after other forms of retaliation had been experienced by the whistle-blower and because they represented a more drastic form of retaliation than did other varieties discussed. Although all of the data were self-reported and were collected after all of the discrete events in the process had occurred, some temporal sequence was at least implied in the questionnaire items, for example, some questions inquired whether the whistle-blower had filed a subsequent complaint after suffering the first round of reprisal and following his or her initial allegation of wrongdoing.

When retaliation was treated as one of several independent variables, it was found to be significantly associated with some of the five dependent variables, but not others. Findings for each of the dependent variables are summarized below and in figure 5–5.

The first dependent variable, involuntary exit, was associated

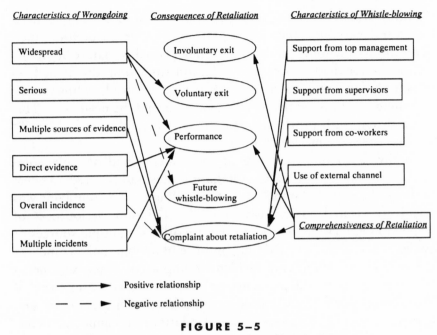

FIGURE 5–5

Long-term Consequences of Whistle-blowing

with retaliation, even when the effects of other independent variables were considered. That is, respondents who suffered retaliation were more likely to be forced to transfer to another department, or leave the organization altogether.

In contrast, the only significant predictor of voluntary exit was observation of widespread wrongdoing, involving multiple groups. Retaliation was unrelated to voluntary exit. These findings suggest that the observation of entrenched wrongdoing, rather than retaliation, affects whistle-blowers' choices to leave, perhaps because widespread wrongdoing may indicate that the organization is tolerant of, or dependent on, wrongdoing. Obviously, further research is needed to determine the causal pattern of relationships among these variables.

Performance was also related to widespread wrongdoing. Whistle-blowers were less likely to feel that their performance had declined when they had direct evidence of widespread wrongdoing, ' had observed multiple incidents, or had suffered retaliation. These whistle-blowers may have concentrated on maintaining or improving their performance out of fear of additional retribution.

Future whistle-blowing activities were reported to be influenced by several variables. Individuals who had observed multiple incidents of wrongdoing said they would probably ignore it in the future, rather than report it. Retaliation (including threatened retaliation), however, was unrelated to their avowed willingness or unwillingness to blow the whistle again, should the need arise. This is consistent with previous research (Miceli et al., 1988; Near & Jensen, 1983; Parmerlee et al., 1982).

Finally, a small percentage of respondents had actually complained to someone about the retaliation they had suffered, in effect blowing the whistle on the retaliation. Filing such a complaint was positively related to extensiveness of retaliation, seriousness of wrongdoing, lack of support from co-workers, multiple sources of evidence about the wrongdoing, and use of an external channel for the initial whistle-blowing incident. Filing a complaint was negatively related to overall incidence of wrongdoing, education level of the whistle-blower, and lack of support from both supervisors and mangers. Whether this was a causal relationship cannot be determined on the basis of the results from this single study, but it should be noted that the first experience of retaliation preceded the complaint about it, at least insofar as the respondents reported the consequences of events. Because the report is dependent on the respondents' cognitive interpretation and recall of the events and their order, causality cannot be inferred, that is, some respondents may have "remembered" the retaliation somewhat differently as a result of filing a formal complaint or retaliation.

These results imply that the organization's response to whistle-blowing, in terms of retaliation, has several effects, some of which may be unintended (Near & Miceli, 1986). First, being the victim of retaliation did not seem to have the expected effect, namely, deterrence of future whistle-blowing. In some cases, it even encouraged whistle-blowers to complain about the retaliation they had already suffered. Second, victims of retaliation claimed to maintain or improve job performance, at least in their perception. Third, extensiveness of retaliation was associated with involuntary exit or firing from the organization. In some sense, involuntary exit may be the most extreme case of retaliation.

An additional finding (Near & Miceli, 1986) was that the retaliation response is not as common as implied by media reports on whistle-blowing. Less than a quarter of the responding whistle-blowers reported that they experienced any retaliation. This figure is comparable to that observed in later studies of federal employees (Miceli & Near, 1989), and internal auditors (Near & Miceli, 1988). On the other hand, it is somewhat lower than the 40 percent retaliation rate reported by women who filed external complaints of sex discrimination against their employers (Parmerlee et al., 1982) and the rate near 100 percent reported by Soeken and Soeken (1987). Differences in the studies' methodology may have contributed to the observed differences in retaliation rates. Although all involved mailed surveys that were quite lengthy (more than fifteen pages), the two later studies involved only persons who remained in the federal system after blowing the whistle. Potentially, many federal whistle-blowers who experienced retaliation may have left to seek private employment. In addition, the last two studies involved random samples of respondents drawn from specified populations, while the first sample represented a "convenience" sample that was neither random nor systematic. However, it is unlikely that methodology accounted for all of the difference in retaliation rates.

These findings suggest that the characteristics of the complaint, complainant, or employing organization may be related to retaliation. For example, whistle-blowing on many types of activities is role-prescribed for federal employees and for internal auditors, and rewards—financial and otherwise—exist. The comparison of results between these samples does not clearly support the notion that legal protections for whistle-blowers prevent retaliation. On the one hand, it is possible that any rate less than 100 percent may be a function of somewhat effective legal proscription of retaliation. On the other hand, in the case of all of the sampled populations, there is some legal protection for whistle-blowers. In fact, in the case of the sex discrimination complainants, there is specific legislation banning retaliation, yet these respondents experienced the highest retaliation rate. The "employment at will" doctrine still governs the relationship between most employers and their employees, thereby allowing employers to terminate employment for any reason and at any time (Blackburn, 1984). However, certain kinds of reasons for termination—discrimination on the basis of protected union activity or on the basis of sex, race, religion, or age—are prohibited under federal law (Hoerr et al., 1985). In addition, several states have recently passed laws specifically protecting whistle-blowers, and courts in a number of states have issued decisions that grant increased protection to whistle-blowers (Blackburn, 1984; Dworkin & Near, 1987). According to a recent *BusinessWeek* report (Hoerr et al., 1985), legislators in twenty-one states are currently sponsoring bills that would specifically protect whistle-blowers from retaliation and termination (Near, Dworkin & Miceli, in press). Of course, such legislation may be difficult to enforce, but it does restrict the employer's legal use of the employment at will doctrine (Near, Dworkin & Miceli, in press). Future additional restrictions on this doctrine have been anticipated by some authors (Ewing, 1983). A full discussion of legal prohibitions on retaliation is provided in chapter 6.

Long-term Consequences for the Organization

Ewing (1983) argued that managers should regard whistle-blowing in a positive light—that is, as an event that provides both the impetus to change and the information required in order to implement the change. For a variety of reasons described in chapter 1, he and others have predicted that the incidence of whistle-blowing will increase. Therefore, managers must learn to live with and even to encourage it. As noted by Staw (1980), this plea for managerial sensitivity to whistle-blowing fits well with recent calls for more participative organization structures (as in Ouchi, 1981) that will encourage greater acceptance of change and, therefore, innovation (Kanter, 1983). From the perspective of theory development, however, the study of whistle-blowers as change agents offers a unique opportunity (Near & Miceli, 1987).

How the organization's top managers view the alleged wrongdoing and the whistle-blowing incident will depend to a large extent on whether they see the whistle-blower as a dissident or a reformer, whether they view the whistle-blowing as an attempt at overall organizational change, and whether this change is believed to be desirable. If executives see only the specifics of the particular whistle-blowing incident, they are likely to act to contain the damage and maintain organizational stability. If, on the other hand, they view it as an opportunity for positive reform, they may be more open to change. Among the possible benefits to an organization are improved performance in the long term, an organizational environment or "culture" that is prosocial or encouraging of responsible social action, and the development of mechanisms for future dispute management (Farrell & Petersen, 1989). More negative outcomes for the organization might include financial costs resulting from the whistle-blowing, increased management turnover, and a loss of cohesion within the organization (Farrell & Petersen, 1989), although it is less clear whether the latter results from the retaliation or from the observation of wrongdoing in and of itself, which may prove alienating to organization members (Near & Miceli, 1986). Unfortunately, we have no indication at this time of the conditions under which any of these benefits or costs are more likely to occur.

Organizational theorists have tended to view change as incremental at best (for example, Lindblom, 1959; Quinn, 1980) and harmful at worst (for example, Benson, 1977). In fact, organizational change is obviously unavoidable. The real question is whether effective change tends to assume a form that is gradual and evolutionary, as represented by many organization development authors (such as Greiner, 1972), or sudden and dramatic (for example, Miller & Friesen, 1984). Whistle-blowing represents a specific case of attempted organizational change that may be examined from the perspective of these two frameworks.

In fact, the admittedly preliminary research on whistle-blowing has focused on the whistle-blower: what drives this person to commit this risky act, why and how the organization responds, and so on. An equally important, but thus far largely neglected question, is: Does whistle-blowing promote healthy and effective change when that change is sudden and quantum, or when it is long-term and gradual? The answer is important for two reasons: to address the particular question of the effects of whistle-blowing, and to elucidate the general processes of organizational change. In other words, the study of the whistle-blowing process may serve to suggest a more general model of organizational dissidence as an impetus for change, with particular relevance for theories about the conditions under which such change is likely to be effective. Only with research attention to these two questions can we develop the base of empirical findings that would provide an appropriate response to Ewing's more pragmatic question about how managers should respond to whistle-blowing. Because virtually no research has begun to address these concerns, this area may offer the most fertile ground yet for empirical examination of the whistle-blowing process. From the perspective that whistle-blowers offer an opportunity for organizational reform, the theoretical questions are: How do whistle-blowers promote organizational reform? and Through what change processes is reform brought about? The pragmatic question is: How can whistle-blowers be more effective in serving their role so that organizations may in fact benefit from whistle-blowing?

Summary

In this chapter, we have attempted to describe consequences of whistle-blowing and their interrelationship. It should be noted, of course, that organizational responses to whistle-blowing may not be consistent, depending on who is doing the responding. The possible responses that we considered included: (1) termination of the wrongdoing and rectification of the situation, (2) retaliation against the whistle-blower, and (3) the whistle-blower's possible actions upon suffering reprisal. Surprisingly, present evidence suggests that the organizational responses are not correlated in obvious ways.

Indeed, at this time, it appears that organizations that do not terminate wrongdoing are not significantly more likely to retaliate against whistle-blowers than are those organizations that do terminate wrongdoing. In short, what we have labeled a "consistent response" in figure 5–3 does not seem to be borne out by existing data as a more likely scenario than an inconsistent response, where organizations terminate and retaliate, or don't terminate and don't retaliate. This may be due to restriction in range of organizational responses, because some of the samples in which data were collected were unique in certain characteristics. A better understanding of the whistle-blowing process will clearly depend on our ability to complete further research on this issue.

What we do know at this point is that individual variables seem to be largely unrelated to whistle-blowing effectiveness. Situational variables directly related to the content of the wrongdoing (that is, unsafe or illegal behavior, and employee theft) were significantly associated with effectiveness in our samples; while other kinds of wrongdoing may be more important in other industries, the point remains that the type of wrongdoing alleged to have occurred seems to be a critical point in influencing effectiveness of the whistle-blowing process. Other situational variables and organizational variables were not consistently related to effectiveness in two samples. Power relationships seemed to have an effect, but here the key variable appeared to be the whistle-blower's credibility; whistle-blowers who were not role-prescribed to blow the whistle were likely to be more effective than those who were, probably because they were trusted to report wrongdoing only when the circumstances were so egregious that the wrongdoing could not be ignored.

Predictors of retaliation have received somewhat more attention than predictors of effectiveness, but here again, the picture is less than clear. The only variables found consistently to be associated with retaliation were support from top management, and from middle management. Unfortunately, casual patterns with these particular variables are especially unclear. Perhaps the most interesting point is that the correlation is not stronger than it is (typically around .50)! This provides at least some reassurance that the phenomena are somewhat distinct.

In conclusion, the whistle-blowing process is definitely complicated, as is once again made clear by the research reviewed in this chapter. Our methods of studying whistle-blowing leave much to be desired, so that many of the findings reported here must be treated as tentative. Perhaps as importantly, other potential predictor variables have yet to receive even cursory examination. Clearly, much work remains to be done here.

6

Legal Approaches to Whistle-blowing

Legal protection of employees who blow the whistle is a relatively recent phenomenon. The adoption of employment at will during the nineteenth century laissez-faire, industrialization era gave employers the power to fire an employee at any time for any reason so long as that employee was not hired for a specific term. Since virtually all employees were hired for an indefinite period, they enjoyed no job protection. Whistle-blowers were not exempted from this rule. Employment at will, while remaining strong well into the 1980s, slowly began to be eroded in the 1930s as exceptions were carved out to protect specific types of employees or to promote specific goals (see table 6–1, column 3, Violations Covered).[1] These congressionally created exceptions, while not enacted to protect whistle-blowers, were written in such a way that whistle-blowers could be encompassed within their protections. It was not until the late 1970s that whistle-blowers, as a distinct entity, began to enjoy broad legal protection.

While legal protection of whistle-blowers has developed slowly, the focus of that protection, until very recently, has consistently centered on retaliation. Both the federal model of protection, and the later state model are designed to protect employees from, or to compensate them when they have suffered, retaliation. As studies cited elsewhere in this book illustrate, retaliation is not the ordinary response to whistle-blowing, and fear of retaliation is not a primary deterrent to whistle-blowing. Thus, the legal focus has not been particularly effective in either protecting or encouraging whistle-blowing. In recognition of this failure, a third model has begun to emerge. This new model focuses on rewards as a way to encourage whistle-blowing and give adequate compensation to those willing to take the risks associated with it.

In this chapter we will examine the structure of the different legal models and illustrate how these structures are inconsistent with the social-psychological research on whistle-blowing. This examination will serve the dual purposes of pointing out the various legal protections enjoyed by whistle-blowers, as well as illustrating why these protections are ineffective in achieving the primary legal goal of correcting and preventing organizational misconduct.

The Federal Model

The National Labor Relations Act of 1935 (NLRA) (see table 6–1, page 253) was the first legislation which encompassed protection of whistle-blowers. The law, designed to protect employees engaging in union-related activities, contained a section protecting employees who testified or filed charges concerning illegal unfair labor practices (NLRA, Col. 4). Thus, while protection of whistle-blowers was merely an incidental means of enforcement of employees' organizational rights, the employer's power to retaliate against union-related whistle-blowing was significantly curtailed. This act established the federal whistle-blower protection model, which would be followed in most important aspects for over forty years.

The right to organize and bargain collectively established by the NLRA was later used to eliminate employment at will for most unionized employees. This was accomplished through bargaining for "just cause" firing provisions in labor contracts. Since retaliation for legitimate whistle-blowing would generally not provide just cause, unionized whistle-blowers eventually gained widespread protection.

Coverage Under the Federal Model

Since most of the subsequent federal acts encompassing whistle-blowers were enacted to carry out or ensure a non-whistle-blowing purpose, the protection afforded is similarly narrowly focused. Thus, employees are protected only if their whistle-blowing pertains to the particular area regulated by the act (table 6–1, col. 3), or the employees are within the group covered by the act (table 6–1, col. 2), such as miners under the Federal Mine Health and Safety Act. Acts designed to achieve similar purposes tend to offer the same kinds of coverage since the later acts are often based on an earlier act that served as a prototype. For example, many of the laws protecting the environment, such as the Clean Air Act, Superfund, the Solid Waste Disposal Act, and the Water Pollution Control Act are patterned after the Federal Mine Health and Safety Act passed in 1969 (see table 6–1, page 252), and many features of antidiscrimination laws resemble Title VII.

While the coverage in terms of employees and topics tends to be narrow, the type of whistle-blowing activity which is covered tends to be broadly based. Thus, most acts protect whistle-blowers who are about to commence, as well as those who are commencing or have commenced, some protected whistle-blowing activity. These activities range from reporting, to assisting in investigations, to testifying, to initiating proceedings (table 6–1, col. 4). Depending on the coverage of the particular act, other protected activity can include opposition to activities made unlawful by the act (Title VII or the Age Discrimination in Employment Act [ADEA]), or unlawfully being denied benefits and making claims therefor (Job Training and Partnership Act, Longshoreman's and Harbor Worker's Compensation Act, and Fair Labor Standards Act [FLSA]). Several of the acts have a "catch-all" phrase, such as "any other action to carry out the purposes of this subchapter,"[2] which gives the secretary and the courts broad latitude in interpreting covered activities.

Because of the narrow focus of the federal model, whistle-blowers do not enjoy generalized federal protection in the reporting of wrongdoing. While the awarding or denial of protection can encourage whistle-blowing regarding those issues that Congress selects as the most important, it does not give employees the message that they are to be generalized watchdogs against organizational wrongdoing. Under this model, whistle-blowing is seen more as an aberrational act valued only if it pertains to certain activities.

Procedure

The NLRA established another important precedent for federal whistle-blower protection by providing an administrative proce-

dure to handle whistle-blower complaints and to determine remedies. The focus of these complaints must be retaliation; the federal
model takes a very narrow focus toward facilitating whistle-blowing
or ensuring the correction of the reported wrongdoing. As discussed
in earlier chapters, correction of wrongdoing, and well-established,
known procedures for reporting the wrongdoing are more important than nonretaliation in facilitating whistle-blowing. Thus, this
model does little to encourage whistle-blowing.

Because the federal statutes were designed to address agendas
other than whistle-blowing, they generally do not contain sections
designating appropriate channels for reporting the wrongdoing.
Rather, they imply appropriate channels in defining what activity is
protected. Because of this failure to specify, disputes arose regarding
whether internal whistle-blowing was statutorily protected. With
few exceptions, courts have interpreted the statutes to protect both
internal and external whistle-blowers.[3] This interpretation allows
the whistle-blower to choose the complaint recipient, and to follow
the usual tendency to first report internally.

The procedure that is statutorily spelled out is the proper channel
for whistle-blowers to use after suffering retaliation. As Column 6
(How Pursued) of table 6–1 shows, virtually every act subsequent
to the NLRA provides for an administrative procedure to deal with
whistle-blower complaints of retaliation. Most commonly, the
whistle-blower who has suffered retaliation files a complaint with
the Secretary of Labor, who investigates the charges and, if a violation is found, orders corrective measures (table 6–1, cols. 6 and
9). If the orders are not complied with, the secretary can file suit in
the appropriate federal district court. Many of the acts establish a
time limit within which the secretary must complete the investigation.[4] If either party feels aggrieved by the secretary's actions, he or
she may appeal to federal court for review.[5]

One of the biggest problems with most of these acts is that they
give the whistle-blower very little time within which to file a claim
(table 6–1, col. 7, Statute of Limitations). The most common period
is thirty days after the adverse job action has occurred. The practical effect of such a short time period is to prevent many whistle-
blowers from pursuing their claims, for it is only the extremely
knowledgeable or aggressive employees who will realize that they
have a claim and be motivated to act within that time frame. The

Fair Labor Standards Act is a notable exception. It gives the employee two years after the violation to file a claim, and three years if the violation was willful. The very short statutes of limitations are one of the reasons why many whistle-blowers who are covered by these federal laws now bring claims under wrongful firing theories in state courts, where the applicable tort statute of limitations is generally one or two years. Another reason is the greatly expanded damages generally available in wrongful firing suits.

Remedies and Penalties

As in the NLRA, reinstatement and lost wages and benefits are the main remedies provided to whistle-blowers under the subsequent federal acts (table 6–1, col. 8, Employee Remedies). Virtually all the acts also allow for the recovery of costs, including attorney fees, of bringing the claim. Some of the later acts also provide for the awarding of compensatory damages, and a few, of exemplary damages (Asbestos Hazard Emergency Response Act of 1986, Fair Labor Standards Act [liquidated damages], Age Discrimination in Employment Act [liquidated damages]).[6] Several allow the court to award exemplary damages if the secretary files suit in federal court after the employer's failure to follow the secretary's remedial order (table 6–1, page 252, col. 6). In addition to these specifically mentioned remedies, many of the acts contain "catch-all" phrases such as "other appropriate relief." Because of this, and courts' interpretations of remedies available under specific acts, it is impossible to determine the exact extent of remedies available without reference to the individual act's interpretive history.[7]

What is clear is that the remedies available under most acts are much more limited than would be available in a tort suit for wrongful firing, where in addition to any lost wages and benefits, the plaintiff is likely to get an award for the emotional distress caused by the retaliatory action, and punitive damages, in addition to other damages peculiar to the particular case. Today, the average award in such suits is approaching $1 million.[8] Even under the federal acts where compensatory and exemplary damages are allowed, damages are likely to be less than would be recoverable in a wrongful firing suit. Juries determine damages in a wrongful firing suit, while under these federal laws the damages determination is made administratively or judicially. In general, juries are more pro-plaintiff and more generous. Plaintiffs, therefore, are likely to file a state wrongful firing claim in addition to, or in exclusion of, the federal claim. This has created a new battleground for whistle-blowers and their employers, for the employers try to force the whistle-blowers to pursue only the more limited federal remedy. Thus, the first step in many whistle-blowing cases today is a lawsuit over where, and under what theory, the suit may be pursued. The issue of whether a wrongful firing claim is preempted by the statutory law is discussed later in this chapter.

A final feature of some of the federal laws is penalties imposed on the retaliator (table 6–1, col. 9). The Fair Labor Standards Act, for example, allows for the imposition of fines up to $10,000 and/or imprisonment, and the Longshoreman's and Harbor Worker's Compensation Act allows for fines up to $5,000 (that cannot be paid by insurance). In general, however, the only sanction against the retaliator is the order of the secretary to abate the violation. It is clear that Congress does not see employer sanctions as a major weapon in the fight against retaliation for whistle-blowing.

Protection of Federal Workers

Most of the laws in table 6–1 pertain to all employees, whether public or private (col. 2). The Civil Service Reform Act (CSRA) (table 6–1, page 251), however, applies only to federal workers, and most federal civil servants file their whistle-blowing claims under this act. The act differs in some significant ways from the traditional federal model, and these differences are ones that should help encourage whistle-blowing.

The CSRA specifically protects whistle-blowing to any recipient. It also provides a recipient for the whistle-blowing if the employee chooses to report outside his or her employer-agency. This recipient, the Office of Special Counsel (OSC), is charged with protecting federal employee whistle-blowers and with handing their CSRA claims. Further, it is charged with investigating and pursuing reports of wrongdoing. Because this act provided for remedying of the wrongdoing, for specific protection of internal whistle-blowers, anonymous whistle-blowing, and an advocate to pursue claims for employees who suffered retaliation, it should have been especially effective in encouraging whistle-blowing. This, however, proved not to be the case.

When the OSC "lost sight of its mission" and failed to carry out its mandate,[9] retaliation increased and whistle-blowing declined.[10] In order to correct these problems, and to further encourage whistle-blowing to help cut down on waste, corruption, fraud, and wrong-doing, Congress passed the Whistleblower Protection Act of 1989 (WPA) to augment the protections provided by the CSRA.[11]

The Whistleblower Protection Act strengthens the Office of the Special Counsel by making it independent, charging it specifically to protect whistle-blowers, and requiring that the head be an attorney qualified to carry out the office's functions. The act increases protection for whistle-blowers in several ways. It allows employees to pursue their own cases against agencies if the Office of Special Counsel refuses to take the case to the Merit Systems Protection Board. It eases the burden of proof necessary for employees to prove they were harassed due to their whistle-blowing, and prevents the Office of Special Counsel from responding to inquiries from prospective employers about employees who have sought its help.[12]

It is questionable whether the changes the WPA makes to the CSPA will have the desired effect. These changes do not allow for damages for employees nor significantly extend the statute of limitations. Thus, many whistle-blowers will still be foreclosed from bringing claims, and those that do will be unable to receive compensation for their actual losses. As discussed later, studies of whistle-blowing legislation with these defects have shown that they do not encourage whistle-blowing. An important factor in the effectiveness of the revisions will be the aggressiveness with which the Special Counsel pursues his or her charge. If the system does work as a way for concerned employees to anonymously bring complaints that will be investigated and pursued to resolution, then whistle-blowing may be encouraged. At a minimum, those federal employees already inclined to blow the whistle will receive somewhat better protection.

In addition to statutory law, some public employees may also seek protection under the Constitution. In 1968, in the landmark case of *Pickering v. Board of Education*,[13] the U.S. Supreme Court set the precedent for such protection by holding that a public school teacher could not be fired for exercising his first amendment right to speak on issues of public importance. A constitutional cause of action was made more attractive by the Supreme Court's subsequent recognition of the right to seek damages for governmental interference with certain constitutional rights.[14] However, in 1983 the Supreme Court severely limited the right of federal employees to pursue first amendment damage claims. In *Bush v. Lucas*,[15] a case in which a federal worker was unconstitutionally demoted for whistle-blowing, the Court held that workers entitled to full CSRA protections were precluded from pursuing constitutional damage claims. While a few courts have carved out limited exceptions to the *Bush* decision, most federal whistle-blowers must rely on CSRA.[16]

State Laws Protecting Whistle-blowers

In the 1980s the focus of whistle-blower protection shifted from the federal arena to the states. This was the result of two events: the erosion of the doctrine of employment at will, and the passage of whistle-blower protection statutes by a majority of states. Of these, erosion of employment at will has been the most far-reaching and effective.

Erosion of Employment at Will

Until very recently the doctrine of employment at will meant that private, nonunionized employees who were hired for an indeterminate period had no common law protection from arbitrary, unjust firings, including firings because they blew the whistle. While one court changed the doctrine to protect a whistle-blower as early as 1959,[17] it has only been in the past few years that such protection has been recognized in a majority of states. The change reflects a growing acceptance by the courts of the idea that the job is so important a right that it should not be taken away arbitrarily. Unlike the earlier federal legislation discussed before, which protected certain groups of employees from specific types of actions, such as employees engaging in union-related activities (the NLRA), or minorities who suffered discrimination (Title VII), the judicially created exceptions apply to all employees. They also apply to all employers regardless of size or type of work.

While employment at will has been eroded under three judicially created theories, whistle-blowers are primarily concerned with the public policy exception to employment at will.[18] This theory holds that employers should not be able to use their power as employers to subvert public policy as established by the legislature or the courts. Firing an employee because she or he claimed a legislatively created benefit like workers' compensation, exercised a right such as voting, or refused to break the law on behalf of the employer, would be an act in violation of public policy because it attempts to prevent what the laws have created (or do what the law has prohibited) for the public good. Likewise, when a whistle-blower is retaliated against for reporting or trying to stop illegal or unsafe acts of the employer, this is considered to be a firing in violation of public policy.[19] The courts are fairly conservative in what they recognize as protected whistle-blowing, however, and if the whistle-blower cannot point to a well-established and clearly expressed law that is being violated, he or she is likely to not be protected.[20]

A firing in violation of public policy is brought as a wrongful discharge in tort. Under a tort cause of action, the employee is entitled to damages for all losses suffered including emotional harms. In addition, as mentioned above, a whistle-blower fired in violation of public policy is likely to get punitive damages. Punitive damages are assessed in cases where the defendant's actions have been especially wrongful. Using one's power as an employer to subvert the law is generally considered to be especially wrongful. Punitive damages are not based on the amount of actual damages suffered, but on how much the jury thinks it would take to teach the defendant not to commit similar acts and to deter others who might act similarly. When the defendants are large corporations, this is often determined to be hundreds of thousands to millions of dollars.[21] Thus, whistle-blowers who have suffered retaliation have a financial incentive to bring their claims in tort rather than, or in addition to, the statutory laws.

The Statutory Model

The 1980s also saw whistle-blower protection extended to employees through state statutes.[22] While a few states statutorily protected public employees before this time, the first protection of private employees was not until 1981. The state statutes were often passed after some public scandal that could have been prevented had employees successfully blown the whistle. By 1986, Michigan, Connecticut, Maine, California, Louisiana,[23] New York, and New Jersey had enacted statutes protecting private as well as public employee whistle-blowers. In addition, Arizona, Delaware, Florida, Kansas, Kentucky, Texas, Utah, and Washington had statutes protecting public employee whistle-blowers (table 6–2, col. 1). Despite the fact that most whistle-blowers could seek tort remedies by 1987, the statutory protection trend continued. As column 1 of the table indicates, as many states passed acts in 1987 and 1988 as in the previous six years, and additional states are considering legislation. These state statutes follow the federal model in its almost exclusive focus on retaliation.

Coverage Under the State Model

While the focus of all the acts is retaliation, there is little consensus as to how the protection for, or from, retaliation ought to be structured. The only thing on which there is total agreement is that, at a minimum, public employees ought to be protected. As does Congress, stage legislatures clearly see whistle-blowing as a way to control waste of public funds, abuse of authority, mismanagement, and violation of laws by those in the public sector. Sixteen states protect public employees only; four states protect employees of contractors with the state as well as state employees; one state (Louisiana) protects all employees but only for environmental whistle-blowing; one state (Montana) protects all employees through a codification of common law theories; and twelve states give general protection to private and public employee whistle-blowers (table 6–2, col. 2).

In general, the type of whistle-blowing protected is no broader than, and is often narrower than, what would be protected under common law theories. Legislatures do not want to leave much to the whistle-blower's discretion. Most states want to encourage whistle-blowing only when the employer is violating a state or federal law, rule, or regulation (table 6–2, col. 3, Violations Covered).[24] Only three states protect employees who report violations of codes of conduct or ethics,[25] and only seven protect employees who refuse to carry out or participate in an activity which violates the law.[26] The protections of refusals to act are generally more narrowly drawn than the reporting protections, but they bring these statutes more closely in line with the protections offered by the common law and the federal statutes.

A third of the states try to further limit the whistle-blower's discretion by requiring that the violation be more than of a minimal or technical nature, or the safety risk be imminent or specific, or the waste of public funds be "gross" (table 6–2, col. 3, Violations Covered). Ohio's statute is most restrictive in this regard. While the employee's discretion may be limited, most states require only that the employee act in good faith or under a reasonable belief in order to be protected (col. 4, Standard Required); the whistle-blower does not have to be correct in the assertion that the employer is violating a law, rule, or regulation. However, two states require that employees try to ascertain the accuracy of their allegations before making them.[27] Pennsylvania and West Virginia seem to have adopted the "altruism" point of view of whistle-blowing discussed in chapter 2, for they will not protect whistle-blowers who act out of a desire for personal gain or benefit.[28] Because of the limitations put on the whistle-blowers' discretion, whistle-blowers are more likely to seek protection under the common law's broader protection.

Procedure

A similar lack of consensus is shown regarding how the whistle-blowing should be reported (table 6–2, col. 5, How Reported). Fifteen states require that the whistle be blown to an external recipient. Some states require that the reporting be to a specific entity such as the office of auditor of accounts (Delaware), some to one of several governmental agencies, and many to a "public body." Whatever the entity, there is a clear preference for reporting to a governmental unit as opposed to a private organization such as a newspaper or activist group. The requirement that employees blow the whistle only externally in order to be protected forces the employee to become an adversary of the employer, denies the employer any chance to correct possible unknown problems, and as previously discussed, is likely to increase retaliation. It also serves little useful purpose.[29] Legislators concerned that internal reporting allows the employer to continue harmful or illegal activity can control for this by requiring the employer to act within a reasonable amount of time before external reporting occurs.[30]

Only six states require that the reporting first be internal.[31] Most of these states also require that the employee give the employer a reasonable chance to correct the problem before reporting externally. As discussed, internal reporting is preferable for the organization and the employee. It gives the organization the opportunity to correct the problem and avoid the negative publicity, investigations, and administrative and legal actions that usually follow external whistle-blowing while also maintaining good rapport with the whistle-blower and other ethically-focused employees.

Remedies and Penalties

As in the federal laws, the most commonly provided-for state remedy (table 6–2, col. 7, Employee Remedies) is reinstatement, back pay and lost benefits, and injunctive relief. Less than half the states allow suit for damages, some of them allowing punitive damages only, some allowing actual damages only, and some not specifying between the two. As was previously discussed, the failure to allow suit for the full range of damage means that the employee is denied an adequate remedy for the harms caused by a retaliating employer, and the statutes are unlikely to encourage employees to act because of this inadequacy. A few states try to protect the organization's interests by requiring the employee to pursue any administrative or internal remedies before bringing suit.[32]

Nineteen states provide for sanctions against the employer (table 6–2, col. 8, Employer Sanctions) in addition to remedies provided to the employee. In general, however, these sanctions are so minimal as to provide little disincentive to retaliate against a whistle-blower. The most common fine is $500, and in other states cannot exceed $1,000. A few of the statutes provide for suspension or discharge of the offender, and three make violation a criminal misdemeanor. When, as in Oregon, the misdemeanor can result in a year's imprisonment, a disincentive may occur.

Effectiveness of the State Whistle-blowing Statutes

State statutes were designed to encourage whistle-blowing by ensuring employees in enacting states that they had a remedy if their employers fired or otherwise retaliated against them for their reporting activities. A study of the first private employee whistle-blower statutes indicated, however, that the statutes did not have the desired effect.[33] In a four-year period, only three appellate cases in the three states studied involved employees who sought protection under the statutes, and these whistle-blowers met with limited success. When this experience was compared to suits brought by whistle-blowers in comparable states without protection statutes but which recognized a common law right to sue for firings in violation of public policy, the number of suits was comparable to or higher than those in the states with statutory protection. Thus, the statutes did not seem to either encourage whistle-blowing or encourage employees to seek protection under the statute.

A follow-up examination of cases brought under these same statutes showed little change. While the number of cases increased somewhat, no plaintiff won a recovery, and most of the plaintiffs used the statutes for purposes not intended by the legislature, such as avoiding an adverse arbitration decision,[34] or attempting to blackmail the employer.[35] In only one case did an act at least partially work in the way the legislature intended.[36] Whistle-blowers were only successful in collecting against their employers when they based their suits on the common law or another act.

One explanation for the limited impact of the statutes may be that the remedies they provide whistle-blowers are inadequate, especially when compared to the remedies provided by common law wrongful firing claims. Statutory remedies in every state with the early statutes offered less damages than if the employee sued under the common law. Remedies such as reinstatement, back pay, and benefits do not present much of an incentive when the employer and other employees are likely to be hostile, career advancement is likely to be severely limited, and the emotional and physical upheaval of being unemployed and pursuing a lawsuit goes uncompensated. In addition, the statutes created procedural difficulties such as ninety-day statutes of limitations, which do not exist in a common-law suit, and requirements of external reports. Finally, as illustrated in previous chapters, statutes which focus exclusively on retaliation fail to provide adequate incentives to spark whistle-blowing. When the whistle-blowing statute is interpreted as preempting the right of a whistle-blower to pursue a common law remedy, as some courts have held,[37] then the passage of a protective statute may even be harmful to whistle-blowers, for it prevents them from collecting the common law remedies that compensate them for the full range of injuries suffered.

Preemption

When laws such as the NLRA and the FLSA were first passed, they were seen as progressive legislation that offered much-needed relief to unprotected employees. The ability to retain or regain one's job and recover lost benefits and wages was certainly a large step forward for the employee. As noted, the erosion of employment at will now gives whistle-blowers who have suffered retaliation the opportunity to sue for damages, including punitive damages, rather than settling for the statutory remedies of reinstatement, and lost wages and benefits. In addition, the extended statute of limitations makes this a more realistic cause of action for many employees. Employers naturally prefer the administrative resolution of the dispute with its generally lower transaction costs, reduced recoveries, and time-barring of many suits. Thus, a common employer response to a whistle-blower's wrongful firing suit is to challenge the right of the employee to bring the suit by arguing that the cause of action is preempted by a federal or state statute which offers protection to the whistle-blower. These arguments have met with mixed success.

The federal preemption argument is based on the Supremacy Clause of the U.S. Constitution, which states that the states cannot enact or enforce laws which undermine federal laws.[38] In addition, in our system of laws, statutes take precedence over the common law. Thus, federal statutory law can preempt state statutory or common law, and state statutory law can preempt state common law. An area can be preempted because Congress or the state legislature has expressly so stated, or it can be impliedly preempted through extensive statutory coverage of the area.[39] In addition, to the extent that state law conflicts with the federal law, or because the state law "stands as an obstacle to the accomplishment and execution" of the federal laws, preemption can occur.[40] In areas where the states have traditionally regulated, the courts give close scrutiny to any federal preemption argument.

Since most of the federal statutes were not passed to protect whistle-blowers, Congress has not specifically preempted state whistle-blowing cases under them. Thus, preemption must be impliedly based. In determining whether a cause of action is preempted, the court must determine the extent to which allowing parallel remedies will undermine the policies underlying the statutes, and strike an appropriate balance between conflicting policies. The Supreme Court, in striking this balance, has recently found employees' causes of action not to be preempted.[41] Many lower courts have made similar holdings.[42]

The preemption argument is most likely to be successful if made about a whistle-blowing statute because the legislature has most clearly indicated its intent regarding the appropriate remedy for whistle-blowers. Thus, some state courts in states with whistle-blower protection statutes have denied wrongful firing claims to whistle-blowers.[43] Even in these states, however, if whistle-blowers can cast their claims not as a wrongful firing tort, but as a tort of defamation, intentional infliction of emotional distress, or some other tort which is not clearly employment-based, they still may be allowed to sue.[44] There seems to be a trend to not deny whistle-blowers the full range of remedies by allowing them to sue for wrongful firing, especially if their only other remedy is reinstatement and lost wages and benefits. However, the decisions are sufficiently mixed at this point that the recent decisions regarding each act, and jurisdiction, must be checked to determine the likelihood of preemption.

New Models of Whistle-blower Protection

Despite the lack of evidence indicating that whistle-blowing statutes fulfilled their intended purpose, the lack of consensus about who, how, and what to protect, and the fact that most employees have adequate protection under the common law, the trend toward legislative protection continues. Additional states are considering legislation, and a bill has been introduced in Congress to protect the private whistle-blower.[45] The federal bill is designed to "fill in the gaps" and would only apply to private employees who have no remedies under other laws. Like the previous statutes, it focuses on retaliation. It is also narrow in its coverage, for it only protects whistle-blowing about activities that threaten the public health or safety. Like the CSRA, it requires that such information be referred to the appropriate federal agency for investigation.[46]

A New Federal Model?

In addition to the traditional retaliation-focused statute, a new model seems to be emerging. Perhaps in recognition of the failure of earlier statutes to spark whistle-blowing, this new model uses rewards as an incentive while also protecting the employee who suffers retaliation. This is best exemplified by the revisions to the False Claims Act (table 6–1, last page). The act, originally passed in 1863 in response to contractors cheating the government, was revised in 1986 to make recoveries easier and more generous, and thereby encourage more whistle-blowing regarding government contractor fraud. Under the act, the whistle-blower files a *qui tam* suit on behalf of the government.[47] The Justice Department can join in the suit if it so desires. If it does join in the suit, the whistle-blower gets up to 25 percent of the judgment if the case is successful; if the government does not join the suit, the whistle-blower gets up to 30 percent of the judgment.[48] The law also protects the whistle-blower from retaliation.

The revised False Claims Act has the potential of becoming one of the most popular whistle-blower statutes, and one which may actually spark whistle-blowing. Justice Department studies estimate that fraud has been as much as 10 percent of the federal budget, or around $100 billion a year.[49] Damages under the act can be trebled. The statute of limitations in these cases is ten years. Thus, there is a great financial incentive (and time) for whistle-blowers and their lawyers to file claims. As discussed in chapter 7, even settlements can be significant. Since the 1986 revisions the number of cases filed has increased twenty-fold.[50] Whether this volume will continue depends on the success of the first suits, which have yet to go to trial.

While the False Claims Act offers the largest rewards, many other recently proposed acts also incorporate significant rewards. For example, the savings and loan "bailout" bill, the Financial Institutions Reform, Recovery and Enforcement Act, has a section offering rewards to whistle-blowers; Congress has proposed doubling the award for disclosure of fraud or waste by government employees; and the State Department has recently doubled to $4 million the reward possible for providing information that helps catch terrorists.[51]

Rewards for whistle-blowing are almost exclusively a federal idea. Only two states offer rewards (table 6–2, col. 7), and these rewards are not significant enough to have much impact. South Carolina gives the employee a reward of 25 percent of the savings in one year that results from the whistle-blowing, up to $2,000. Oregon allows whistle-blowers to collect $250 if this amount is greater than the damages suffered because of the whistle-blowing.[52]

As discussed in other chapters, research on the effectiveness of rewards as incentives to blow the whistle is limited, and it remains to be seen whether significant rewards will spur activity.[53] However, Congress seems to have assumed their effectiveness, and their use is likely to continue.

A New State Model?

On the state level, a different, possibly conflicting development is occurring. This is a movement to specifically protect whistle-blowers under proposed legislation designed to extend just-cause firing protection to all employees. It is exemplified by Montana's "just cause" statute passed in 1987. The law protects all employees against wrongful discharge while limiting damages to lost wages and benefits for a period not to exceed four years. The statute defines one type of wrongful discharge as discharge which "was in retaliation for the employee's refusal to violate public policy or for reporting a violation of public policy."[54] Employees can collect punitive damages for termination in violation of public policy if actual fraud or malice in the discharge can be shown. It should be relatively easy for an employee who is fired for reporting an employer's violation of public policy to show malice. Thus, while most employees receive greatly reduced damages under the act, most whistle-blowers still can collect punitive damages.

While Montana is the only state to so far adopt such a statute, the idea is receiving much discussion.[55] At least twelve other states, including California, Illinois, Michigan, New York, and Pennsylvania, have or are considering similar legislation. The Massachusetts legislature, which had a bill introduced in 1989, was urged by Labor Secretary Paul Eustace to pass the legislation, in part, to protect whistle-blowers.[56] In addition, the National Conference of

Commissioners on Uniform State Laws, the body that proposes model legislation, such as the Uniform Commerical Code, for states to enact, has completed a draft "just cause" law. The Commissioners' proposals are likely to receive close consideration by many state legislatures.

If rewards for whistle-blowing are an effective spur, then "just cause" bills, which severely limit damages, are likely to have a negative impact on whistle-blowing. Their impact may be the same as the early private employee whistle-blower protection statutes just discussed. However, "just cause" statutes would also eliminate the tort law alternative. In addition to limiting damages, "just cause" laws often narrow the definition of protected whistle-blowing.[57]

Wide adoption of state "just cause" bills may result in a situation where employees again primarily rely on federal statutes for protection, especially if those statutes incorporate reward incentives. Adoption will also cause the preemption issue to become more important.

Summary

As this review of enacted and proposed legislation and laws indicates, it is highly risky for an employer to retaliate against a whistle-blower. The legislative coverage, while varying widely, is increasingly pervasive. Even if the employer is in a state which does not legislatively protect its employees, and is not covered by a federal law, it is highly likely that a whistle-blower will be able (and will prefer) to pursue remedies under the common law. A common law suit, with its potential for large damages, publicity, and disruption, can be very costly.

Since wrongdoing is endemic to organizations, and whistle-blowing is likely at some point to occur, organizations are well advised to take a proactive, positive approach along the lines suggested in chapter 7. Probably the best approach would be to set up internal complaint procedures where concerned employees could report, and make sure that those procedures provide for speedy and impartial review. Employees should be kept informed of the action taken on their complaints. Whistle-blowers should not be retaliated against for filing reports; indeed, the employer may want to consider rewarding such behavior. Another preventative step would be to have all firings reviewed by someone of authority other than the person doing the firing. This would not only help prevent retaliatory firings for whistle-blowing, but would also help liability exposure to employment at will suits or proceedings under a just cause statute like Montana's. At a minimum, the only legally rational approach for an employer to take is to approach whistle-blowing in a nonretaliatory manner.

TABLE 6-1

Federal Whistle-blowing Statutory Sections

Act	Coverage	Violations Covered	Standard	How Pursued	Statute of Limitations	EE Remedies	ER Sanctions
Civil Service Reform Act 5 USC 2302 as amended by the Whistle-blower Protection Act of 1989 5 USC 1201	EE or applicant for a position in competitive service, a career app'tee position in senior exec. serv. or pos. in the excepted serv. (with exceptions)	race, relig, sex, nat'l origin, age, handicap, marital status, pol. affil. discrim., or conduct which does not adversely affect perf. of EE or others; reprisal for appeal; personnel act. viol. merit system principles; coerce pol. act. or reprisal for failure to take pol. act.; solicit or consider recomm. or stmt. unless based on pers. know. or records & is relevant; obstruct, neg. infl., or give illegal preference to appl.; nepotism; disclose viol. of law, rule or reg., or mismgt, gross waste of funds, abuse of authority, sub. & spec. danger to pub. health or safety	reasonable belief	file complaint with the Office of Special Counsel, which shall investigate & where approp., bring petitions for stays, corrective act, file a complaint or make recommend. for discip. action to Merit Systems Protection Board, and disclose to Att'y Gen. or agency head	file with M.S.P.B. 60 days after termination of invest. by O.S.C. or 120 days after orig. complaint if not notified by O.S.C.	stay of personnel action; approp. corrective action, costs & att'y fees	removal, reduction in grade, debarment from fed. employment up to 5 yrs., suspension, reprimand or fine up to $1,000

Table 6–1 Federal Statutes (continued)

Act	Coverage	Violations Covered	Whistleblower Actions Covered[1]	Standard[2]	How Pursued[3]	Statute of Limitations	EE Remedies	ER Sanctions
Clean Air Act[4] 42 USC 7622	any EE or person acting pursuant to EE's request	violation of purposes of Act	commencing, causing or testifying in proceeding under Act or assisting or participating in proceed. or action to carry out purposes of Act	EE who causes deliberate viol. of Act without direction of ER not covered	file complaint with Sec. of Labor; Sec. will notify person named in complaint, and complete invest. within stated time; if cause found & Sec. issues order which is not complied with, Sec. will file civil action in US dist. ct.	30 days after adverse job action	reinstatement, wages & benefits, compensatory dams., costs, expenses & att'y fees; if Sec. files suit in fed. ct, exemplary dams., injunctive relief; other appropriate relief	Sec. orders person who committed viol. to take affirm. action to abate viol.
Comprehensive Env. Response. Compensation & Liab. Act (Superfund)[5] 42 USC 9610								
Energy Reorganization Act[6] 42 USC 5851								
Federal Surface Mining Act[7] 30 USC 1293								
Occup. Safety & Health Act 29 USC 660[8]								
Safe Drinking Water Act[9] 29 USC 300-j-9								
Solid Waste Disposal Act[10] 42 USC 6971								
Surface Transportation Act[11] 49 USC 2305								

252

Act	Protected Persons/Conduct	Prohibited Conduct	Protected Activity	Burden of Proof	Where to File	Time Limit	Remedies	Other Remedies
Toxic Substances Control Act[12] 15 USC 2622								
Water Pollution Control Act 33 USC 1367								
National Labor Relations Act 29 USC 158(a)(4)	EE having the right to unionize, etc., or not to unionize	unfair rep. by unions or interfer. w/ EE rts.; race, color, relig., sex or nat'l origin disc.; or disc.; discharge on organ. membership; unfair labor prac., interfer. with organ. of EE incl. discrim., domination & refusal to barg.	filing charges or giving testimony under Act	NLRB's gen. couns. must make prima facie showing that protected conduct was motivating factor; ER has burden of demons. that same action would have occurred even in the absence of protected conduct	file charge at nearest NLRB office	6 mos. (unless in armed forces)	reinstatement, back pay, reimburse union & NLRB for exp. in investigating, prepar., present., & conducting case, att'y fees	cease & desist order, union access to plant bulletin bd's, ER notif. EE's of their rts., union access to EE in non-working areas during non-working time, etc.
Labor Management Relations Act 29 USC 158(a)(3)	viol. of contracts b/w ER & labor organ. rep. EEs, or between labor organs.				suit in US dist. ct.			

Table 6–1 Federal Statutes (continued)

Act	Coverage	Violations Covered	Whistleblower Actions Covered[1]	Standard[2]	How Pursued[3]	Statute of Limitations	EE Remedies	ER Sanctions
Fair Labor Standard Act 29 USC 215(a)(3)	non-exempt private and public EEs whose occup. relates to interstate commerce; (exempt EEs incl. salaried professionals, execs., admin., & outside sales EEs)	viol. of act	file complaint or cause proceed. or testify relating to Act, or service on indus. comm.		EE files own act. or for other EE for dams. in state or fed. ct.; rt. to be party plaintiff ends on Sec. of Lab. filing act. where legal & equit. relief sought; Sec. may bring act. to recover amt. of unpd. min. wages or overtime plus equal amt. of liq. dams.	2 yrs. after viol.; if willful viol., 3 yrs.	approp. legal or equitable relief incl. employment, reinstatement, promotion, backpay plus equal amount as liq. dams., att'y fees & costs	willful violator subject to fine up to $10,000 or imprison. up to 6 mo., or both; imprison. if prev. convicted of viol.; ct. may order civil remedies
Longshoreman's & Harbor Worker's Compensation Act 33 USC 948(a)	EE	EE claimed compensation from ER or testified in a proceeding under Act		person adjudicated to have filed false claim not protected	file claim with secretary after ER refuses to pay		reinstatement, lost wages unless no longer qualified to perform duties	fine of $1,000–$5,000 as determined by dep. comm'r, deposited in special fund; if not pd, suit in US dist. ct.;

EE Retirement Income Security Act 29 USC 1132	participant, beneficiary or fiduciary of covered plan	administrator's failure to recover benes. due, to enforce rts., to clarify rts. to future benes. under plan's terms; breach of fiduc. duty: failure or refusal to comply with request for info. which admin. req'd to furnish to partic. or bene.; viol. of Act or terms of plan	complaint served on Sec. of Labor & Sec. of Treasury by certified mail; litigation subject to control of Att'y. Gen.; civil suit by Sec., participant, benef. or fiduciary	recovery of benefits due; clarification of future benes.; interest; enforce rts; injunctive relief or other app. prop. relief; att'y fees & costs	ER alone (not carrier) liable for penalties & pymts. adm. who refuses to provide info. requested may be personally liable for up to $100/day from date of failure or refusal; liq. dams. not in excess of 20% of that allowed by fed. or state law

Table 6–1 Federal Statutes (continued)

Act	Coverage	Violations Covered	Whistleblower Actions Covered[1]	Standard[2]	How Pursued[3]	Statute of Limitations	EE Remedies	ER Sanctions
Federal Mine Health & Safety Act 30 USC 815(c)	miner, miners' rep., or applicant for employment in mine	interfere with exercise of stat. rts. of miner or rep. because s/he filed compl. related to Act incl. danger or safety or health viol. in mine; or EE is subject of med. eval. & potential transfer; or instituted proceed., testified, or exercised rt. under Act		not frivolous	file compl. w/ Sec., who investigates; if Sec. finds viol., Sec. files rpt. with Comm'n & suggests relief; Comm'n offers hearing then issues order; if Sec. decides no viol., EE may file before Comm'n	60 days after viol.; 30 days after Sec's. finding of no viol. to file with Comm'n	immed. reinstatement pending final order if Sec. finds complaint not frivolously brought, costs, expenses & att'y fees	Comm'n can require violator to abate viol.
Migrant and Seasonal Agricultural Workers Prot. Act 29 USC 1855	migrant or seasonal agricultural worker	discrim. in viol. of Act	file compl, institute or testify in proceed. or exercise of rt. for protection for self or others under Act	with just cause	file complaint with Sec., who investigates; if viol. determined, Sec. institutes action in US dist. ct.	180 days after adverse job action	all approp. relief incl. reinstatement with back pay or dams.; injunction	

Statute	Covered Employee	Violation	Protected Activity	Procedure	Time	Remedy
Asbestos School Hazard Abatement Act 20 USCA 4018	state or local EE	asbestos problem in schl. bldgs. in juris. of agency	bringing to attention of public asbestos problems			
Safe Containers For International Cargo Act 46 USC 1506	reporting EE	violation of Act	reporting existence of viol. of Act to Sec. or his agents	file complaint with Sec. of Labor, who may inves.; if viol., Sec. files act. in US dist. ct.	60 days	injunction, reinstatement, backpay, other approp. relief
Title VII 42 USC 2000 e-4(a) Amended by Civil Rights Act of 1991[14]	any EE, applicant, union member or applicant[13]	unlawful employment practice within meaning of Act	opposition to practice unlaw. under Act, or charging, testifying, assisting, or partic. in any manner in invest, proceed. or hearing under Act	writ. charge submitted to EEOC or any design. rep. of Comm'n with stmt. disclosing whether proceed. have been commenced before state or local agency	180 days	injunction, reinstatement, hiring, backpay, other equitable relief; limited compensatory punitive damages for intentional discrimination

Table 6–1 Federal Statutes (continued)

Act	Coverage	Violations Covered	Whistleblower Actions Covered[1]	Standard[2]	How Pursued[3]	Statute of Limitations	EE Remedies	ER Sanctions
Age Discrimination in Employment Act 29 USC 623(d)	EE or applicant; union member or applicant[15]	violation of Act	oppos. any prac. lawful under Act or has made a charge, testified, assisted, or partic. in any manner in invest., proceed., or hearing under Act		suit by Sec. of Labor after conciliation fails, or suit by plaintiff after notice to Sec.	180 days to file notice with Sec.	appropriate legal or equit. relief incl. reinstatement, promotion, unpd. compen., att'y fees	liquidated damages for willful viol. equal to backpay
Job Training and Partnership Act 29 USC 1574(g)	participant, or any indiv. in connection w/ admin. of program (fed. fiscal controls & fund acctg. procedures)	viols. of Act; unlawful denial of benefit to which indiv. is entitled under Act or Sec's. reg.	filed complaint, instituted or testified in proceed. or investig. related to Act; unlaw. denied benefit		if Sec. determines viol., Sec. shall take action or order corrective measures	30 days	necessary corrective measures	

258

False Claims Amendments Acts of 1986 31 USC 287	any EE	false claims for fed. funds	investigating, initiating, testifying or assisting in action filed under Act	lawful actions	suit in US dist. ct. on behalf of gov't; notify Justice Dep't	reinstatement, 2 times back-pay, int., special dams. incl. costs & att'y fees; all relief necess. to make EE whole.

[1] The actions covered typically include "about to" commence, testify or assist in proceedings or actions.

[2] The F.S.M.A. and the S.T.A. do not exempt deliberate violators from coverage.

[3] Superfund, the F.S.M.A., the S.W.D.A., and the W.P.C.A. provide for an opportunity for a public hearing of record at the request of either party.

[4] Actions covered include actions for enforcement or administration of requirement under Act or implementation plan.

[5] No provision for suit in fed. dist. ct.; whistleblower acts covered incl. providing info. to state or fed. gov't; compensatory damages not mentioned.

[6] The E.R.A. whistleblower actions include activities under the Atomic Energy Act of 1954, as do the violations covered, and the standard.

[7] The F.S.M.A. does not provide for a suit in federal district court, and does not mention compensatory damages.

[8] Covered viols. incl. state health stnds; if Sec. determines viol., Sec. files act. in US dist. ct.; besides reinstate. & back pay, only remedy mentioned is "other appropriate relief."

[9] Whistleblower actions incl. acts. re state drinking water regs. or underground injection control programs; Sec. can order exemplary damages.

[10] Whistleblower actions incl. acts re implementation plans; no provision for suit in fed. dist. ct., & no mention of compensatory damages.

[11] The statute of lims. is 180 days; exemplary dams. are not mentioned in dist. ct. suit; Sec. can order immed. relief with the prelim. finding.

[12] The Secretary can order exemplary damages.

[13] Coverage also incls. any indiv. discrim. against by employment agency, jt. labor-mgt. comm. controlling apprenticeships or other training or retraining, incl. on-the-job training programs.

[14] The Americans with Disabilities Act, which is being phased in during 1992–1994, was also amended by the Civil Rights Act. The ADA, in a manner similar to Title VII, protects against discrimination on the basis of disability, a record of disability, or perceived disability.

[15] Employment agency, jt. labor-mgt. comm. controlling apprent. or other training or retrainng programs, prohib. from discrim. against "any indiv."

TABLE 6-2
State Chart

State & Statutory Cite Yr. Passed/Revised	Employees (EE) Covered	Violations Covered	Standard Required	How Reported	Statute of Limitations	Employee Remedies	Employer (ER) Sanctions
Alaska Stat. §39.90.100 1989	public	viol. of state, fed., or mun. law, reg. or ordinance; danger to pub. health or safety, gross mismanagement, substantial waste of funds or clear abuse of authority; matter accepted for invest.		to a pub. body or in ct. action; ER can req. in writ. personnel policy that EE first submit writ. rept. to it unless EE reas. believes won't be prompt action, is already known to super., is emerg. or fears reprisal or disc.		civil action incl. punitive damages; can't be declared ineligible to bid on pub. contracts, receive land under state law, or rec. other rt., priv., benefit	civil fine up to $10,000; person attempting to prevent report or public inquiry subject to fine up to $10,000
Ariz. Rev. Stat. Art. 9, §38-531	public	viol. of law, mismgt., gross waste of money or an abuse of authority	reasonable belief	to a public body (incl. bd. of dirs. of non-profit & county hosps)			offender suspended without pay up to 30 days, or dismissed
Cal. Lab. Code §1102.5[1] 1988	all	viol. of or noncompliance with state or fed. statute or reg.	reasonable belief	to government or law enforcement agency			

260

Colo. Rev. Stat. §24-50.5-101 1988	public	actions of state agencies that are not in the public interest	knowingly false claim or disregard for truth or falsity not protected	good faith effort to give info. to super., app'ting authority or member of gen. assem. before disclosure; disclose by writ. evid. to any person or testimony before gen. assem. comm.		state personnel board investigates & hears; EE may sue if no grounds found; reinstate., backpay, lost service credit, record expungement, costs	offense noted on offender's personnel record; reimbursement to EE paid out of ER agency's funds
Conn. Gen. Stat. §31-51 m(a)-(d) 1987 (private) 1985 (public)	all	*private EE:* viol. or suspected viol. of state or fed. law or reg.; *public EE:* corruption, uneth. pracs., viol. of state law or reg., mismgt., gross waste of funds, abuse of author. or danger to pub. safety	knowingly false not protected	*private EE:* to public body; *public EE:* must report to inspector general.[2]	90 days (private) 30 days (public)	*private EE:* exhaust admin. remedies; then suit for reinstate., backpay, benefits, ct. costs, att'y fees; *public EE:* file appeal with EE review bd. or follow collective barg. contract proced.	
Del. Code Tit. 29 §5115 1983	public	viol. or suspected viol. of state or fed. law or reg.	known to be false not protected	must report to office of auditor of accounts	90 days	injunctive relief, actual damages	

Table 6–2 State Chart (continued)

State & Statutory Cite Yr. Passed/Revised	Employees (EE) Covered	Violations Covered	Standard Required	How Reported	Statute of Limitations	Employee Remedies	Employer (ER) Sanctions
Fla. Stat. §112.3187 (1) to (10) 1986	public; EE of independent contractor of state agency	malfeas., viol. or suspected viol. of fed., state or local law, rule or reg. creating substantial & specific danger to pub. health, safety, or welfare	knowingly false not protected	sworn complaint to approp. agency or fed. entity with authority to investigate, police, manage or remedy violation	90 days	exhaust contractual or admin. remedies, then suit for reinstatement, benefits, seniority, lost wages, damages, costs & att'y fees, injunction	
Hawaii Rev. Stat. §378-61 1987	all	viol. or suspected viol. of state, local or fed. law or rule	knows to be false not protected	to a public body	90 days	reinstate., benefits, seniority, lost wages, damages, costs, att'y fees, injunction	up to $500 fine
Ill. Personnel Code (Private) Ch. 127. §19 c.1(1),(2)(1987) (public) §1(a) & (b) (1988)	all	viol. of law, rule or reg., mismgt., gross waste of funds, abuse of authority, substan. and specific danger to pub. health or safety	reasonable belief				

Ind. Code §20-12-1-8 §22-5-3-3 1987	public; EE of state educational instit.; EE of ER under state contract	viol. of federal law or reg, state or local law, rule or ordinance, or misuse of pub. resources, viol. of st. or fed. law or rule, ordinance of a pol. subdivis., misuse of pub. resources	reasonable attempt to ascertain correctness before disclose	*public EE*: in writ. to super. or app'ting author. unless he is one in viol., then his super. or app't-ing author. or state comm'n; if no good faith effort made to correct in reas. time, can submit writ. rpt. to any-one; *pub. contract EE*: in writ. to ER, then like public EE		
Iowa Code §79.28 1989	public	viol. of law or rule, mismgt., gross abuse of funds, abuse of authority or substantial and significant danger to pub. health or safety	reasonable belief	member of gen. assem., legis. service or fiscal bureau, citizens' aide, computer support bur. or respective caucus staffs of gen. assem.	injunctive relief, reinstatement, backpay, any other equitable relief ct. deems approp., att'y fees & costs	offender commits simple misdemeanor

Table 6-2 State Chart (continued)

State & Statutory Cite Yr. Passed/Revised	Employees (EE) Covered	Violations Covered	Standard Required	How Reported	Statute of Limitations	Employee Remedies	Employer (ER) Sanctions
Kan. Stat. §75-2973 1984	public	viol. of state or fed. laws, rules or reg.	knows to be false or reckless disregard for truth not protected	can't prohibit from or require notice of EE discussing with legis. or rpting. to anyone			
Ky. Rev. Stat. §61.102. 1986	public; some EEs of public contractors	actual or suspected viol. of law, statute, exec. order, reg., mandate, rule or ord. of US or KY, or mismgt., waste, fraud or endang. of pub. health or safety	good faith; knows to be false or reckless disregard for truth not protected	att'y general, auditor of pub. acc'ts, gen. assem. or EEs, judiciary law enforcement, or any other approp. body or author.; no notice can be req'd	90 days	injunctive relief, reinstatement, back wages, benefits, seniority, punitive damages, costs & att'y fees	willful violator guilty of class A misdemeanor
La. Rev. Stat. §30:2027 1981	all	viol. of state, fed. or local environmental statute, ordinance or reg.	good faith; deliberate violators not protected			triple damages, inc. lost wages & antic. wages from lost promotion, lost prop., benes., phys. or emot. damages, costs & att'y fees	

264

Statute	Covered	Protected conduct	Standard	Procedures	Time limit	Remedies	Penalties
Me. Rev. Stat. Tit. 26, §831 1983	all	viol. of state or fed. law or rule, risk to health or safety[a]	good faith; reasonable cause to believe	first to super. & allow reas. time to correct unless EE has spec. reason to believe ER won't correct; then to pub. body; may bring complaint to human rts. comm'n		reinstatement, back wages, benefits & seniority, costs, att'y fees	offender liable for $10.00/day fine for each day of willful violation
Md. Ann. Code Art. 64A, §12G 1988	public and applicants	viol. of law, rule or reg, gross mismgt., waste of funds, abuse of author., sub. & specific danger to pub. health or safety	reasonable belief	file complaint with sec. of personnel	1 year after EE knew or should have known	provides remedies supplemental to ordinary state EE grievance procedures	
Mich. Comp. Laws §15.361 1981	all	viol. or suspected viol. of state or fed. law, reg. or rule	knows to be false not protected	public body	90 days	actual damages, att'y fees, reinstate., back wages, benefits, senior., inj. relief	civil fine of no more than $500

Table 6–2 State Chart (continued)

State & Statutory Cite Yr. Passed/Revised	Employees (EE) Covered	Violations Covered	Standard Required	How Reported	Statute of Limitations	Employee Remedies	Employer (ER) Sanctions
Minn. Stat. §181-931 1987	all	viol. or suspected viol. of any fed. or state law or rule.[a]	good faith; knows to be false or reckless disregard for truth not protected	ER, gov'tal body or law enforcement official		if involuntarily term., in 5 days request in writ. reason from ER; ER has 5 days to respond; dams., costs & disburse., att'y fees, equit. relief	failure to notify EE of reason for dismissal results in civil penalty of $25/ day up to $750
Mo. Stat. §105.055 1987	public	viol. of any law, rule or reg., or mismgt., gross waste of funds or abuse of authority, sub. or specific danger to pub. health or safety, operations of agency with legis.	reasonable belief; knows to be false, reckless disregard or disclosure of EE's own wrongdoing not protected	appeal to state personnel advisory board or appropriate agency or review board	30 days	modification or reversal of action and appropriate relief	violator suspended on leave without pay for up to 30 days; dismissal and ban from employ. for up to 2 yrs.

Citation	Coverage	Protected activity	Standard	Procedure	Time	Remedies
Mont. Code Ann.[3] Part 9, §39-2-901 1987	all	viol. of pub. policy re health, safety or welfare established by constitution, statute or administrative rule		exhaust internal procedures or 90 days from initiating internal procedure; ER must notify EE of written procedures within 7 days of termination	1 year	arbitration by mutual agree., or suit for up to 4 yrs. of benefits & int.; pun. damages for ER's fraud or malice in discharge; att'y fees if prevailing party's offer to arb. was refused
N.H. Rev. Stat. §275-E:1 1988	all	viol. of law or rule of state, local entity, or US[a]	good faith report of what has reasonable cause to believe	must first rpt. to super. & allow reas. oppor. to correct unless specific reason to believe won't promptly remedy		exhaust internal procedures, then hearing with comm'ner of labor; reinstate., benefits; seniority, injunctive relief
N.J. Rev. Stat. §34:19-1 1986	all	activity, policy or practice in viol. of law, rule or reg.[a]	reasonable belief	written notice to super. first & reas. oppor. to correct unless reas. fear phys. harm in emergency sit.; then pub. body	1 year	injunction, reinstatement, benefits, seniority, lost wages, costs & att'y fees, punitive damages; civil fine up to $1,000 for first viol., & up to $5,000 for subsequent viols.

Table 6–2 State Chart (continued)

State & Statutory Cite Yr. Passed/Revised	Employees (EE) Covered	Violations Covered	Standard Required	How Reported	Statute of Limitations	Employee Remedies	Employer (ER) Sanctions
N.Y. Labor Law §740 (1984) N.Y. Civil Service Law §75-b (1986) N.Y. Labor Law §215 (1967)	all	*private EE*: viol. of law, rule or reg. which creates & presents a sub. & specific danger to pub. health or safety;[a] *public EE*: same as private, plus improper gov't act.	good faith	*private EE*: first to super. & give ER reas. oppor. to correct, then pub. body; *public EE*: first to app'ting author. & give reas. time to take approp. act. unless imminent serious danger to pub. health or safety, then gov'tal body; *unionized EE*: comm'ner or author. rep.	1 year	*private EE*: injunction, reinstate., benefits, seniority, lost wages, costs & att'y fees; *public EE*: arb. if req'd. otherwise, same as private EE; *unionized EE*: reinstate., lost comsen, lost compensation, damages, att'y fees	civil fine from $200 to $2,000 for offender with union contract
N.C. Stat. §126-84 (1989)	public	viol. of state or fed. law, rule or reg., fraud, misappropriation of state resources, or substantial & spec. danger to the pub. health & safety		report verbally or in writing to super, dep't head, or other approp. authority	1 year	damages, injunction, or other remedies agst. person or agency commiting viol. incl. reinstate, backpay, benefits, seniority, costs & att'y fees	if ct. finds ER willfully viol. act, EE entitled to treble damages, costs & att'y fees

268

Ohio Rev. Code §4413.51 (1988) §124.341 (1986)	all	viol. of state or fed. statute, ord. or reg. that ER has authority to correct & EE believes is a criminal offense likely to cause imminent risk of phys. harm or hazard to pub. health or safety, or is a felony; viol. by fellow EE	reasonable belief; reasonable & good faith effort to determine accuracy	orally report to super. or other respon. officer of ER, then file writ. detailed rept; if no reas., good faith effort to correct in 24 hrs., file det. writ. rept. with local prosecut. author., peace officer, or app. prop. pub. official with regulatory author.[4]	180 days	reinstatement, back wages, benefits, seniority, costs & att'y fees, injunctive relief	ER must respond in writing to EE notifcation within 24 hours or next business day about effort to correct or absence of hazard; interest on backpay for willful viol.
Or. Rev. Stat. §240.740 (1983) §659.510 (1989)	public; EEs of pub. corp. or contractor performing pub. services except constructing pub. improvements[5]	viol. of fed. or state law, rule or reg.; gross waste of funds, abuse of author., sub. & spec. danger to pub. health or safety, mismgt.; subject to warrant for arrest; require notice or in any way attempt to prevent discl.	reasonable belief	independent agency; rpt. to super. or agency designee re arrest warrant vulner. & super. shall notify state police	90 days	appeal under ORS §240.560 & 659.035; injunctive relief; actual dams. or $250, whichever is greater	misdemeanor, fine up to $500, or up to 1 yr. in jail, or both; ineligible for appointment for 5 yrs.

269

Table 6–2 State Chart (continued)

State & Statutory Cite Yr. Passed/Revised	Employees (EE) Covered	Violations Covered	Standard Required	How Reported	Statute of Limitations	Employee Remedies	Employer (ER) Sanctions
Pa. Stat. Ann. Tit. 43, §1421	all	viol. or imminant viol., which is not merely technical or minimal, of a fed., state or local statute or reg. or a code of conduct or ethics designed to protect interests of pub. or ER, or waste	good faith: without malice or consideration of personal benefit and reasonable cause to believe is true	superior or agent of employer or appropriate authority	180 days	damages, reinstatement, back wages, seniority, costs, art'y fees, injunctive relief	offender liable for civil fine up to $500; public EE who tried to discourage disclosure of criminal activity can also be suspended up to 6 months
R.I. Gen. Laws §36-15-1 1984	public; EE of ER rec. more than $200,000 in pub. funds in preceding 12 mos.[6]	viol. or imminent viol. of state, fed. or local law, rule or regulation	reasonable belief; knowingly false not protected	to a public body	3 years	injunctive relief, actual damages, reinstatement, back wages, fringe benefits, seniority, litigation costs	

Statute	Coverage	Protected activity	Condition	Reporting requirement	Time limit	Remedies	Penalty
S.C. Code Ann. §8-27-10 1988	public	viol. of any state or fed. law, or reg. or gov'tl criminality, corruption, waste, fraud, gross negligence or mismgt.	acts without probable cause not protected		1 year[7]	25% of 1 yr. of savings resulting from report, up to $2,000; reinstatement, lost wages, actual damages, costs & att'y fees	
Tex. Pub. Offices Code Ann. Art. §6252-16a 1983	public	viol. of law	good faith		90 days[8]	injunctive relief, actual & punitive damages, ct. costs, att'y fees, reinstate., lost wages, benefits, seniority	offending supervisor subject to civil penalty up to $1,000
Utah Code Ann §67-21-1 1985	public	waste of pub. funds, property, manpower, or viol. of local, state or fed. law, rule or reg.[9a]	reason to know report is malicious, false or frivolous not protected	writ. notice, or formally inform ER unless reas. believe prob. won't be solved in reas. & timely manner; give suff. time to take approp. action, or follow ER's admin. estab. procedures	180 days	reinstatement, backpay, benefits, seniority, damages, costs & att'y fees, injunctive relief	violator liable for civil fine of up to $500, damages

Table 6–2 State Chart (continued)

State & Statutory Cite Yr. Passed/Revised	Employees (EE) Covered	Violations Covered	Standard Required	How Reported	Statute of Limitations	Employee Remedies	Employer (ER) Sanctions
Wash. Rev. Code §42.40.010 1982	public	improper gov'tl act., viol. of state law or rule, abuse of author., sub. & specific danger to pub. funds	good faith	office of state auditor	2 years	judicial review, att'y fees	
W. Va. Code §6c-1-1 1988	public	waste or wrongdoing of more than merely tech. or minimal nature of fed., state or local statute, reg., or ord., or of code of conduct or ethics designed to protect the pub. or ER's interests	good faith; without malice or consideration of personal benefit, and reasonable belief in truth	employer or approp. authority	180 days	injunctive relief, reinstatement, back wages, benefits, seniority, actual damages, costs & att'y fees	violator subject to civil fine up to $500, suspension up to 6 months

Wisc. Stat. §230-80 1984	public	violation of state or fed. law, rule or reg., mismgt., abuse of author., sub. waste of pub. funds, danger to pub. health & safety	reasonable belief; disclosure for anything of value not protected unless for award offered by gov't to get info. to improve admin. or oper.	written notice to super. or approp. gov'tal unit, law enforcement agency, state or fed. dist. att'y, grand jury or judge, or att'y,, collective barg. unit or legislator	60 days	may file written complaint to commission; sue

[a] Refusal to participate in violation also protected.

[1] Additional rules & protections exist for EEs or applicants of local agencies under §53296.

[2] There are different reporting requirements for public service company and nuclear power EEs.

[3] Montana's statute is a general wrongful discharge statute.

[4] If viol. of Air Pollution Control, Solid and Hazardous Waste, Safe Drinking Water, or Water Pollution Control law that is a criminal offense, EE can directly notify appropriate pub. official or agency. EE protected from retaliation for checking for accuracy for, or making inquiry related to writ. report.

[5] Additional rules & protections exist for EEs or applicants of local agencies under §532.96.

[6] Law also applies to EE of ER subject to Title 23, Ch. 19.1, who disposes of toxic waste in violation of chapter.

[7] Job action within year from time EE reports is presumed to be violation of act. ER must rebut this presumption.

[8] It is a rebuttable presumption that suspension or termination within 90 days of report is in violation of act.

[9] ER can't make rules unreasonably restricting EE's ability to document waste or viol.

273

Notes

1. The Federal Chart contains the most commonly used federal whistle-blower protection laws. Other federal laws might be implicated depending on the special circumstances of particular cases. For example, a black employee who suffers retaliation for reporting the employer's discriminatory contracting practices might be able to sue under the Civil Rights Acts of 1866 and 1871 in addition to Title VII. These acts do not have specific whistle-blower sections, but they can encompass retaliatory job actions as deprivations of rights guaranteed by these laws. The advantage of suing under them is that recovery of damages such as punitive damages is possible, and there are certain procedural benefits. If whistle-blowers consult with knowledgeable and creative attorneys, a variety of additional federal laws might be used.

2. Safe Drinking Water Act, 42 U.S.C. Sec. 300j–9(i)(1)(C).

3. See, e.g., Kansas Gas & Elec. Co. v. Brock, 780 F.2d 1505 (10th Cir. 1985), cert denied, 478 U.S. 1011 (1986); Mackowiak v. University Nuclear Systems, Inc., 735 F.2d 1159 (9th Cir. 1984).

4. See, e.g., Safe Drinking Water Act, 42 U.S.C. Sec. 300j–9(i)(2)(b) (thirty days after receipt of complaint); Surface Transportation Act, 49 U.S.C. Sec. 2305(c)(2)(A) (sixty days after receipt of complaint).

5. See, e.g., Federal Mine Health and Safety Act, 30 U.S.C. Sec. 815(C)(3); Energy Reorganization Act, 42 U.S.C. Sec. 5851(c).

6. Liquidated damages under the ADEA and the FLSA are equal to the amount of back pay awarded. They are awarded for willful violations under the ADEA. Under the FLSA, the defendant must show good faith with reasonable grounds for believing that its actions were lawful in order to escape liability. M. Player, Federal Law of Employment Discrimination 278 (1981).

7. For example, a few courts have allowed compensatory damages under Title VII of the Civil Rights Act of 1964 and the ADEA, although most courts limit remedies to reinstatement and wages and benefits lost. See, e.g., Kennedy v. Mountain States Telephone & Telegraph Co., 449 F. Supp. 1008 (D. Colo. 1978); Beesley v. The Hartford Fire Insurance Co., 717 F. Supp. 781 (D. N. Ala. 1989).

8. According to a study reported in 1989, the average award in wrongful firing cases was $732,000. BNA Communicator (Spring 1989), p. 3, col.

3. In a Rand Corporation study of wrongful firing cases that went to trial in California between 1980 to 1986, the average award was $646,855. Awards have continued to rise since then. *Wall Street Journal,* 7 Sept. 1989, B1, col. 3.

9. R. McMillion, "Aiding Whistle-blowers," *A.B.A. J.* (March 1989): p. 121 (quoting Rep. Patricia Schroeder). The office viewed its role as protecting the merit system rather than the whistle-blower. Up to 90 percent of federal employee whistle-blowers lost their appeals. *Focus On . . . Whistle-blower Law,* Indiv. Empl. Rts., vol. 3, p. 4 (Bureau of National Affairs, Oct. 25, 1988).

10. *Focus On . . . Whistleblower Law;* Devine & Aplin, "Abuse of Authority: The Office of Special Counsel and Whistleblower Protection," 4 *Antioch L.J.,* 25–26 (1986).

11. Whistleblower Protection Act of 1989 Sec. 2(a), 5 U.S.C. Sec. 1201 note (1989).

12. This last measure is designed to prevent the whistle-blower from becoming a "pariah," unable to find another job because he or she blew the whistle. This protection is partially based on the experience of Elaine J. Mittleman, who was unable to get a job at the Department of Commerce because the Office of Special Counsel, which had refused to defend her in her whistle-blowing claim against the Department of the Treasury, prevented her from getting the needed security clearance. "Whistleblower Protection," *Nat'l L. J.* (3 April 1989): p. 39, col. 1.

13. 391 U.S. 563 (1968). In Connick v. Myers, 461 U.S. 138, 142 (1983), the Court further refined this right by holding that the public employee's first amendment right is protected if the interest of the employee as a citizen "in commenting on matters of public concern" outweighs the interest of the state in its role as an employer "in promoting the efficiency of the public services it performs through its employees."

14. Bivens v. Six Unknown Agents of Federal Bureau of Narcotics, 403 U.S. 388 (1971) (damages remedy available for fourth amendment violations).

15. 462 U.S. 367 (1983).

16. *See, e.g.,* Kotarski v. Cooper, 799 F.2d 1342 (9th Cir. 1986); Spagnola v. Mathis, 809 F.2d 16 (D.C. Cir. 1986) (rehear *en banc* and partially vacated, 809 F.2d 40 (D.C. Cir. 1987). For a general discussion *see,* Note, *The Scope of Bush v. Lucas: An Examination of Congressional Remedies for Whistleblowers,* 88 *Col. L. Rev.* 587 (1988).

17. Peterman v. International Brotherhood of Teamsters, 174 Cal. App.2d 184, 344 P.2d 25 (1959).

18. There have been numerous law review articles which examine this development. *See, e.g.,* Blades, *Employment At Will v. Individual Freedom: On Limiting the Abusive Exercise of Employer Power,* 67 Colum. L. Rev. 1404 (1967); Murg & Scharman, *Employment At Will: Do the Exceptions Overwhelm the Rule?,* 23 B.C.L.R. 329 (1983); Peirce, Mann &

Roberts, *Employee Termination at Will: A Principled Approach*, 28 *Vill. L. Rev.* 1 (1982).

19. *See, e.g.*, Palmateer v. Int'l Harvester Co., 85 Ill.2d 124, 421 N.E.2d 876 (1981); Peterman v. International Brotherhood of Teamsters, 174 Cal. App.2d 184, 344 P.2d 25 (1959).

20. *See, e.g.*, Pierce v. Ortho Pharmaceutical Corp., 84 N.J. 58, 417 A.2d 505 (1980); Geary v. United States Steel Corp., 456 Pa. 171, 319 A.2d 174 (1974).

21. For a discussion of punitive damages in wrongful firing claims *see*, Mallor, *Punitive Damages for Wrongful Discharge of At Will Employees*, 26 *Wm. & Mary L. Rev.* 449 (1985).

22. One thing is evident from a quick perusal of the State Chart—there is great variation in what the states choose to protect and how they choose to protect it. Due to space limitations, only certain statutory features could be included, and all aspects of every statute could not be indicated. For example, many states, following the federal lead, consider giving testimony requested by a public body to be a protected form of whistle-blowing. Some states protect it within the whistle-blowing statute; others protect it in other statutes. Since space was at a premium, and indicating whether it was protected in the statute would give an incomplete picture, this information was omitted from the chart. Other information, such as whether the state allows the employer to collect costs and attorney fees if plaintiff's suit was without merit (a handful do); whether the employer must pay the employee for the time spent giving official testimony (a few states address this issue); or whether plaintiffs must prove their case by a higher standard than "beyond a reasonable doubt" (few states addresss the burden of proof issue at all; a few which do require proof by clear and convincing evidence) also had to be omitted. Thus, the particular state statute must be referred to in order to get a complete picture of the protection offered.

23. Louisiana's statute only protects whistle-blowing relating to environmental violations.

24. A minority of the states also state that public employees should blow the whistle on waste of public funds, mismanagement and abuse of authority, and actions which present a threat to public health or safety. With the plethora of laws which exist, it is unlikely that these last would not be encompassed within "a violation of a law, rule or regulation."

25. Pennsylvania, West Virginia, and Connecticut.

26. Maine, Minnesota, Montana, New Hampshire, New Jersey, New York, and Utah.

27. Indiana and Ohio.

28. Wisconsin only protects those acting for gain if the award is offered by the government to improve administration or operations.

29. For a discussion of the possible reasons external reporting is legislatively mandated, *see* Dworkin & Callahan, *Internal Whistle-blowing: Protect-*

ing the Interests of the Employee, the Organization, and Society, 29 Amer. Bus. L. J. 267 (1991).

30. *See* the statutes of Alaska, Indiana, Maine, Montana, New Hampshire, New Jersey, New York, Ohio, and Utah.

31. These states are Indiana, Maine, New Hampshire, New Jersey, New York, and Utah. The remaining states allow the employee to choose whether the recipient will be internal or external.

32. Colorado, Connecticut, Florida, Minnesota, and New Hampshire. Alaska allows the employer to require the employee to go internally.

33. Dworkin & Near, *Whistleblowing Statutes: Are They Working,* 25 Amer. Bus. L. J. 241–264 (1987). The states were Michigan, Connecticut, and Maine. The comparison states were Illinois, Hawaii, and Arizona, respectively.

34. Hopkins v. City of Midland, 158 Mich. App. 347, 404 N.W.2d 744 (1987); Tuttle v. Bloomfield Hills School Dist., 156 Mich. App. 527, 402 N.W.2d 54 (1986).

35. Walcott v. Champion Int'l Corp., 691 F. Supp. 1052 (W.D. Mich. 1987). The other unsuccessful cases were Dickson v. Oakland Univ., 3 Indiv. Empl. Rts. Cases 1550 (Mich. Ct. App. 1988) (policeman's firing for overzealous enforcement of law construed not to be firing because of whistle-blowing), and Poole v. Maine Coal Products, 3 Indiv. Empl. Rts. Cases 1007 (Maine 1987) (Whistleblower's Protection Act narrowly interpreted to make whistle-blower's burden of proof harder, thereby causing loss of suit).

36. Tyrna v. Adamo, Inc., 407 N.W.2d 47 (Mich. Ct. App. 1987). The court found that the Occupational Safety and Health Act (OSHA) did not preempt the employee's right to sue under the whistle-blower act for a firing involving the reporting of a safety violation. OSHA provides no private right to sue, it merely protects the employee from being fired in retaliation for making a safety claim. Thus, while the employee had a remedy, it was not one she liked, and the Michigan court let her proceed under the whistle-blower law.

37. *See, e.g.,* Covel v. Springles, 141 Mich. App. 76, 366 N.W. 2d 76 (1985); Pratt v. Brown Machine Co., 3 Indiv. Empl. Rts. Cases (BNA) 1121 (6th Cir. 1988).

38. U.S. Const. art. VI, Cl. 2.

39. Rice v. Santa Fe Elevator Corp., 331 U.S. 281 (1947).

40. Hines v. Davidowitz, 312 U.S. 52 (1941).

41. *See, e.g.,* Alexander v. Gardner-Denver Co., 415 U.S. 36 (1974) (Title VII and parallel federal and state law claims can be brought as well as suits under private contracts); Barrentine v. Arkansas-Best Freight Systems, 450 U.S. 728 (1981) (FLSA); Belknap Inc. v. Hale, 463 U.S. 491 (1983) (NLRA); Silkwood v. Kerr-McGee Corp., 464 U.S. 238 (1984); Lingle v. Norge Civ. of Magic Chef, Inc., 486 U.S. 199 (1988). In English v. General Electric Co., 496 U.S. 72 (1990), the latest case on this issue, the

Supreme Court again found no preemption when a whistle-blower sued for intentional infliction of emotional distress and the employer claimed her suit was preempted by the Energy Reorganization Act.

The passage of the Civil Service Reform Act is likely to reinforce the Supreme Court's finding that public employees must rely on the Federal Civil Service Reform Act and cannot sue under the first amendment.

42. *See, e.g.,* Garibaldi v. Lucky Food Stores, Inc., 726 F.2d 1367 (9th Cir. 1984), *cert. denied,* 471 U.S. 1099 (1985) (whistle-blower's wrongful discharge claim not preempted by NLRA); Stokes v. Bechtel, 614 F. Supp. 732 (N.D. Calif. 1985). *But see,* Snow v. Bechtel Constr. Inc, 647 F. Supp. 1514 (C.D. Calif. 1986).

43. *See, e.g.,* Covel v. Springles, 141 Mich. App. 76, 366 N.W. 2d 76 (1985); Pratt v. Brown Machine Co., Indiv. Empl. Rts., vol. 3, Cases 1121 (6th Cir. 1988). Some of the state statutes state that the act should not diminish or impair employee rights under a collective bargaining agreement. *See, e.g.,* the statutes of Connecicut, Michigan, and New Jersey. This language has been used to find a state tort cause of action was not preempted. *See, e.g.,* Tuttle v. Bloomfield Hills School Dist., 402 N.W.2d 481 (1986).

44. *See, e.g.,* Holien v. Sears, Roebuck & Co., 298 Or. 76, 689 P.2d 1291 (1984). State preemption decisions outside of the whistle-blower statute context are mixed. Compare: Reed v. Municipality of Anchorage, 4 Indiv. Empl. Rts. Cases 1613 (Alaska 1989); Lepore v. National Tool & Mfg. Co., 4 Indiv. Empl. Rts. Cases 871 (N.J. 1989); Ryherd v. General Cable Co., 4 Indiv. Empl. Rts. Cases 596 (Ill. 1988); Brevik v. Kite Painting, 2 Indiv. Empl. Rts. Cases 1284 (Minn. 1987) (no preemption) with Netzel v. UPS, 2 Indiv. Empl. Rts. Cases 1301 (Ill. App. 1987); Corbin v. Sinclair Mktg. Inc., 684 F.2d 265 (Colo. App. 1984) (preemption).

45. S. 436, 101st Cong., 1st Sess. (1989). A similar bill, H.R. 3368, 101 Cong., 1st Sess. (1989) was introduced in the House by Rep. William Ford. In addition, two bills intended to protect whistle-blowing about federal contractors were introduced in this session. H.R. 1861, 101st Cong., 1st Sess. (1989); H.R. 2579, 101st Cong., 1st Sess. (1989).

46. The Department of Labor would be in charge of investigating complaints.

47. *Qui tam* is a Latin phrase meaning "he who sues for the king as well as for himself." When the suit is filed, the government has sixty days to decide if it will join the suit. During this time, the suit is under seal.

48. The penalty in a case can go up to $10,000 per fraudulent incident plus three times the amount of the fraud. By 1989 the Justice Department had joined in 29 cases, refused in 73, and not made decisions in the others. T. Gest, "Why Whistle-blowing Is Getting Louder," *U.S. News & World Report,* 20 Nov. 1989, 64.

49. R. Thompson, *Stealth Law,* 8 Cal. Law. 33 (Oct. 1988).

50. R. Wartzman and P. Barrett, "Government Could Stifle False Claims Act," *Wall Street Journal,* 27 Sept. 1989, p. B1, col. 4.

51. 34 *Res Gestae* 121 (Mar. 1989); Kasich, *Incentives Bill Moves Forward,*

8 *Reports to the 12th District* 2 (July 1990); *Wall Street Journal*, 17 Oct. 1990, p. A20, col. 4.

52. Wisconsin allows the whistle-blower to collect a reward offered by the government to get information to improve administration or operations. No reward is offered in the statute, however.

53. For a discussion of the likely effectiveness of rewards as incentives for whistle-blowing *see* Callahan and Dworkin, *Do Good and Get Rich: Financial Incentives for Whistleblowing and the False Claims Act*, *Villanova L. Rev.* (in press).

54. *Mont. Code Ann.* Sec. 39–2–904 (1987).

55. *See, e.g.,* Tompkins, *Legislating the Employment Relationship: Montana's Wrongful-Discharge Law*, 14 *Empl. Rels. L.J.* 387 (1988).

56. Indiv. Empl. Rts., vol. 4, col. 4 (Feb. 14, 1989).

57. Indiv. Empl. Rts. Manual, Sec. 540:433; *see, e.g.,* Indiv. Empl. Rts., vol. 3, p. 4 (Aug. 16, 1988).

7

Some Implications for Practice

In the preceding chapters in this book, we presented a model of whistle-blowing and reviewed research pertaining to the model. Our goal was to inform the reader of the present state of scientific knowledge regarding whistle-blowing. But for this chapter, we have a different goal; here we attempt to identify the implications of existing research for practice.

More specifically, this chapter has three purposes. First, we describe the implications of research on whistle-blowing and offer some suggestions for organizational leaders who wish to reduce wrongdoing and encourage valid whistle-blowing. Second, we include some suggestions for organizations that can provide support for whistle-blowers, such as professional associations and religious institutions. Third, we advise organization members who are contemplating blowing the whistle and who wish to bring about positive change quickly without jeopardizing their career or their well-being.

Our suggestions are based on conclusions drawn mostly from the empirical literature on whistle-blowing. Ideally, advice should be based on a comprehensive body of knowledge, but the weaknesses and limitations of the literature have been described earlier in this book. We do, however, include the chapter because we believe the researchers should generate or disseminate ideas that may help practitioners improve organizational practice. At the same time, researchers are obliged to limit their recommendations to those with a sound theoretical and empirical base. Further, even where research has demonstrated that certain practices may be efficacious, generalizability of findings is an important issue. The conditions in any particular organization may be quite different from connections prevailing in the research settings—the organizations or the laboratories—involved in the study in question. Thus, implementation of change must be done with sensitivity to the conditions of the organizations in which the change may take place.

These considerations pose a dilemma for whistle-blowing researchers, because as noted earlier in this book, the theoretical and empirical exploration of whistle-blowing has only recently begun. We choose to resolve this dilemma by doing three things. First, we allow ourselves some room to speculate, with the caveat that our recommendations should be viewed as tentative and in need of confirmation. We encourage organizational leaders and whistle-blowers to use their knowledge of their own particular circumstances to modify these recommendations where it is appropriate, and to monitor and (we would hope!) to share their experiences with the academic and industrial communities. Second, we draw from literature not expressly concerned with whistle-blowing where we believe it is relevant, as we have done in other chapters. Third, we try to help readers to evaluate the potential usefulness of the recommendations by briefly showing their basis, which we draw from the research previously cited. We would encourage interested readers to refer to previous discussion in this book, where additional detail concerning the research is required. We now turn our attention to actions organizations may take.

Implications for Organizations in General

Our presumption through this discussion is somewhat normative in nature. We presume that most leaders of organizations want to encourage valid whistle-blowing or eliminate the need for its occurrence. Such leaders want to create a climate of fairness and respect for their organizations' members, for a variety of reasons. Some of these reasons may be based on ethical principles. Organizational leaders may believe that creating such climates is inherently good, and behaving unfairly, unethically, or illegally cannot be morally justified.

Other reasons may reflect business judgments about the long-run costs of wrongdoing to the organization. Organizations characterized by lower levels of wrongdoing and the appropriate exercise of rights and execution of responsibilities are attractive to more productive and satisfied employees. As noted earlier, there is some preliminary evidence that the climate for whistle-blowing is associated with higher levels of employee satisfaction (Gorden et al., 1988; Zalkind, 1987). Further, as described in chapter 1, the organization that engages in or ignores wrongdoing risks fines, court expenses, negative publicity, additional restrictions imposed by regulators, and other tangible and intangible costs that may be associated with lawsuits. In any case, our suggestions for organizational practice are based on a belief that effective organizations generally do not engage in wrongdoing and want to correct it when it becomes apparent.

We also presume that most organizations' leaders would like to determine ways to reduce the need for whistle-blowing and to encourage their members' use of internal channels to inform them when wrongdoing does occur. We presume that these leaders would prefer to avoid whistle-blowing that makes the complaint known to parties outside the organization. Furthermore, we presume that organizational leaders would like to discourage the gadfly who threatens to file complaints when no reasonable basis exists, and who is disruptive in attempting to assert or challenge authority indiscriminately. They do not want interference with legitimate attempts to improve employee performance or discipline employees who engage in inappropriate behavior, including wrongdoing that ironically may be the target of another whistle-blowing complaint!

While our presumptions are not necessarily true in every case, we believe that they are reasonable. With these presumptions in mind, we offer a number of suggestions that we believe are not at odds with the limited research and legal developments to date. Obviously, our list is not exhaustive, but rather it represents a first step toward providing action-oriented advice. We use a broad classification scheme to categorize actions that can be taken, as shown in figure 7–1.

Essentially, figure 7–1 shows that organizations may adopt actions in support of strategies to create positive climates for correcting wrongdoing that are either proactive or reactive. That is, they may attempt to create conditions to prevent wrongdoing (proactive) or to respond effectively when wrongdoing and whistle-

Strategy to Create Positive Climate for Correcting Wrongdoing	Supportive Actions		
	Strategic	Structure and Communication	HRM
Proactive	•Managing issues •Monitoring legal developments •Defining wrongdoing	•Developing codes	•Training managers •Training employees •Rewarding ethical behavior •Staffing
Reactive	•Defining appropriate responses	•Establishing and supporting designated complaint recipients •Supporting and training informal complaint recipients •Encouraging the use of alternative communication and resolution mechanisms •Communicating the wish to respond •Establishing a supportive culture	•Training managers •Training employees to respond to wrongdoing •Rewarding appropriate responses •Staffing

FIGURE 7–1

Actions Organizations Can Take to Encourage Valid Whistle-blowing

blowing occur (reactive). Organizations could adopt both types of strategies simultaneously. A second dimension used to classify actions taken to support the strategies concerns the nature of the action. We have divided these, somewhat arbitrarily, into (1) strategic actions, (2) structure and communication actions, and (3) human resource management (HRM) actions. Obviously, because many of these actions are related, our classification scheme serves as a crude organizational device rather than a precise taxonomy. We begin our discussion by examining proactive approaches.

Proactive Approaches: Avoiding the Need for Whistle-blowing

One objective that the organization may embrace is to avoid the need for whistle-blowing, because it will eliminate associated costs, as described in chapter 1. Of course, this strategy will require eliminating wrongdoing, which is not an easy task. Further, eliminating wrongdoing will not necessarily eliminate whistle-blowing, because of (a) variations in individual perceptions of and views about wrongdoing, and (b) changing environmental conditions, which may raise new questions about what constitutes wrongdoing. Therefore, when we speak of avoiding the need for whistle-blowing, we must remind ourselves that we will never be able to do so entirely. Nonetheless, organizations that take steps in that direction may realize beneficial consequences.

Eliminating wrongdoing will depend on a causal analysis in particular cases, and this issue cannot be addressed here because of its idiosyncratic nature and because of the limitations on our scope, that is, our focus on whistle-blowing. Instead, we will not address the various causes of different types of wrongdoing, and we will make only general statements about preventing wrongdoing.

STRATEGIC ACTIONS. Policies or strategies to prevent wrongdoing must be formulated at the highest levels of the organization. From there, it will be possible to devise supportive actions involving the management of human resources and the continued communications of policies and information concerning wrongdoing. What we propose is much like an environmental scanning approach described in textbooks as part of the strategic planning process. More specifically, strategic actions can be classified as those involving management of issues, monitoring legal developments, and defining wrongdoing.

Managing Issues. Earlier, we described research pertaining to issues management, a process that prepares the organization for circumstances that may produce wrongdoing and whistle-blowing, and enables it to respond (Meyers & Garrett, 1988). Ideally, issues managers should scan the environment for potential problems and conflicts that may produce conditions for whistle-blowing. Taking action to address these problems before organization members perceive that problems exist may be helpful.

Monitoring Legal Developments. Some labor attorneys believe that many violations of the law, particularly discrimination laws, result from a lack of knowledge of legal developments rather than an intent to harm (Finney, 1988a). They suggest that managers should set up their own tracking or scanning systems for learning about new developments in the legal arena. In so doing, organization members can avoid inadvertent wrongdoing. There are many sources of information on laws pertinent to the workplace. For example, the Society for Human Resource Management ([SHRM], formerly the American Society for Personnel Administration) publishes a monthly newsletter, *Resource*, that provides information on recent cases, paraphrased for managers who are not legal experts. It also describes pending legislation and recently passed federal statutes, guidelines, and regulations issued by government agencies, such as the Internal Revenue Service, and other legal developments. Local chapters of SHRM also publish newsletters with similar types of information.

Defining Wrongdoing. Organizational leaders should discuss and clarify their beliefs about what constitutes wrongdoing. Frank discussions considering alternative views may help identify potential problem areas. The results of these discussions should be used to guide the development and implementation of polices, as we describe later.

At the opposite extreme, wrongdoing very narrowly or specifically may actually be counterproductive. Organizations may be tempted to increase standardization, giving certain individuals "checklists" for wrongdoing, but this may lead to overreliance on such devices and inattention to unusual signals. At least one study provides a basis for concern. Pincus (1989) found that a "red flags" questionnaire did improve data acquisition in fraud detection, but it didn't improve fraud risk assessment. She speculated that the questionnaire users may not have considered all relevant cues. Or, they may have paid insufficient attention to one set of information cues, namely, the negative indicators, which tended to be associated with risk assessment. In any event, the definition of wrongdoing may best be viewed as a changing, on-going process rather than an attempt to devise a set of narrow rules to be followed rigidly.

STRUCTURE AND COMMUNICATION

Developing Policies and Codes of Ethics. Notwithstanding the concern about inappropriate rigidity in defining wrongdoing, codes of ethics should spell out more specifically than they currently tend to do (a) what activities are considered wrongful and (b) what behaviors are desired. This should include activities that primarily harm parties other than the organization or its stockholders (such as discrimination, safety violations, or pollution). Such a policy should increase consensus about what constitutes wrongdoing and is more in keeping with the true notion of codes of ethical behavior, than is the "anything goes so long as it doesn't hurt me" approach that seems to typify codes. This policy is consistent with Mathews's (1987a) finding that many codes emphasized wrongdoing against the organization but said little about other types of wrongdoing. Mathews (1987a) also found that the presence of specific categories of code content was associated with a higher number of corporate violations (with the exception of the "conflict of interest" category). She speculated, however, that codes may have been written in response to prior illegal activity, so wrongdoing may have caused the specificity rather than the reverse.

Consistent with this advice are the implications of a study by Bennett-Alexander (1988), who reviewed recent U.S. Supreme Court decisions involving sexual harassment. According to Bennett-Alexander (1988), employers should have a specific policy dealing with sexual harassment rather than a general anti-discrimination policy. She suggested that policy writers refer to Equal Employment Opportunity Commission guidelines for information about what constitutes a violation, and actions that can be taken to prevent and combat discrimination.

A policy that specifies and provides examples of questionable activities may be more easily understood by organization members than is a general statement, and may lead to fewer unfounded complaints. The process of devising such a policy may also provide a developmental benefit—enhanced communication among organizational members who participate in policy formation, and increased awareness may result.

However, we would caution organizations about two events. First, simply having the policy is not likely to be effective; the policy should become part of the organizational culture and reward system (Jansen & Von Glinow, 1985). For example, Osigweh (1987) argued that firms should provide training to help organization members take the initiative in reporting wrongdoing, rather than sanctioning whistle-blowing behavior. In a similar vein, Sashkin and Morris (1987) focused heavily on the need for management to model values they wish employees to emulate, rather than simply communicating policies and procedures to which they do not appear committed. McAfee and Ricks (1987) provided further support for this view by reviewing social learning theory and its implications for modeling moral behavior, when managers wish to encourage such behavior among employees. Second, an exclusive focus on activities specifically described or illustrated in the policy foster inattention to other, possibly more harmful activities. Even the most knowledgeable policy writers cannot anticipate every event that may face organizational members in the future. The organization should instead strive to develop a culture and reward system that helps its members make ethical decisions. This leads us to consider human resource management actions that can be taken to bring about this culture and reward system.

HUMAN RESOURCE MANAGEMENT ACTIONS

Management Education, Development, and Training. Some authors have argued that business schools as well as employing organizations must play a greater role in influencing managerial ethical values (Osigweh, 1988). Courses, case discussions, or exercises may heighten managers' awareness of ethical issues. One case was recently published in the *Harvard Business Review* (Seymour, 1988). While this advice seems reasonable, we know of no research that systematically examines the impact of such programs on wrongdoing; we therefore encourage further examination of this issue.

Training Employees to Prevent Wrongdoing. One practitioner magazine has recommended that organizations train all employees to be considerate of each other's rights ("Control your liability . . .," 1988). This could conceivably ensure that co-workers are not the source of rights violations and may also communicate that organizations will not tolerate certain behaviors.

Employee notices, such as posters, also can be used to keep awareness levels high ("Control your liability . . .," 1988). For example, Pacific Gas & Electric San Luis Obispo posts notices imploring workers to tell supervisors or the Nuclear Regulatory Commission immediately—without fear of retribution—if they see something amiss (Sheler, 1981). Once again, though we have no quarrel with the sentiment behind this advice, we are unaware of behavioral research establishing a link between training (or reminders) and wrongdoing. It is conceivable that heightened awareness training may even have some adverse effects. Our own research (Miceli & Near, 1985) suggests that awareness of wrongdoing may be associated with more negative reactions about organizational response, so the organization should prevent demoralization while increasing employees' awareness of wrongdoing.

Rewarding Ethical Behavior. We noted earlier that several authors (such as Jansen & Von Glinow, 1985) have called for organizations to reward behavior that follows codes of ethics or other prescriptions. Such advice is consistent with prescriptions derived from motivation theories (such as reinforcement theory and expectancy theory) described in chapter 2. Obviously, it is difficult for organizations to put this prescription into practice. Further research should examine the effects of specific characteristics of ethical behavior reward systems.

Staffing. It is with special care that we consider the implications of research on whistle-blowing for staffing practice. If observers of wrongdoing have different demographic characteristics (or other traits that would be present at the time of hiring decisions) than do nonobservers, then it would be possible to identify potential observers of wrongdoing. These individuals may be more vigilant and potentially more conscientious about not committing wrongdoing. On the other hand, implications of the same research may lead less scrupulous organizations to avoid hiring individuals who could not be pressured into wrongdoing. While it is probably true that other recommendations and suggestions in this chapter may be turned around to devise an organization condoning wrongdoing, it seems particularly disconcerting that individuals who resist wrongdoing could be denied jobs. Perhaps it is reassuring that the research had identified few stable individual characteristics typical of observers; some research suggests that low tolerance for ambiguity and the ability to separate wrongdoing cues from their context may lead to greater observation. Although we must be careful not to conclude that personal characteristics are unimportant merely because many have not been investigated, at this time we cannot clearly state that personal characteristics strongly influence vigilance. However, we do have evidence that the environment within the organization is critical, and we would encourage organizations to continue their efforts to create climates that support ethical behavior.

Reactive Strategies: Responding to Wrongdoing and to Whistle-blowing

STRATEGIC ACTIONS

Defining Appropriate Responses to Perceived Wrongdoing. As noted in chapter 4, Barnett et al. (1990) found that, in those organizations that had developed policies, personnel executives perceived that internal whistle-blowing increased, and external whistle-blowing decreased, following policy implementation. Organizations where there was no such policy were likely to experience lower levels of internal whistle-blowing. Existence of a policy was related to perceived managerial responsiveness to complaints, which in turn was related to higher levels of internal whistle-blowing. This research suggests that establishing policies that define appropriate responses to perceived wrongdoing can encourage internal whistle-blowing.

Prescribing Roles. Research suggests that role prescriptions are critically important in encouraging whistle-blowing (Miceli, Dozier & Near, 1991). But role prescriptions must go beyond defining certain jobs as "watchdog" roles. They must specify what types of activities are considered wrongdoing and what the incumbent should do when wrongdoing is observed. For example, an internal auditor may be expected to observe and report wrongdoing, but does this extend beyond financial malfeasance to perceived racial discrimination? What should the auditor do if management fails to respond to the charges?

At the same time, theory on interactional justice (Bies, 1987) suggests that the unique advantages of role prescriptions may be lost if *all* organization members are expected to observe and report wrongdoing (Near et al., in press). There are costs to requiring individuals to monitor and report wrongdoing, particularly those who have not traditionally viewed this as a function for which they were responsible. These costs must not be overlooked. Johnson (1990, p. 80), for example, emphasized the cost of monitoring wrongdoing in arguing against requiring scientists to detect and report misconduct: "Hobbling all scientists to restrict the activity of a few is not the solution . . . each activity in which a scientist must engage reduces the time available for research. The result is less research." He weighed these costs against the cost of allowing wrongdoing to continue, which he viewed as low because "it would appear from the evidence available that the problem [of fraud in scientific research], which is a real one, is localized" (p. 79). As a solution, he proposed limiting vigilance to the areas of research where "the monetary reward for particular results is very high (e.g., pharmaceutical development and testing) [which] are the most likely to produce fraudulent research or testing." As valid as these points may be, Johnson presented no data in support of his views, and clearly, research is needed to establish the cost-benefit tradeoffs of requiring close monitoring as well as to establish alternatives beyond simply ignoring the problem.

STRUCTURE AND COMMUNICATION

Establishing and Supporting Designated Complaint Recipients. Establishing or designating internal communications mechanism for reporting wrongdoing is consistent with the empirical finding that greater knowledge of effective internal channels of complaint is associated with higher levels of internal whistle-blowing (Miceli & Near, 1985; Miceli et al., 1988). Consistent with this, Beauchamp and Bowie (1983) recommended that there be a clear process of receiving complaints. On the other hand, research suggests that different potential recipients or types of communication attempts may be needed to evoke reporting from different persons, for example, persons with internal loci of control (informative communications), and persons with external loci of control (persuasive communications) (Dozier & Miceli, 1985). We next consider several formal complaint recipients that could be selected.

Mathews (1987a) found that according to the codes of ethics, employees should discuss ethical questions with the corporation's legal counsel or with the employees' supervisors. But the issue of trust and access is important in the case of legal counsel. If the attorney is unknown to the employee or is far away geographically, it is unlikely that the employee will feel comfortable raising sensitive issues with him or her, in part because the employee has no evidence of the trustworthiness and effectiveness of the attorney in stopping wrongdoing. Further, many employees are lower in professional or organizational status than are corporate attorneys, and these employees may feel intimidated by them.

In the case of the supervisor, employees may feel reluctant to report wrongdoing, because the supervisor may be directly involved in the wrongdoing. Or the employees may believe that the supervisor, as a member of the "management team," will feel compelled to defend organizational actions or may actually believe, because of the effectiveness of prior socialization processes (Glazer & Glazer, 1987), that the activity is acceptable. Thus, it is not surprising that the author of the study of sexual harassment cases recommended that organizations provide "a procedure for victims to report complaints, including a means to circumvent their immediate supervisor if that is who is presenting the problem" (Bennett-Alexander, 1988, p. 188). More importantly, perhaps, the Equal Employment Opportunity Commission requires this procedure in its guidelines (*EEOC Guidelines on Discrimination Because of Sex*, 29 CFR Sections 1604.11[e], 1985). The U.S. Supreme Court gives these guidelines great deference (*Meritor Savings Bank, FSB v. Vinson*, 477 U.S. 57, 1986).

There may be better alternatives to recommend in certain situations. Shingler (1987) described communication systems developed and partially administered by a research institute for organizations within the federal government. The Battelle Memorial Institute developed a safety reporting system that was instituted in the Federal

Aviation Administration in 1976. A second Battelle system was introduced into the National Aeronautic and Space Administration in 1987 at the Kennedy Space Center, following the explosion of the space shuttle Challenger. According to Michael Hanley, the project manager, the system enables anyone working on the shuttle project to alert NASA to any potential safety problem while maintaining anonymity. The program is designed to reduce the fear that whistle-blowing will lead to reprisals, a theme that had been sounded in the aftermath of the Challenger disaster.

The research on codes of ethics suggests that it may be beneficial for organizations to consider establishing "internal watchdog committees" (Matthews, 1987) or ombudspersons offices that have some power and independence from the organization. Ethics committees "can help to remove the label of deviance from whistle-blowing" and encourage it through the institution of rewards and discouragement of retaliation (Mathews, 1988, p. 106). Unfortunately, Mathews (1987) found that only 12 percent of the codes of conduct she examined directed employees to such parties. However, there is anecdotal evidence that such organizational units can be helpful, and recently, as discussed in chapter 4, Barnett et al. (1990) presented empirical evidence implying that organizations with trusted, independent, powerful complaint recipients have experienced positive outcomes. These outcomes might include lower levels of wrongdoing, a higher rate of internal whistle-blowing where wrongdoing does occur, or a climate that is viewed as procedurally just and fair. One feature of the procedures examined by Barnett et al. (1990) was the existence of appeal procedure, which is consistent with the literature on procedural justice (Greenberg, 1987).

Bennett-Alexander (1988) cautioned that victims are not always required by law to use internal complaint channels before turning to an external party. Employees may sue or complain to an equal employment enforcement agency without first providing the organization with an opportunity for self-correction. This suggests that employers must make concerted efforts to encourage employees to use these internal channels. Our own research indicates that wrongdoing involving harm to the public or organization members, or wrongdoing involving employee theft are more likely to result in whistle-blowing via external channels (Miceli, Near & Schwenk, 1991). Therefore, managers who can reduce these types of wrongdoing may succeed in encouraging whistle-blowers to use internal channels. Unfortunately, there is little empirical research directly examining methods of encouragement. We do know that practically all wrongdoing that is eventually reported externally is first reported internally. This suggests that responsiveness to an initial complaint is a key factor in avoiding external reporting.

Complaint recipients should conduct impartial investigations, using defined standards of judgment; they should provide a fair hearing procedure and reach the most objective and responsible decision possible (Beauchamp & Bowie, 1983). However, complaint recipients are sometimes perceived as taking too much time to investigate and respond to employee complaints (for instance, see Hostetler, 1987). To the extent that this occurs, would-be whistle-blowers may be discouraged from reporting wrongdoing internally, and ultimately, outsiders may become involved.

Supporting and Training Informal Complaint Recipients (other than supervisors). Employee Assistance Programs (EAPs) are maintained by organizations to help their members with performance problems stemming from psychological problems, alcoholism, drug abuse, family stresses or other personal problems. Organization members may be referred by their supervisors, or they may go on their own. Since some problems may actually stem from workplace issues, potential whistle-blowers may sometimes view the EAP counselor as a complaint recipient. If this occurs, counselors need to know how to handle the complaint as well as the complainant. Unfortunately, EAPs may provide opportunities for victimizing an already vulnerable party; there have been alleged abuses of the psychiatric examination policy in the military (Kennedy, 1987). The clear implication is that EAPs should not be used to harass whistle-blowers. Counselors should be trained in procedures to be used when they suspect referral for that purpose, and when employees refer themselves in response to possible stress from pursuing a complaint.

One potential complaint recipient who may be overlooked is the trainer or internal organizational development consultant. These individuals may have opportunities to hear expressions of employee concerns. During training or focus group sessions, for example, suspicions of wrongdoing may be expressed, even when these issues are not the planned topic for the sessions. Trainers may be surprised at such expressions and they may not know how to handle them, particularly where confidentiality has been promised to participants. Therefore, organizations should develop policies for responding to these incidents, and they should train the trainers accordingly.[a]

Similarly, if the organization employs outside consultants, including external audit teams, additional opportunities for expression of concerns exist. Consultants may have difficulty resolving ethical dilemmas about whether to report information given to them in confidence by employees, and development of policies for such instances should be undertaken.

Encouraging the Use of Alternative Communication and Resolution Mechanisms. Generally, there has been little research concerning the specific steps organizations can take to encourage whistle-blowing through alternative communication mechanisms. However, given that research does underscore the importance of responsiveness, it seems reasonable to propose that facilitating upward communications through alternative systems would have beneficial consequences for organizations and their members. Several alternative communication mechanisms, which were originally established for other purposes, may be used to communicate and resolve concerns about illegal, unethical, or illegitimate activities.

Suggestion systems are a mechanism whistle-blowers may use to communicate their concerns. Although many suggestions may not constitute whistle-blowing, organization members who feel free to contribute suggestions and view the system as responsive may feel more comfortable reporting unethical or illegal behavior through the suggestion system than to other recipients. This may be particularly true where anonymous suggestions are accepted. Suggestion systems are widely used. For example, each agency and department in the federal government now maintains a suggestion system of some sort. The Office of Personnel Management estimates that the program saves $2 billion per year. However, participation rates vary by agency (Burnett, 1988). This suggests that merely having a system is not sufficient; organizations must provide encouragement for their use. Moreover, to accommodate individual differences in

[a] We are indebted to Judy Tansky for this suggestion.

communication preferences, suggestion systems can allow for either verbal or written media. IBM has an "open door" policy under which employees "are urged to carry complaints all the way up the corporate ladder. IBM receives up to 18,000 letters a year from workers making confidential complaints under a 'Speak Up' program" (Sheler, 1981, p. 82). As another example, Bank of America in San Francisco: "encourages its employees to submit complaints or reports through its 'Open Line' program. The program's coordinator contacts the whistle-blower at home to gather information and then confronts the accused person for a response. All of this says a bank official, is done in 'complete confidence' " (Sheler, 1981, p. 82).

Another method that has been proposed to resolve whistle-blowing complaints is to use arbitration. Traditionally, arbitration serves as the last step of a grievance procedure in unionized settings. Both parties agree to allow the arbitrator to decide the grievance. Arbitration is used not only in private sector organizations but also in public sector organizations, including nineteen states and a large number of federal agencies ("Control your liability . . .," 1988). The primary reasons for its popularity are cost savings and efficiency: "Relative costs and speed are demonstrably 10 to 50 times better for proceedings of the American Arbitration Association for civil court proceedings." ("Control your liability . . .," 1988, p. 3). The association estimates the costs to be $200 to $1,500 per case with two to three months for resolution. This can be contrasted with the case of Bertrand Berube, a federal whistle-blower; resolving concerns he raised cost $200,000 to $700,000 and exhausted six years in the court system. Reducing the time in resolution may also reduce opportunities for retaliation against the whistle-blower and the stress of uncertainty imposed on all parties. Obviously, organizations must look closely at how the arbitration process can be adapted to accommodate questions of unethical behavior in addition to disputes concerning more traditional issues, such as excessive absences, pay disputes, or other issues.

In-house review panels also can frequently settle complaints more cheaply than court cases ("Control your liability . . .," 1988). In 1983, General Electric's Columbia, Maryland, plant initiated a panel process for its hourly employees. Although viewed as radical when it was originated, the system continues with only minor refinements since it began (Finney, 1988b). The company encourages employees with complaints to first try to resolve it "on a one-to-one basis with the supervisor." If that is unsuccessful (about one-third of the time), the next step is to bring the complaint to the peer review panel, composed of five individuals. Three are hourly employees, drawn at random from about sixty hourly employees. The other two are management representatives who are permanently assigned to the panel. These panelists are specially trained in dispute resolution techniques. The eight-hour training course covers "listening skills, legal, and moral implications of serving on the panel, types of questions that are either useful or dangerous, and the importance of confidentiality" (Finney, 1988b, p. 45). Both sides present their cases. The panel may seek additional information from anyone. The panel may modify the complaint. When the panel reaches a decision (by secret ballot), it issues a statement explaining that decision. General Electric reports that the number of grievances has "far outpaced the number of complaints filed in the previous five years during the so-called 'open door' policy when employees were free to complain to management" (Finney, 1988b, p. 46). A survey shows that 82 percent of the plant's staff was satisfied with the peer review process. The company attributes the success of the program to the placing of power in the hands of the hourly employees, which removes the "management insulation" of the supervisor from the consequences of unfair practices.

Communicating the Wish to Respond. As noted in chapter 4, the notion of increasing the likelihood of positive outcomes following whistle-blowing is both intuitively and theoretically appealing. Previous research has shown that most observers are reluctant to come forward *not* primarily because they fear retaliation, but rather because they don't believe their actions will make a difference (MSPB, 1981). An organization that promises to respond under certain conditions may convince would-be whistle-blowers that they will be heard. This finding has many implications. Organizations can publicize, through employee newsletters or posters, how problems were solved as a result of reports. Employees should also be informed as to why action is *not* taken when action would be inappropriate. Further, organizations can institutionalize their commitment to ethical responsibility, by including dimensions of ethical behavior on job descriptions and performance appraisals and by ensuring that the compensation system supports such behavior (Raelin, 1987).

If organizations fail to respond when employees share concerns and expect certain responses, they are not tapping all sources of information about problems that can be corrected. Further, they may inadvertently demoralize employees who may feel that their input is ignored on this occasion, and perhaps these employees may grow cynical about participation in other areas as well. This would seem particularly noteworthy in an era of increasing employee participation; in fact, a panel of top Ohio manufacturers recently concluded that employee involvement, not technology, is critical to remaining competitive (Lietzke, 1990). Finally, employees who believe their input is ignored may experience a loss of perceived control, which has been shown to relate to satisfaction and performance, and which may result in attempts to restore control through undesirable means (Greenberger et al., 1991).

Establishing a Supportive Culture. Keenan (1990a, p. 15) argued that organizations "need to embark upon the development of an ethically focused culture. This includes the need to: (1) institute and reinforce norms and practices which encourage employees to report illegal or wasteful activities; (2) communicate an adequate degree of information to employees about procedures for reporting these activities; (3) protect employees from retaliation for reporting such wrongdoings; and (4) provide incentives and reward those who bring forth legitimate concerns about possibly illegitimate situations and behaviors." In addition, reducing bureaucracy where it interferes with organizational functioning and communications may result in higher levels of whistle-blowing (Miceli, Near & Schwenk, 1991).

In chapter 4, we reviewed research showing that organizational climates that are less defensive and more participatory are associated with whistle-blowing. For example, Blackburn (1988) found that employees who voiced concerns viewed top management more positively and perceived a more participatory climate, than did those who were silent. Such climates may also produce higher employee satisfaction in general. Thus, in day to day dealings with employees, organization leaders must show their respect and concern for employees and their inputs.

HUMAN RESOURCE MANAGEMENT ACTIONS

Training Managers to Respond to Whistle-blowers. Advice to managers traditionally focuses on avoiding retaliation. Obviously, we endorse this view, but the research shows consistently that retaliation is not the primary factor in the decision to blow the whistle, though certainly, retaliation can be devastating and must be avoided. Therefore, we emphasize alternative suggestions that may have greater impact.

Managers need to understand that the types of people who blow the whistle are those who may be very valuable for other reasons to the organization. We found that whistle-blowers see themselves as high performers who are relatively well paid and who feel compelled to report wrongdoing by their own sense of moral behavior (Miceli, Near & Schwenk, 1991). These are not dispensable employees. Consequently, managers who tend to dismiss such complaints by denigrating the whistle-blower should be cautioned that such perceptions may not be valid. Instead, managers in organizations that have taken care to devise fair and effective responses to whistle-blowers should be trained as to the company's procedures for handling such issues.

On the other hand, the possibility of abuse by employees who claim to be whistle-blowers but are merely disgruntled poor performers is real, though as we reported in chapter 2, research in the federal sector suggests that managers do not perceive this to be a serious hindrance to their taking appropriate actions to coach or discipline such employees. Nonetheless, steps can be taken to protect managers from such abuses. According to a recent article in a leading human resource management practitioner journal, attorneys have provided advice that will enable managers to respond to complaints more effectively whether they are valid or not ("Control your liability . . .," 1988). These recommendations are consistent with the literature on procedural justice (for example, Greenberg, 1987), which suggests that consistent, unbiased application of standards will be perceived as more fair. First, it is recommended to leave a "paper trail" in performance appraisal. Second, managers should institute a progressive disciplinary system built into the performance appraisal process. Third, where firing is contemplated, managers should refer questions to a "termination czar," who will "objectively review any termination process to make sure the documentation is complete" and "that the termination was driven by appropriate reasons" (p. 44). Finally, supervisors should be trained to be considerate of employee rights.

Training Employees to Respond to Wrongdoing. It is important to indicate what organization members should do when they observe questionable activity. In a study by Miceli, Near, and Schwenk (1991), whistle-blowers claimed their actions concerning the specific activity observed were required by the job, and this variable was among the most important in differentiating whistle-blowers from bystanders. This finding provides preliminary empirical evidence that establishing "watchdog" roles for organizational members, touted in the popular press and anecdotal accounts as critical, may indeed be effective in increasing whistle-blowing.

Rewarding Appropriate Responses to Perceived Wrongdoing. The research is rather consistent in its showing that the most powerful reward an organization may be able to offer potential whistle-blowers is its willingness to correct wrongdoing. However, organizations may offer more direct incentives, such as cash awards, to encourage individuals to come forward. For example, Sheler (1981) reported that Hughes Tool Co. of Houston offered rewards of up to $10,000 leading to the arrest and conviction of oil-field thieves, who may also be members of the organization. General Motors has offered cash rewards to get information about leaks of sensitive future product information ("GM to offer . . .," 1987). Several retail chains, including Bloomingdale's and Alexander's Inc., are using rewards to get information on employee theft (Solomon, 1987).

One law permitting whistle-blowers to receive monetary rewards is the False Claims Amendments Act of 1986 ("Doctor may profit . . .," 1987). In one pending case, a physician left a clinic and sued it and a former colleague for allegedly defrauding Medicare by billing for procedures that were more expensive than those actually performed. Under the False Claims Amendments Act of 1986, if successful, the whistle-blowing physician could receive from 15 percent to 25 percent of the judgment, which in this case could extend to $6.3 million in civil damages and penalties ("Doctor may profit . . .," 1987).

Curiously, whistle-blowers and would-be whistle-blowers are frequently quoted as claiming that the financial incentives played (or would play) no role in their decision to blow the whistle, as in the case just described ("Doctor may profit . . .," 1987, p. 3). In the MSPB studies (MSPB, 1981, 1984), very few organization members said that cash awards would encourage them to blow the whistle. However, self-reports about hypothetical incentives are not necessarily reliable.

Unfortunately, research on the effectiveness of such incentives is woefully lacking. While it may seem straightforward that adding "rewards" would increase the likelihood of whistle-blowing, there are two reasons why this may not be true. First, whistle-blowing may have conflicting consequences. For example, if the whistle-blower is viewed by others as having blown the whistle primarily to get the bonus, they may view the person as a "fink," ostracizing him or her from the group. Other negative consequences may be that important information may be withheld because organization members are not sure whether any member might be motivated by the prospect of a bonus for reporting wrongdoing. These consequences may outweigh the positive consequences brought about by the bonuses.

Second, many conditions must be present in order for such an event as the awarding of a whistle-blowing bonus to be reinforcing in the sense that it increases whistle-blowing, or rewarding in the sense that it increases the satisfaction or well-being of the whistle-blower. As the compensation literature attests, many questions must be addressed; for example, what constitutes a "just noticeable difference" that is large enough to spur one to change behavior? (Heneman, 1985). There is some evidence that the possibility of large awards has spurred whistle-blowing. Before the False Claims Act was revised in 1986 to facilitate large rewards, cases under the False Claims Act averaged ten per year. By late 1989, the number of suits filed since the revisions became effective was 198 (France, 1990; Wartzman & Barrett, 1989). Therefore, we strongly recommend that further research examine the characteristics of awards programs and their effectiveness.

Other rewards such as written commendations may be useful (Mathews, 1988). For example, First Interstate Bank of California in Los Angeles maintains a code of ethics, and bank officials encourage employees to report suspected violations (Sheler, 1981). The senior vice president in charge of personnel noted that "if an officer seems to be too close to a customer, making bad loans, we want to know. . . . Commendations are placed in whistle-blowers' files acknowledging the 'tough decision' to report a co-worker" (Sheler, 1981, p. 82). Organization members may appreciate this recognition. However, research is needed to identify the conditions under which this may actually produce negative reactions, such as hostility or ridicule from others.

Staffing. As noted earlier, because of the potential for abuse, we have strong reservations about the process of identifying characteristics of persons who may be most likely to complain about wrongdoing. With this ethical concern in mind, we cautiously remind the reader that slightly older individuals are more likely to blow the whistle but this may be largely a function of long service with the organization rather than age. Men are more likely to blow the whistle than women, but obviously, equal employment opportunity laws would proscribe discrimination in hiring even if the research suggested an overwhelmingly strong gender-whistle-blowing connection, which it does not. As we noted in chapter 4, whistle-blowers may have a lower need for approval from others. Research has not examined the effects of self-esteem or confidence that might influence whistle-blowing; potentially, these would lead to other desirable organizational behaviors as well, so organizations may want to consider seeking such candidates.

The research conducted to date suggests that events occurring after hire may be more important than characteristics present at the time of hire in influencing whistle-blowing. Higher-paid individuals who are more satisfied and committed and who are better performers are more likely to blow the whistle. So are those who hold supervisory positions, who know where to report wrongdoing, and who believe that they are expected to report certain incidents. These individual characteristics suggest that strategies other than staffing strategies may be most likely to enhance employee response to wrongdoing.

Implications for Organizations Not Employing the Whistle-blower

To this point, we have focused on implications of the research for organizations that employ the whistle-blower. But whistle-blowers may interact with other organizations who could potentially affect the process. Among these organizations are professional associations such as the California Society of Professional Engineers, which was involved in the San Francisco Bay Area Rapid Transit system case (Perrucci et al., 1980). Others are religious institutions, business schools, and consulting firms.

Glazer and Glazer (1987, pp. 206 and 211) took professional and religious organizations to task for failing to provide support for ethical resisters, but did not suggest actions these organizations could take. Near and Miceli (1988) recommended that professional associations actively support career networking of their members. This activity would enable individuals who observe wrongdoing but fear losing their jobs to be aware of career opportunities in other organizations.

Professional and religious organizations could also provide positive recognition in newsletters, or they could invite whistle-blowers to speak about their experiences. Potentially, they could offer financial support of some type. Conversations at meetings may serve to strengthen members' sense of professional responsibility and support from colleagues, conditions proposed by Perrucci et al. (1980) to lead to whistle-blowing.

As noted earlier, many authors (such as Osigweh, 1988) have recommended that business schools add courses on ethics in management practice to their curricula. There is a great deal of interest in this area, and many programs are being developed. For example, Arthur Andersen, a large CPA firm, provides materials and training for faculty members who wish to incorporate ethics training into their classroom instruction. Obviously, more research is needed to help identify ways in which all organizations that may come into contact with whistle-blowers can provide support for valid whistle-blowing.

Implications for Would-be Whistle-blowers

Whistle-blowers and their counselors are frequently asked what advice they would give to other observers of wrongdoing who are contemplating blowing the whistle. Unfortunately, in the case of the Soeken and Soeken (1987) interview-based study, about one-third of the whistle-blowers advised others not to blow the whistle at all! For those who decide to blow the whistle, former whistle-blowers have offered advice that has appeared in numerous articles in practitioner magazines. We will now summarize some of the advice typically offered and then consider whether there is at this time any basis in the research supporting this advice.

First, an observer of wrongdoing should listen to his or her conscience (Soeken & Soeken, 1987). Second, documentation is important (Soeken & Soeken, 1987). Whistle-blowers should "keep a detailed diary of all significant developments—a fact, a verbal warning, or some sudden insight into events. A diary can be invaluable when preparing to testify and can help resolve credibility disputes ... [they should] obtain and copy all available and necessary records before making complaints. After you expose a problem, the flow of information may be cut off because you are viewed as a threat" (Shepherd, 1987b, p. A6).

Third, whistle-blowers should try to obtain support from their families, co-workers, other whistle-blowers, reporters, and members of Congress (Shepherd, 1987b; Soeken & Soeken, 1987). Fourth, whistle-blowers should first work within the system, as by talking about the problem with their supervisors (Shepherd, 1987b). Fifth, whistle-blowers should obtain solid legal advice (Soeken and Soeken, 1987); "you need to know the odds of success in court, potential retaliation, and the price tag of proving that you are right" (Shepherd, 1987b, p. A6).

Sixth, observers should plan their actions carefully (Soeken & Soeken, 1987) and always be on their best behavior with supervisors and administrators who might retaliate (Shepherd, 1987b). Seventh, according to Soeken and Soeken (1987), retaliation should be expected, as should financial loss and mental anguish. Thus, they recommend blowing the whistle anonymously.

Unfortunately, at this time, evidence is not consistent in supporting all of the foregoing advice in every case. Would-be whistle-blowers would benefit from advice in two areas: how to blow the whistle effectively, and how to avoid retaliation subsequent to whistle-blowing. This advice is based on empirical findings described in chapter 5 but is presented here in an effort to suggest pragmatic steps to individuals considering whether to report wrongdoing they have observed. Admittedly, the empirical results on which these recommendations are based are limited, and in some cases our conclusions must be speculative; advice to whistle-blowers available elsewhere has been based largely on conclusions derived from case studies of famous whistle-blowers, making it somewhat speculative in nature as well.

Whistle-blowing is effective when it results in termination of the wrongdoing and—where applicable—when wrongs that have been committed are somehow rectified. It is important to note that this may require repeated reporting of the wrongdoing to different individuals over a long period of time. Thus, we argue that effectiveness really represents a range of possible organizational responses, with the "best" response being rapid and complete resolution of the wrongdoing (that is, termination and rectification). More research has been completed concerning predictions of retaliation than is the case with predictions of effectiveness. While the results should not be viewed as definitive, we can still draw tentative conclusions where consistent findings point to a pattern. With these points in mind, then, we can comment on the above suggestions to potential whistle-blowers.

First, the advice concerning listening to one's conscience appears to be consistent with research showing that whistle-blowers often feel morally compelled to act, but at this time there is no evidence that people who appear to act out of social or moral responsibility are perceived differently by other organization members. Second, similarly, the research reviewed here shows that corroborative evidence sometimes increases whistle-blowing, but it does not bolster the case greatly. Having direct evidence of wrongdoing on complaints by multiple whistle-blowers does not influence effectiveness, nor does co-worker agreement that wrongdoing has occurred.

Third, there has been little research concerning the support of others besides managers in the organization. Parmerlee et al. (1982) found that co-worker support made little difference in avoiding retaliation. The benefits to be derived from support of other parties awaits further research.

Fourth, working within the system wherever possible seems to make sense, but using external channels to blow the whistle has little or no impact on whistle-blowing effectiveness or retaliation; our research indicated no effect in either study in which this was examined. It may be that the appropriateness of this advice heavily depends on the nature of the system itself. Consistent with this speculation, in one study, at least, blowing the whistle in an organizational culture supportive of whistle-blowing increased the likelihood of success. Thus, would-be whistle-blowers may want to judge the organization before blowing the whistle. Perhaps there are alternatives to whistle-blowing that may work more effectively in some organizations.

Unfortunately, we know of no research investigating the efficacy of obtaining sound legal advice. Given the expense and potential benefits of doing so, it would be most interesting to see whether hiring an attorney is cost-effective, and if so, at what point in the process the attorney should intervene.

The sixth and seventh suggestions concerned avoiding retaliation. Many authors of anecdotal cases and studies of whistle-blowers who were nonrandomly selected (for example, Soeken & Soeken, 1987; Parmerlee et al., 1982) agree that retaliation is both likely and severe. But comparative survey-based studies of large samples of randomly selected whistle-blowers and other organization members show that retaliation occurs in a small proportion of cases and it generally takes the form of more subtle harassment than firing or physical threats (for example, Graham, 1983; Miceli & Near, 1989). Thus, we must disagree that retaliation is inevitable; more likely, the whistle-blower and his or her complaint will be ignored. It is also unclear whether blowing the whistle anonymously will be advantageous in every situation. Some complaint recipients may not be trustworthy and may reveal a confidence; others may refuse or be unable to follow up on a complaint if they cannot identify the complainant.

However, the advice that whistle-blowers attempt to retain the support of supervisors and management appears sound. The pattern of results is quite clear. Whistle-blowers are more likely to avoid retaliation if they have support from top and middle management. Unfortunately, this assessment was provided after the whistle-blowing occurred, so we have no way of knowing how many organization members who enjoy management support lose that support when they blow the whistle; probably this varies with the individual case, so our best advice is for would-be whistle-blowers to be aware of the problem and to try to take proactive actions to maintain their managerial support throughout the course of the whistle-blowing process. Curiously, other variables relating to the whistle-blower, the wrongdoing situation, the organization, and power relationships were not shown to be related to reprisal in any systematic way in the five studies reviewed in chapter 5.

Research on effectiveness suggests some other considerations for potential whistle-blowers. First, whistle-blowers may be more effective when the problem's resolution will benefit the organization, for example, employee theft in a private firm or unsafe behavior in a public agency. Thus, alternatives to whistle-blowing may be necessary if this is not the case. On the other hand, the organization's dependence on the wrongdoing for its performance seems not to be consistently related to its decision to terminate the wrongdoing; thus, would-be whistle-blowers should not assume that organizations will necessarily resist termination of wrongdoing from which they draw benefits.

Second, members' power in the organization may affect their ability to blow the whistle effectively. Research has indicated that whistle-blowers receiving higher pay are more effective than those who aren't; in contrast, those for whom whistle-blowing is prescribed by the job are less likely to be effective. Third, the powers of the complaint recipient and the wrongdoer have not been found consistently to be related to effectiveness. Thus, perhaps observers of wrongdoing should try to avoid being intimidated by the apparent stature of the wrongdoer, and they should not rule out reporting to a complaint recipient who might seem rather powerless at first.

Summary

This chapter provided suggestions to organizations and individuals who may be involved in whistle-blowing. Our advice, which was in many cases quite speculative, was based on the research and legal developments described in earlier chapters of this book.

It can be argued that organizations should strive to eliminate wrongdoing, because an organization in which no wrongdoing occurs will have no need for whistle-blowers. But reality dictates that this ideal state of affairs will not always be possible, and that it is more realistic to strive for a high probability of whistle-blowing following wrongdoing, perhaps by establishing and supporting a climate for reporting wrongdoing, than to try to eliminate whistle-blowing. If there is a common theme in our advice, it is that organizations must emphasize responsiveness to whistle-blowers if they are to achieve these desired goals. The previous emphasis on avoiding retaliation, while certainly understandable, simply will not go far enough to encourage whistle-blowing.

We drew a rough classification scheme which separated proactive and reactive actions into those involving strategies, structure and communication, and human resource management actions. Proactive actions reflect a wish by organizational leaders to avoid or prevent wrongdoing. Managers can scan the environment, define wrongdoing, and develop codes of conduct. Then, they can train employees to prevent wrongdoing. They can provide rewards for ethical behavior. Reactive actions concern steps that can be taken once wrongdoing has been observed or reported. Defining appropriate responses to wrongdoing, designating complaint recipients, and providing support and training for these recipients would be beneficial. Informal complaint recipients should not be overlooked. Organizations must communicate their wish to respond and establish supportive cultures. They can train managers and employees to respond appropriately to wrongdoing and provide rewards for these responses. Finally, organizations can attempt to select a diverse set of employees who will be willing to challenge authority where it is appropriate.

Professional or religious organizations can help whistle-blowers by providing emotional, professional, or financial support. For example, they can provide a vehicle for networking, which may reduce a professional's dependence on the employer. Business schools can provide assistance with training in ethics or related topics as can consulting firms.

Advice to organization members contemplating blowing the whistle has been offered many times before. Here, we attempted to consider the existing advice in light of the research findings reviewed earlier. Unfortunately, in many cases the research is too preliminary to make definitive statements. However, it appears that taking steps to obtain supervisory and managerial support is advisable. Would-be whistle-blowers should also examine the organization carefully for potential responsiveness, because it appears that in some organizations whistle-blowing is likely to be much more effective than in others.

In conclusion, there remain a great many questions of practical and theoretical importance concerning whistle-blowing. In this book, we have attempted to sort out some controversies and summarize what is known about the process. But perhaps more to the point, we hope that this book has stimulated the thinking of those persons and organizations who will help us move forward to addressing these critical unanswered questions. Finally, we hope that this book has provided something useful for those organizations and individuals who are experiencing whistle-blowing.

References

Adams, J. S. (1965). Inequity in social exchange. In L. Berkowitz (ed.), *Advances in experimental social psychology* (Vol. 2, pp. 267–299). New York: Academic Press.

Allen, V. L., and Wilder, D. A. (1980). Impact of group consesus and social support on stimulus meaning: Mediation of conformity by cognitive restructuring. *Journal of Personality and Social Psychology* 39:1116–1125.

Anderson, J., and Spear, J. (1987, Oct. 11). Whistleblowing no longer popular. *Newark [OH] Advocate*: 4A.

Anderson, J., and VanAtta, D. (1987, May 17). Whistleblowers need aid. *Newark [OH] Advocate*: 4A.

Andrews, S. D. W. (1981). Student development and the goals of higher education: A conceptual framework for selecting teaching strategies. *Exchange* 6 (2):5–114.

Asch, S. E. (1951). Effects of group pressure upon the modification and distortion of judgments. In H. Guetzkow (ed.), *Groups, leadership, and men* (pp. 177–190). Pittsburgh: Carnegie Press.

Ashkanasy, N. M. (1985). Rotter's internal-external scale: Confirmatory factor analysis and correlation with social desirability for alternative scale formats. *Journal of Personality and Social Psychology* 48 (5):1328–1341.

Baker, M. (1983). Employer response to professional complaints and alarms: Can corporate scientists and engineers speak out? Working paper. New York: Educational Fund for Individual Rights.

Baldwin, J. D., and Baldwin, J. I. (1981). *Behavior principles in everyday life.* Englewood Cliffs, NJ: Prentice-Hall.

Bandura, A. (1977). *Social learning theory.* Englewood Cliffs, NJ: Prentice-Hall.

Banfield, E. C. (1975). Corruption as a feature of governmental organization. *The Journal of Law and Economics* 18:587–605.

Barnard, C. I. (1938). *The functions of the executive.* Cambridge: Harvard University Press.

Barnett, T. R., Cochran, D. S., and Taylor, G. S. (1990). *The relationship between internal dissent policies and employee whistleblowing: An exploratory study.* Paper presented at the 50th annual meeting of the Academy of Management, San Francisco.

Bateman, T. S., and Organ, D. W. (1983). Job satisfaction and the good soldier: The relationship between affect and employee "citizenship." *Academy of Management Journal* 36:587–595.

Batson, C. D. (1983). Sociobiology and the role of religion in promoting prosocial behavior: An alternative view. *Journal of Personality and Social Psychology* 45:1380–1385.

Batson, C. D., Duncan, B., Ackerman, P., Buckley, T., and Birch, K. (1981). Is empathic emotion a source of altruistic motivation? *Journal of Personality and Social Psychology* 40:290–302.

Baucus, M. S., and Near, J. P. (1991). Can illegal corporate behavior be predicted? An event history analysis. *Academy of Management Journal* 34:9–36.

Baucus, M. S., Near, J. P., and Miceli, M. P. (1985, Aug.). *Organizational culture and whistle-blowing*. Paper presented at the 45th annual meeting of the Academy of Management, San Diego, CA.

Bavelas, A. (1968). Communication pattens in task-oriented groups. In D. Cartwright and A. Zander (eds.), *Group dynamics: Research and theory* (pp. 503–511). New York: Harper & Row.

Beauchamp, T., and Bowie, N. (1983). *Ethical theory and business*. Englewood Cliffs, NJ: Prentice-Hall.

Becker, H., and Fritzsche, D. J. (1987). A comparison of the ethical behavior of American, French and German managers. *The Columbia Journal of World Business* 22 (4):87–95.

Bennett-Alexander, D. (1988, June). Sexual harassment in the office. *Personnel Administrator* 33 (6):174–188.

Benson, J. K. (1977). Innovation and crisis in organizational analysis. *Sociological Quarterly* 18 (1):3–16.

Berkowitz, L., and Connor, W. H. (1966). Success, failure, and social responsibility. *Journal of Personality and Social Psychology* 4:664–669.

Bernstein, C., and Woodward, R. (1974). *All the president's men*. New York: Simon & Schuster.

Berry, B. (1990). *The sanctioning of physicians: A theory of response to professional threats*. Paper presented at the annual meeting of the American Sociological Association.

Bickman, L., and Rosenbaum, D. R. (1977). Crime reporting as a function of bystander encouragement, surveillance, and credibility. *Journal of Personality and Social Psychology* 32 (2):296–302.

Bies, R. J. (1987). The predicament of injustice: The management of moral outrage. In L. L. Cummings and B. M. Staw (eds.), *Research in organizational behavior* (Vol. 9, pp. 289–320). Greenwich, CT: JAI Press.

Bies, R. J., and Shapiro, D. L. (1988). Voice and justification: Their influence on procedural fairness judgments. *Academy of Management Journal* 31:676–685.

Biggart, N. W., and Hamilton, G. G. (1984). The power of obedience. *Administrative Science Quarterly* 29:540–549.

Biondo, J., and MacDonald, A. P., Jr. (1971). Internal-external locus of control and response to influence attempts. *Journal of Personality* 39:407–419.

Black, D. C. (1976). *The behavior of law.* New York: Academic Press.

Blackburn, J. D. (1984). A comparison of statutory protections of public and private sector whistle-blowers. Unpublished working paper, The Ohio State University, College of Business, Columbus, Ohio.

Blackburn, M. S. (1988, Aug.). Employee dissent: The choice of voice versus silence. Unpublished doctoral dissertation, The University of Tennessee, Knoxville.

Blau, P. (1964). *Exchange and power in social life.* New York: Wiley.

Bok, S. (1980). Whistle-blowing and professional responsibilities. In P. Callahan and S. Bok (eds.), *Ethics teaching in higher education* (pp. 277–295). New York: Plenum Press.

———. *Secrets: On the ethics of concealment and revelation.* New York: Pantheon Books.

Bourgeois, L. (1985). Strategic goals, perceived uncertainty, and economic performance in volatile environments. *Academy of Management Review* 28:548–573.

Bowman, J. S., Elliston, F. A., and Lockhart, P. (1984). *Professional dissent—An annotated bibliography and resource guide.* New York: Garland Publishing.

Brabeck, M. M. (1984). Ethical characteristics of whistle-blowers. *Journal of Research in Personality* 18:41–53.

Braithwaite, J. (1982). Challenging just deserts: Punishing white-collar criminals. *Journal of Criminal Law and Criminology* 73:723–745.

Brehm, J. W. (1972). *Responses to loss of freedom: A theory of psychological reactance.* Morristown, NJ: General Learning Press.

Brief, A. P., and Motowidlo, S. (1986). Prosocial organizational behaviors. *Academy of Management Review* 11:710–725.

Burnett, C. (1988, June 8). Reactions to incentives mixed. *Columbus [OH] Dispatch*: 7A.

Callahan, E. S. (1990). Employment at will: The relationship between societal expectations and the law. Unpublished manuscript, Department of Law and Public Policy, Syracuse University.

Campbell, A. K. (1980, Mar. 12). Testimony before the Subcommittee on Post Office and Civil Service, U.S. House of Representatives, as cited in Merit Systems Protection Board (1981).

Cavanagh, G. H., Moberg, D. J., and Velasquez, M. (1981). The ethics of organizational politics. *Academy of Management Review* 6:363–374.

Cheney, G., and Vibbert, S. (1987). Corporate discourse: Public relations and issue management. *Handbook of organizational communication* (pp. 165–194). Newbury Park, CA: Sage.

CIA whistle-blower moves from job. (1987, Mar. 14). *Newark Advocate*, p. 3A.

Clinard, M. B. (1983). *Corporate ethics and crime: The role of middle management*. Beverly Hills: Sage.

Clinard, M. B., and Yeager, P. (1980). *Corporate crime*. New York: The Free Press.

Cochran, P. L., and Nigh, D. (1986, Aug.). *Illegal corporate behavior: An empirical examination*. Paper presented at the 46th annual meeting of the Academy of Management, Chicago.

Cole, R. E. (1981, July). The Japanese lesson in quality. *Technology Review*, pp. 29–40.

Colt, C. (1981). Protesting sex discrimination against women. In A. Westin (ed.), *Whistle blowing! Loyalty and dissent in the corporation* (pp. 55–68). New York: McGraw-Hill.

Control your liability to keep out of court. (1988, Mar.). *Personnel Administrator* 33 (3):44.

Costanzo, P. R., and Shaw, M. E. (1966). Conformity as a function of age level. *Child Development* 37:967–974.

Costigan, J. I., and Schmeidler, M. A. (1984). Exploring supportive and defensive communication climates. In J. E. Jones and W. Pfeiffer (eds.), *The 1984 Annual Developing Human Resources* (pp. 112–119). San Diego, CA: University Associates.

Cressy, D. R. (1976). Restraint of trade, recidivism, and deliquent neighborhoods. In J. F. Short (ed.) *Delinquency, crime and society*. Chicago: University of Chicago Press.

Crosby, F. (1982). *Relative deprivation and working women*. New York: Oxford University Press.

——— (1984). Relative deprivation in organizational settings. In B. M. Staw and L. L. Cummings (eds.), *Research in organizational behavior* (Vol. 6, pp. 51–93). Greenwich, CT: JAI Press.

Daft, R. L. (1978). A dual-core model of organizational innovation. *Academy of Management Journal* 21:193–210.

Davidson, W. N., and Worrell, D. L. (1988). The impact of announcements of corporate illegalities. *Academy of Management Journal* 31:195–200.

Dertke, M. C., Penner, L. A., and Ulrich, K. (1974). Observers' reporting of shoplifters as a function of the thief's race and sex. *Journal of Social Psychology* 94:213–221.

Devine, T. M., and Aplin, D. G. (1986). Abuse of authority: The office of the special counsel and whistleblower protection. *Antioch Law Journal* 4 (5):5–71.

Doctor may profit in a medicare fraud suit against ex-colleague. (1987, Sept. 10). *New York Times*: 3.

Doeringer, P. B., and Piore, M. J. (1971). *Internal labor markets and manpower analysis*. Lexington, MA: D.C. Heath.

Donahue, P. (1983). *Transcript 10283*. Cincinnati: Multimedia Entertainment, Inc.

Dozier, J. B. (1988). Is whistle-blowing helping behavior? A laboratory study of team members' reporting of an unethical team leader. Unpublished doctoral dissertation, The Ohio State University, Columbus.

Dozier, J. B., & Miceli, M. P. (1985). Potential predictors of whistle-blowing: A prosocial behavior perspective. *Academy of Management Review* 10:823–836.

Dworkin, T. M., and Near, J. P. (1987). Whistle-blowing statutes: Are they working? *American Business Law Journal* 25 (2):241–264.

Eagly, A. H. (1983, Sept.). Gender and social influence: A social psychological analysis. *American Psychologist* 38:971–981.

Edelhertz, H. (1978). The nature, impact, and prosecution of white collar crime. In J. M. Johnson and J. D. Douglas (eds.), *Crime at the top: Deviance in business and the professions* (pp. 44–65). Philadelphia: Lippincott.

Eisenhardt, K., and Bourgeois, L. (1988). Politics of strategic decision making in high velocity environments: Toward a midrange theory. *Academy of Management Journal* 31:737–770.

Elliston, F. A. (1982a). Anonymity and whistle-blowing. *Journal of Business Ethics* 1:167–177.

——— (1982b). Civil disobedience and whistle-blowing: A comparative appraisal of two forms of dissent. *Journal of Business Ethics* 1:23–28.

Emerson, R. M. (1954). Deviation and rejection: An experimental replication. *American Sociological Review* 19:688–694.

——— (1962). Power-dependence relations. *American Sociological Review* 27:31–41.

Emler, N., Renwick, S., and Malone, B. (1983). The relationship between moral reasoning and political orientation. *Journal of Personality and Social Psychology* 45:1073–1080.

Employees greater threat to banks than robbers. (1985). *Columbus [OH] Dispatch* 155 (199): H1.

England, P. (1979). Women and occupational prestige: A case of vacuous sex equality. *Signs* 5:252–265.

Enz, C. A. (1986). *Power and shared values in the corporate culture.* Ann Arbor, MI: UMI Research Press.

——— (1988). The role of value congruity in intraorganizational power. *Administrative Science Quarterly* 33:284–304.

Enz, C. A., and Fryxell, W. (1987, Aug.). *The meaning and measurement of organizational value congruence.* Paper presented at the 47th annual meeting of the Academy of Management, New Orleans, LA.

Enz, C. A., and Schwenk, C. R. (1989). Believing is not succeeding: Value similarity and corporate performance. Unpublished manuscript, Indiana University, Bloomington.

Ethics pay. (1987, Dec. 29). *Wall Street Journal*: 1.

Ewing, D. W. (1983). *Do it my way or you're fired! Employee rights and the changing role of management prerogatives.* New York: John Wiley & Sons.

Fama, E. F. (1980). Agency problems and the theory of the firm. *Journal of Political Economy* 88:288–307.

Farrell, D. (1983). Exit, voice, loyalty and neglect as responses to job dissatisfaction: A multidimensional scaling study. *Academy of Management Journal* 26:596–607.

Farrell, D., and Petersen, J. C. (1982). Patterns of political behavior in organizations. *Academy of Management Review* 7:403–412.

——— (1989). *The organizational impact of whistle-blowing.* Paper presented at the annual meeting of the American Criminology Society, Reno, NV.

Feinstein, S. (1988a, Jan. 12). Labor letter. *Wall Street Journal*: 1.

——— (1988b, May 31). Worker complaints. *Wall Street Journal*: 1.

Ferguson, L. J., and Near, J. P. (1987, Apr.). The whistle-blowing phenomenon: A look at social, situational, and personality influences. *Proceedings of the annual meeting of the Midwest Academy of Management*, pp. 171–175.

——— (1989, Nov.). *Whistle-blowing in the lab.* Paper presented at the annual meeting of the American Criminological Society, Reno, NV.

Ferris, G. R., Russ, G. S., and Fandt, P. M. (1989). Politics in organizations. In R. A. Giacalone and P. Rosenfeld (eds.), *Impression management in the organization*. Hillsdale, NJ: Lawrence Erlbaum.

Festinger, L. (1950). Informal social communication. *Pyschological Review* 57:271–282.

——— (1957). *A theory of cognitive dissonance*. Evanston, IL: Row, Peterson.

Festinger, L., Schachter, S., and Back, K. (1950). *Social pressures in formal groups*. New York: Harper.

Festinger, L., and Thibaut, J. (1951). Interpersonal communication in small groups. *Journal of Abnormal and Social Psychology* 46:92–99.

Finney, H. C., and Lesieur, H. C. (1982). A contingency theory of organizational crime. In S. B. Bacharach (ed.), *Research in the sociology of organizations* (Vol. 1, pp. 255–299). Greenwich, CT: JAI Press.

Finney, M. I. (1988a). A game of skill or chance? *Personnel Administrator* 33 (3):38–44.

——— (1988b). A good idea—five years later. *Personnel Administrator* 33 (3):45–46.

Fiske, D. W. (1982). Convergent-discriminant validation in measurements and research strategies. In D. Brinberg and L. Kidder (eds.), *New directions for methodology of social and behavioral science: Forms of validity in research* (No. 12, pp. 77–92). San Francisco: Jossey-Bass.

Fiske, S. T., and Taylor, S. E. (1984). *Social cognition*. Reading, MA: Addison-Wesley.

Ford, S. (1987, Aug. 17). Counsel denies unfairness to whistleblowers. *Federal Times*: 2, 16.

Forsyth, D. R. (1985). Individual differences in information integration during moral judgment. *Journal of Personality and Social Psychology* 49 (1):264–272.

France, S. (1990, Mar.). The private war on Pentagon fraud. *American Bar Association Journal*: 46–49.

Freidson, E. (1972). *Profession of medicine*. New York: Dodd, Mead.

French, J. R. P., Jr., and Raven, B. H. (1959). The bases of social power. In D. Cartwright (ed.), *Studies in social power* (pp. 118–149). Ann Arbor, MI: University of Michigan Press.

Fritzsche, D. J. (1988). An examination of marketing ethics: Role of the decision maker, consequences of the decision, management position, and sex of the respondent. *Journal of Macromarketing* 8 (2):29–39.

Fritzsche, D. J., and Becker, H. (1984). Linking management behavior to ethical philosophy: An empirical investigation. *Academy of Management Journal* 27:166–175.

Gaerte, D. M. (1990). *An application of the model for judging communicant acceptability to the phenomenon of whistle-blowing*. Paper presented at the annual meeting of the Speech Communication Association.

Gaines, J. (1980). Upward communication in industry: An experiment. *Human Relations* 33:929–942.

Galbraith, J. K. (1973). On the economic image of corporate enterprise. In R. Nader and M. J. Green (eds.), *Corporate power in America*. New York: Grossman.

Gamson, W. A. (1968). *Power and discontent*. Homewood, IL: Dorsey.

GAO says U.S. help for thrifts to top receipts. (1989, Jan. 27). *Wall Street Journal:* A12.

Garrett, D. E. (1987). The effectiveness of marketing policy boycotts: Environmental opposition to marketing. *Journal of Marketing* 51 (2):46–57.

Gelfand, D. M., Hartmann, D. P., Walder, P., and Page, B. (1973). Who reports shoplifters? A field-experimental study. *Journal of Personality and Social Psychology* 25:276–285.

Gellert, D. (1981). Insisting on safety in the skies. In A. Westin (ed.), *Whistle blowing! Loyalty and dissent in the corporation* (pp. 17–30). New York: McGraw-Hill.

Gibb, J. R. (1961). Defensive and supportive communication. *Journal of Communications* 11:141–148.

Giddens, A. (1984). *The constitution of society: Outline of the theory of structuration*. Berkeley, CA: University of California Press.

Glauser, M. J. (1982, Aug.). *Factors which facilitate or impede upward communication in organizations*. Paper presented at the 42nd annual meeting of the Academy of Management, New York.

Glazer, M. P., and Glazer, P. M. (1987). Pathways to resistance: An ethical odyssey in government and industry. In M. Lewis and J. L. Miller (eds.), *Research in social problems and public policy* (Vol. 4, pp. 193–219). Greenwich, CT: JAI Press.

——— (1989). *The whistle-blowers: Exposing corruption in government and industry*. New York: Basic Books.

GM to offer cash rewards to halt information leaks. (1987, Sept. 17). *Wall Street Journal*: 33.

Gorden, W. I., Infante, D. A., and Graham, E. E. (1988). Corporate conditions conducive to employee voice: A subordinate perspective. *Employee Responsibilities and Rights Journal* 1:101–112.

Gouldner, A. W. (1957a). Cosmopolitans and locals: Toward an analysis of latent social roles (part 1). *Administrative Science Quarterly* 2:281–306.

—— (1957b). Cosmopolitans and locals: Toward an analysis of latent social roles (part 2). *Administrative Science Quarterly* 2:444–480.

Graham, J. W. (1983). Principled organizational dissent. Unpublished doctoral dissertation, Northwestern University, Evanston, IL.

—— (1984, Aug.). *Organizational response to principled organizational dissent.* Paper presented at the 44th annual meeting of the Academy of Management, Boston, MA.

—— (1986). *Principled organizational dissent: A theoretical essay.* In L. L. Cummings and B. M. Staw (eds.), *Research in organizational behavior* (Vol. 8, pp. 1–52). Greenwich, CT: JAI Press.

—— (1989, Nov.). *Whistleblowing as organizational citizenship behavior and/or civic duty.* Paper presented at the annual meeting of the American Society of Criminology, Reno, NV.

Green, S. G., and Mitchell, T. R. (1979). Attributional processes of leader, member interactions. *Organizational Behavior and Human Performance* 23:429–458.

Greenberg, J. (1987). A taxonomy of organizational justice theories. *Academy of Management Review* 12:9–22.

Greenberger, D. B., Miceli, M. P., & Cohen, D. (1987). Oppositionists and group norms: The reciprocal influence of whistle-blowers and co-workers. *Journal of Business Ethics* 7:527–542.

Greenberger, D. B., Porter, G., Miceli, M. P., and Strasser, S. (1991). Responses to inadequate personal control in organizations. *Journal of Social Issues* 47:111–128.

Greenberger, D. B., and Strasser, S. (1986). The development and application of a model of personal control in organizations. *Academy of Management Review* 11:164–177.

Greenberger, D. B., Strasser, S., Cummings, L. L., and Dunham, R. B. (1989). The impact of personal control on performance and satisfaction. *Organizational Behavior and Human Decision Processes* 43:29–51.

Greenberger, D. B., Strasser, S., and Lee, S. (1988). Personal control as a mediator between perceptions of supervisory behaviors and employee reactions. *Academy of Management Journal* 31:405–417.

Greiner, L. E. (1972, July/Aug.). Evolution and revolution as organizations grow. *Harvard Business Review* 50:37–46.

Gutek, B. A. (1985). *Sex and the workplace: The impact of sexual behavior and harassment on women, men, and organizations.* San Francisco: Jossey-Bass.

Gutek, B. A., Morasch, B., and Cohen, A. G. (1983). Interpreting social-sexual behavior in a work setting. *Journal of Vocational Behavior* 22:30–48.

Hacker, A. (1978). Loyalty—and the whistle-blower. *Across the Board* 15 (4–9):67.

Hackman, J. R., and Oldham, G. (1980). *Work redesign.* Reading, MA: Addison-Wesley.

Hamilton, V. L., and Sanders, J. (1981). The effect of roles and deeds on responsibility judgments: The normative structure of wrongdoing. *Social Psychology Quarterly* 44:237–254.

Hannan, M. T., and Freeman, J. (1977). The population ecology of organizations. *American Journal of Sociology* 82:929–964.

Hanrahan, J. (1983, Mar.). Whistleblower! How a major defense contract may have cost taxpayers millions and this man his job. *Common Cause* 9 (2):17–23.

Harari, H., and McDavid, J. W. (1969). Situational influence on moral justice: A study of "finking." *Journal of Personality and Social Psychology* 11:240–244.

Heacock, M. V., and McGee, G. W. (1989). Whistleblowing: An ethical issue in organizational and human behavior. *Business and Professional Ethics Journal* 6 (4):35–46.

Heneman, H. G., III (1985). Pay satisfaction. In K. M. Rowland and G. R. Ferris (eds.), *Research in personnel and human resources management* (Vol. 3, pp. 115–139). Greenwich, CT: JAI Press.

Hickson, D. J., Hinings, C. R., Lee, C. A., Schneck, R. E., and Pennings, J. M. (1971). A strategic contingencies theory of intraorganizational power. *Administrative Science Quarterly* 16:216–229.

Hirschman, A. O. (1970). *Exit, voice and loyalty: Responses to decline in firms, organizations, and states.* Cambridge: Harvard University Press.

Hoerr, J., Glaberson, W. G., Moskowitz, D. B., Chan, V., Pollock, M. A., and Tasini, J. (1985, July 8). Beyond unions: A revolution in employee rights is in the making. *BusinessWeek* 29 (2):72–77.

Hollander, E. P. (1958). Conformity, status, and idiosyncrasy credit. *Psychological Review* 65:117–127.

——— (1960). Competence and conformity in the acceptance of influence. *Journal of Abnormal and Social Psychology* 61:361–365.

Hornstein, H. A. (1978). Promotive tension and prosocial behavior: A Lewinian analysis. In L. Wispe (ed.), *Altruism, sympathy, and helping: Psychological and sociological principles* (pp. 177–207). New York: Academic Press.

Hostetler, A. J. (1987, July). NIMH sends fraud case to justice. *APA Monitor* 18 (7):18.

Isen, A. M. (1970). Success, failure, attention, and reaction to others: The warm glow of success. *Journal of Applied Psychology* 15:294–301.

Isen, A., and Levin, A. (1972). Effect of feeling good on helping: Cookies and kindness. *Journal of Personality and Social Psychology* 21:384–388.

Janis, I. L. (1972). *Victims of groupthink: A psychological study of foreign policy decisions and fiascos.* Boston: Houghton, Mifflin.

Jansen, E., and Von Glinow, M. A. (1985). Ethical ambivalence and organizational reward systems. *Academy of Management Review* 10:814–822.

Jensen, J. V. (1987). Ethical tension points in whistle-blowing. *Journal of Business Ethics* 6:527–542.

Jensen, T. C. (1979). Title VII: Impacts of a legal remedy for illegal employment discrimination. Unpublished manuscript, School of Business, Indiana University, Bloomington.

Johnson, D. (1990). Public perceptions, public good, and the modal scientist. *Psychological Science* 1 (2): 79–80.

Johnson, D. A., and Pany, K. (1981, July). Exposé or cover-up: Will an employee blow the whistle? *Management Accounting* 59 (7):32–36.

Johnson, J. (1983). Issues management—what are the issues? *Business Quarterly* 48 (Fall): 22.

Jones, A. P., James, L. R., and Brunni, J. R. (1975). Perceived leadership behavior and confidence in the leader as moderated by job involvement. *Journal of Applied Psychology* 60:146–149.

Jones, J., and Pottmyer, A. (1987, July). Whistleblower: How the system fired, imprisoned and silenced Mark Price. *Utah Holiday* 16 (10):20–41, 64.

Julie, L. (1987, July 14). Testimony before the Subcommittee on Federal Services, Post Office and Civil Service.

Kanter, R. M. (1977). *Men and women of the corporation.* New York: Basic Books.

——— (1983). *The change masters.* New York: Simon & Schuster.

Kasich, J. (1988, Sept.). Kasich federal employee incentives bill approved by House. *Reports to the 12th District* 6 (3):1, 4.

Katz, D. (1964). The motivational basis of organizational behavior. *Behavioral Science* 9:131–146.

Keenan, J. P. (1988a). Communication climate, whistle-blowing, and the first-level manager: A preliminary study. *Academy of Management Best Paper Proceedings* 40:247–251.

——— (1988b). Communication climate, whistle-blowing, and the first-level manager: A preliminary study. Working paper, School of Business-Management Institute, University of Wisconsin, Madison.

——— (1989, November). *Whistleblowing and the senior-level executive: Determinants of feeling obliged to blow the whistle.* Paper presented at the annual meeting of the American Society of Criminology, Reno, NV.

——— (1990a). First-level managers and whistleblowing: An exploratory study of individual and organizational influences. Working paper, School of Business-Management Institute, University of Wisconsin, Madison.

——— (1990b). Upper-level managers and whistleblowing: Determinants of perceptions of company encouragement and information about where to blow the whistle. *Proceedings* of the 33rd annual meeting of the Midwest Academy of Management, Milwaukee.

Kelley, H. H. (1967). Attribution theory in social psychology. In *Nebraska symposium on motivation*. Lincoln, NE: University of Nebraska Press.

Kelman, H. C., and Hamilton, V. L. (1989). *Crimes of obedience: Toward a social psychology of authority and responsibility*. New Haven, CT: Yale University Press.

Kendall, D. W. (1988). Rights across the waters. *Personnel Administrator* 33 (3):58–61.

Kennedy, W. V. (1987, Nov. 29). Military uses exam to curb whistle-blowers. *Christian Science Monitor*: B1.

Kiesler, C. A., Collins, B. E., & Miller, N. (1969). *Attitude change*. New York: Wiley.

Kohlberg, L. (1969). Stage and sequence: The cognitive developmental approach to socialization. In D. Goslin (ed.), *Handbook of socialization theory and research* (pp. 347–480). Chicago: Rand McNally.

Kolarska, L., and Aldrich, H. (1980). Exit, voice, and silence: Consumers' and managers' responses to organizational decline. *Organizational Studies* 1:41–58.

Koshland, D. E., Jr. (1988). Science, journalism and whistle-blowing. *Science* 240:585.

Kurtines, W., and Greif, E. B. (1974). The development of moral thought: Review and evaluation of Kohlberg's approach. *Psychological Bulletin* 81:453–470.

Latané, B. (1981). The psychology of social impact. *American Psychologist* 36:343–356.

Latané, B., and Darley, J. M. (1968). Group inhibition of bystander intervention. *Journal of Personality and Social Psychology* 10:215–221.

——— (1970). *The unresponsive bystander: Why doesn't he help?* New York: Prentice-Hall.

Laurent, A. (1986, Nov. 3). Wieseman explains plans for OSC. *Federal Times*: 8, 20.

Laver, M. (1976). "Exit, voice, and loyalty" revisited. *British Journal of Political Science* 6:463–482.

Levine, J. M. (1980). Reaction to opinion deviance in small groups. In P. Paulus (ed.), *The psychology of group influence* (pp. 375–429). Hillsdale, NJ: Erlbaum.

Levine, J. M., and Ranelli, C. J. (1978). Majority reaction to shifting and stable attitudinal deviates. *European Journal of Social Psychology* 8:55–70.

Lietzke, R. (1990, Oct. 27). Employees called critical to success. *Columbus [OH] Dispatch*: C–1.

Lindblom, C. E. (1959). The science of muddling through. *Public Administration Review* 19:76–88.

Maass, A., and Clark, R. D. (1984). Hidden impact of minorities: Fifteen years of minority influence research. *Psychological Bulletin* 95:428–450.

MacDonald, A. P., Jr. (1970). Revised scale for ambiguity tolerance: Reliability and validity. *Psychological Reports* 26:791–798.

Mainiero, L. A. (1986). Coping with powerlessness: The relationship of gender and job dependency to empowerment-strategy usage. *Administrative Science Quarterly* 31: 633–653.

Malin, M. H. (1983). Protecting the whistle-blower from retaliatory discharge. *University of Michigan Journal of Law Reform* 16:277–318.

March, J. G., and Simon, H. A. (1958). *Organizations.* New York: Wiley.

Martin, J. (1981). Relative deprivation: A theory of distributive justice for an era of shrinking resources. In L. L. Cummings and B. M. Staw (eds.), *Research in organizational behavior* (Vol. 3, pp. 53–107). Greenwich, CT: JAI Press.

Martin, J., Brickman, P., and Murray, A. (1983, Aug.). *Psychological and sociological barriers to collective action in organizations.* Paper presented at the 43rd annual meeting of the Academy of Management, Dallas.

Mathews, M. C. (1987a). Codes of ethics: Organizational behavior and misbehavior. In W. C. Frederick (ed.), *Research in corporate social performance and policy* (Vol. 9, pp. 107–130). Greenwich, CT: JAI Press.

——— (1988). *Strategic intervention in organizations: Resolving ethical dilemmas.* Newbury Park, CA: Sage.

Mautz, R. K., Tiessen, P., and Colson, R. H. (1984). *Internal auditing: Directions and opportunities.* Altamonte Springs, FL: Institute of Internal Auditors Research Foundation.

McAfee, R. B., and Ricks, B. R. (1987). Communicating employee rights and responsibilities: The influence of role modeling. In C. A. B. Osigweh, Yg. (ed.), *Communicating employee responsibilities and rights: A modern management mandate* (pp. 141–148). New York: Quorum Books.

Merit Systems Protection Board (MSPB) (1981). *Whistle-blowing and the federal employee.* Washington, DC: U.S. Government Printing Office.

——— (1984). *Blowing the whistle in the federal government: A comparative analysis of 1980 and 1983 survey findings.* Washington, DC: U.S. Government Printing Office.

——— (1988). *Sexual harassment in the federal government: An update.* Washington, DC: U.S. Government Printing Office.

Meyer, A. D. (1982). Adapting to environmental jolts. *Administrative Science Quarterly* 27:515–537.

Meyers, R. A., and Garrett, D. E. (1988, Aug.). *Contradictions, boycotts, and communication: Reproducing organizational structure.* Paper presented at the 48th annual meeting of the Academy of Management, Anaheim, CA.

Miceli, M. P., Dozier, J. B., and Near, J. P. (1991). Blowing the whistle on data-fudging: A controlled field experiment. *Journal of Applied Social Psychology,* 21:301–325.

Miceli, M. P., & Near, J. P. (1984). The relationships among beliefs, organizational position, and whistle-blowing status: A discriminant analysis. *Academy of Management Journal* 27:687–705.

———— (1985). Characteristics of organizational climate and perceived wrongdoing associated with whistle-blowing decisions. *Personnel Psychology* 38:525–544.

———— (1988a). Individual and situational correlates of whistle-blowing. *Personnel Psychology* 41:267–282.

———— (1988b, Aug.). *Retaliation against role-prescribed whistle-blowers: The case of internal auditors.* Paper presented at the 48th annual meeting of the Academy of Management, Anaheim, CA.

———— (1988c). Whistle-blowers: A challenge to human resources practice. In R. S. Schuler, S. A. Youngblood, and V. L. Huber, *Readings in Personnel and Human Resource Management* (pp. 387–396). St. Paul, MN: West Publishing Company.

———— (1989). The incidence of wrongdoing, whistle-blowing, and retaliation: Results of a natural occurring field experiment. *Employee Responsibilities and Rights Journal* 2:91–108.

Miceli, M. P., Near, J. P., and Jensen, T. C. (1983, June). *Perceived retaliation and the perceived effectiveness of sex discrimination complaints.* Paper presented at the fifth annual convention of the National Women's Studies Association, Columbus, OH.

Miceli, M. P., Near, J. P., and Schwenk, C. R. (1991). Who blows the whistle and why? *Industrial and Labor Relations Review* 45:113–130.

Miceli, M. P., Roach, B., and Near, J. P. (1988). The motivations of anonymous whistle-blowers: The case of federal employees. *Public Personnel Management* 17:281–296.

Miller, D., and Friesen, P. H. (1984). *Organizations: A quantum view.* Englewood Cliffs, NJ: Prentice-Hall.

Moberg, D. J. (1989). *Tactics for resisting change: Bureaucratic opposition to new policies.* Paper presented at the meeting of the Western Academy of Management.

Moberg, D. J., and Meyer, M. J. (1989). An ethical theory of peer relations in organizations. Unpublished paper.

Moscovici, S. (1976). *Social influence and social change.* London: Academic Press.

Moscovici, S., and Faucheux, C. (1972). Social influence, conforming bias, and the study of active minorities. In L. Berkowitz (ed.), *Advances in experimental social psychology* (Vol. 6). New York: Academic Press.

Moscovici, S., Lage, E. and Naffrechoux, M. (1969). Influence of a consistent minority on the responses of a majority in a color perception task. *Sociometry* 32:365–379.

Moscovici, S., and Nemeth, C. (1974). Social influence: II. Minority influence. In C. Nemeth (ed.), *Social psychology: Classic and contemporary integrations.* Chicago: Rand McNally.

Motowidlo, S. (1984). Does job satisfaction lead to consideration and personal sensitivity? *Academy of Management Journal* 27:910–915.

Mowday, R., Steers, R. M., and Porter, L. W. (1979). The measurement of organizational commitment. *Journal of Vocational Behavior* 14:224–247.

Nader, R., Petkas, P. J., and Blackwell, K. (eds.) (1972). *Whistle-blowing: The report on the conference on professional responsibility.* New York: Grossman.

Nassi, A. J., Abramowitz, S. I., and Youmans, J. E. (1983). Moral development and politics a decade later: A replication and extension. *Journal of Personality and Social Psychology* 45:1127–1135.

Near, J. P. (1989, Jan.–Feb.). The editor's chair: Whistle-blowing: Encourage it! *Business Horizons*: 2–6.

Near, J. P., Baucus, M. S., and Miceli, M. P. (1991). Espoused organizational culture for wrongdoing: Relationship to culture-in-use. Manuscript under review.

Near, J. P., and Dworkin, T. M. (1989). Organizational responses to whistle-blowing. Unpublished manuscript, Indiana University, Bloomington.

Near, J. P., Dworkin, T. M., and Miceli, M. P. (in press). Explaining the whistle-blowing process: Suggestions from power theory and justice theory. *Organization Science.*

Near, J. P., and Jensen, T. C. (1983). The whistle-blowing process: Retaliation and perceived effectiveness. *Work and Occupations* 10:3–28.

Near, J. P., and Miceli, M. P. (1985). Organizational dissidence: The case of whistle-blowing. *Journal of Business Ethics* 4:1–16.

——— (1986). Retaliation against whistle-blowers: Predictors and effects. *Journal of Applied Psychology* 71:137–145.

——— (1987). Whistle-blowers in organizations: Dissidents or reformers? In B.M Staw and L. L. Cummings (eds.), *Research in Organizational Behavior* (Vol. 9, pp. 321–368). Greenwich, CT: JAI Press.

——— (1988). *The internal auditor's ultimate responsibility: The reporting of sensitive issues.* Altamonte Springs, FL: The Institute of Internal Auditors Research Foundation.

——— (1990). When whistle-blowing succeeds: Predictors of effective whistle-blowing. *Proceedings* of the 50th annual meeting of the Academy of Management, pp. 175–179.

——— (1991). How to succeed as a whistle-blower: Predictors of effective whistle-blowing. Unpublished working paper, Indiana University, Bloomington.

Near, J. P. Parmerlee, M. A., White, R. W., and Jensen, T. C. (1981, Aug.). *Blowing the whistle on sex discrimination: A comparison of public and private organizations.* Paper presented at the 41st annual meeting of the Academy of Management, Detroit.

Nemeth, C. (1986). Differential contributions of majority and minority influence. *Psychological Review* 93:23–32.

Nuclear Regulatory Commission (NRC) (1979). *Requirements for compliance functions*. Washington, DC: U.S. Government Printing Office.

O'Day, R. (1972). Intimidation rituals: Reactions to reform. *Journal of Applied Behavioral Science* 10:373–386.

Organ, D. W. (1988). *Organizational citizenship behavior: The good soldier syndrome*. Lexington, MA: Lexington Books.

Organ, D. W., and Konovsky, M. (1989). Cognitive versus affective determinants of organizational citizenship behavior. *Journal of Applied Psychology* 74:157–164.

Osigweh, C. A. B., Yg. (1987). Communication, responsibilities, and pro-rights revolution in the industrial workplace. In C. A. B. Osigweh, Yg. (ed.), *Communicating employee responsibilities and rights: A modern management mandate* (pp. 3–40). New York: Quorum Books.

——— (1988). The challenge of responsibilities: Confronting the revolution in workplace rights in modern organizations. *Employee Responsibilities and Rights Journal* 1 (1):5–24.

Ouchi, W. G. (1981). *Theory Z*. New York: Avon.

Paicheler, G. (1976). Norms and attitude change, I: Polarization and styles of behavior. *European Journal of Social Psychology* 6:405–427.

Panel on Government and the Regulation of Corporate and Individual Decisions (1980). *Regulation in the Eighties*. Washington, DC: U.S. Government Printing Office.

Parmerlee, M. A., Near, J. P., and Jensen, T. C. (1982). Correlates of whistle-blowers' perceptions of organizational retaliation. *Administrative Science Quarterly* 27:17–34.

Perrow, C. (1984). *Normal accidents: Living with high-risk technologies*. New York: Basic Books.

Perrucci, R. M., Anderson, R. M., Schendel, D. E., and Trachtman, L. E. (1980). Whistle-blowing: Professionals' resistance to organizational authority. *Social Problems* 28:149–164.

Peters, P., and Branch, T. (1972). *Blowing the whistle: Dissent in the public interest*. New York: Praeger.

Petersen, J. C., and Farrell, D. (1986). *Whistleblowing: Ethical and legal issues in expressing dissent*. Dubuque, IA: Kendall/Hunt.

Pfeffer, J., and Salancik, G. R. (1978). *The external control of organizations*. New York: Harper & Row.

Piaget, J. (1932). *The moral development of the child*. London: Rutledge and Kegan Paul.

Pincus, K. V. (1989). The efficacy of a red flags questionnaire for assessing the possibilty of fraud. *Accounting, Organizations, and Society* 14:153–163.

Pincus, K. V. (in press). Auditor individual differences and fairness of presentation judgments. *Auditing: A Journal of Practice and Theory*.

Podsakoff, P., and Organ, D. (1986). Self-reports in organizational research: Problems and prospects. *Journal of Management* 12:531–544.

Polman, D. (1989, June 15). Telling the truth, paying the price. *Philadelphia Inquirer*, pp. 16–18, 20, 21, 26, 28, 30–32.

Porter, M. (1980). *Competitive strategy.* New York: Free Press.

Porter, L. W., and Steers, R. M. (1973). Organizational, work, and personal factors in employee turnover and absenteeism. *Psychological Bulletin* 80:151–176.

Pottmyer, A. A. (1987, July). Fruits of blowing the whistle. *Utah Holiday* 16:(10), 30.

Powell, D. E. (1990, July 29). Blowing it. *The Miami Herald:* 5–11.

Pratt & Whitney prices spur federal inquiry. (1983, Mar. 27). *Columbus [OH] Dispatch:* A7.

Price, J. L., and Mueller, C. W. (1986). *Handbook of organizational measurement.* White Plains, NY: Pitman Publishing.

Professional Standards and Responsibilities Committee (1985, May). *Deterrence, detection, investigation, and reporting of fraud.* Statement on internal auditing standards, No. 3. Altamonte Springs, FL: The Institute of Internal Auditors.

Quinn, J. B. (1980). *Strategies for change: Logical incrementalism.* Homewood, IL: Richard D. Irwin.

Raelin, J. A. (1987). The professional as the executive's ethical aide-de-camp. *Academy of Management Executive* 1:171–182.

Rafaeli, A., and Sutton, R. I. (1987). Expression of emotion as part of the work role. *Academy of Management Review* 12:23–37.

Reid, J. E., and Associates. (1989). *The integrity interview* (advertising literature). Chicago, IL: John E. Reid and Associates.

Rest, J. (1979). *Development in judging moral issues.* Minneapolis: University of Minnesota Press.

Ricklefs, R. (1984, Nov. 3). Executives apply stiffer standards than public to ethical dilemmas. *Wall Street Journal:* 27.

Rosenberg, J. M. (1988, Feb. 14). Retailers search for more workers. *Columbus [OH] Dispatch:* F2.

Rotter, J. B. (1966). Generalized expectancies for internal vs. external control of reinforcement. *Psychological Monographs* 80:1–28.

Rowe, M. P., and Baker, M. (1984, May–June). Are you hearing enough employee concerns? *Harvard Business Review:* 127–135.

Rusbult, C. E., Farrell, D., Rogerts, G., and Mainous, A. G., III. (1988). Impact of exchange variables on exit, voice, loyalty, and neglect: An integrative model of responses to declining job satisfaction. *Academy of Management Journal* 31:599–627.

Rushton, J. P. (1980). *Altruism, socialization, and society.* Englewood Cliffs, NJ: Prentice-Hall.

——— (1984). The altruistic personality: Evidence from laboratory, naturalistic, and self-report perspectives. In E. Staub, D. Bar-Tal, J. Karylowski, and J. Reykowski (eds.), *Development and maintenance of prosocial behavior: International perspectives on positive morality* (pp. 271–290). New York: Plenum.

Ruth, R. (1989, Jan. 1). Police spying is widespread, Cincinnati whistle-blowers say. *Columbus [OH] Dispatch*: 11D.

Rutkowski, G. K., Gruder, C. L., and Romer, D. (1983). Group cohesiveness, social norms, and bystander intervention. *Journal of Personality and Social Psychology* 44:545–552.

Salancik, G., and Pfeffer, J. (1978). A social information processing approach to job attitudes and task design. *Administrative Science Quarterly* 23:224–253.

Sampson, E. E., and Brandon, A. C. (1964). The effects of role and opinion deviation on small group behavior. *Sociometry* 27:261–281.

Sashkin, M., and Morris, W. C. (1987). Communicating employee responsibilities and rights: The medium and the message. In C. A. B. Osigweh, Yg. (ed.), *Communicating employee responsibilities and rights: A modern management mandate* (pp. 113–118). New York: Quorum Books.

Schachter, S. (1951). Deviation, rejection, and communication. *Journal of Abnormal and Social Psychology* 46:190–207.

Scholl, R., Cooper, E. A., and McKenna, J. F. (1987). Reference selection in determining equity perceptions: Differential effects on behavioral and attitudinal outcomes. *Personnel Psychology* 40:113–124.

Schutt, S. R. (1982, March). White collar crime: The Nation's largest growth industry. *The Accountant's Digest:* 18–20.

Schwenk, C. (1988). *The essence of strategic decision making.* Lexington, MA: Lexington Books.

Schwenk, C., Miceli, M. P., and Near, J. P. (1989, Aug.). *Escalation of commitment in the pursuit of organizational dissent.* Paper presented at the 49th annual meeting of the Academy of Management, Washington, DC.

Seligman, D. (1981, May 18). Rat protection. *Fortune:* 36.

Senneker, P., and Hendrick, C. (1983). Androgyny and helping behavior. *Journal of Personality and Social Psychology* 45:916–925.

Seymour, S. (1988, Jan.–Feb.). The case of the willful whistle-blower. *Harvard Business Review:* 103–109.

Shaw, M. E. (1981). *Group dynamics: The psychology of small group behavior.* New York: McGraw-Hill.

Sheler, J. L. (1981, Nov. 16). When employes [sic] squeal on fellow workers. *U.S. News & World Report:* 81–82.

Shepherd, M. (1987a, Nov.). Before exposing wrongdoing . . . *Kansas City Star/Times:* A6.

——— (1987b, Nov.). Federal whistle-blowers pay a high price. *Kansas City Star/Times:* A1, A6.

Shingler, D. (1987, Oct. 5). Battelle program attracts NASA whistleblowers. *Business First of Greater Columbus* 4 (3):9.

Shotland, R. L., and Goodstein, L. I. (1984). The role of bystanders in crime control. *Journal of Social Issues* 40:9–26.

Shotland, R. L., and Heinold, W. D. (1985). Bystander response to arterial bleeding: Helping skills, the decision-making process, and differentiating the helping response. *Journal of Personality and Social Psychology* 49:347–356.

Shotland, R. L., and Stebbins, C. A. (1980). Bystander response to rape: Can a victim attract help? *Journal of Applied Social Psychology* 10:510–527.

Simon, H. A. (1975). *Administrative behavior* (second ed.). New York: Macmillan.

Sitkin, S. (1986, Aug.). *Selective exposure: Determinants of secrecy behavior among engineers in three Silicon Valley firms.* Paper presented at the 46th annual meeting of the Academy of Management, Chicago.

Skinner, B. F. (1953). *Science and human behavior.* New York: Macmillan.

Smith, C., Organ, D., and Near, J. P. (1983). Organizational citizenship behavior: Its nature and antecedents. *Journal of Applied Psychology* 68:653–663.

Soeken, K. L., and Soeken, D. R. (1987). A survey of whistleblowers: Their stressors and coping strategies. *Proceedings of the Hearing on H. R. 25* (pp. 156–166). Washington, D. C.: U.S. Government Printing Office.

Solomon, D. (1987, Nov. 22). Hotlines and hefty rewards: Retailers step up efforts to curb employee theft. *Wall Street Journal*: B5.

Spector, P. E. (1982). Behavior in organizations as a function of employee's locus of control. *Psychological Bulletin* 91:482–497.

Spencer, B. A., and Wokutch, R. E. (1984, Aug.). *Corporate crime, social responsibility and financial performance.* Paper presented at the 44th annual meeting of the Academy of Management, Boston, MA.

Stang, D. J. (1972). Conformity, ability and self-esteem. *Representative Research in Social Psychology* 3:97–103.

Staub, E. (1974). Helping a distressed person: Social, personality, and stimulus determinants. In L. Berkowitz (ed.), *Advances in experimental social psychology* (Vol. 7, pp. 203–341). New York: Academic Press.

——— (1978). *Positive social behavior and morality: Social and personal influences: Vol. 1.* New York: Academic Press.

Staw, B. M. (1980). Rationality and justification in organizational life. In L. L. Cummings and B. M. Staw (eds.), *Research in organizational behavior* (Vol. 2, pp. 45–80). Greenwich, CT: JAI Press.

——— (1981). The escalation of commitment to a course of action. *Academy of Management Review* 6:249–260.

——— (1984). Organizational behavior: A review and reformulation of the field's outcome variables. In M. Rosenzweig and L. W. Porter (eds.), *Annual review of psychology* (Vol. 35, pp. 627–666). Palo Alto, CA: Annual Reviews, Inc.

Staw, B. M., and Szwajkowski, E. (1975). The scarcity-munificence component of organizational environments and the commission of illegal acts. *Administrative Science Quarterly* 20:345–354.

Swartz, S., and Smith, R. (1988, Dec. 22). Will Drexel now lose clients, staff opposing firm's guilty plea? *Wall Street Journal*: A1, A5.

Tanford, S., and Penrod, S. (1984). Social influence model: A formal integration of research on majority and minority influence process. *Psychological Bulletin* 95:189–225.

Tangney, J. P. (1987, Aug. 6). Fraud will out—or will it? *New Scientist* 115:62–63.

Terpstra, D. E., and Baker, D. D. (1988). Outcomes of sexual harassment charges. *Academy of Management Journal* 31:185–194.

Therpists' sexual misconduct covered up. (1987, Apr. 8). *Columbus [OH] Dispatch*: 2B.

Thompson, J. D. (1967). *Organizations in action.* New York: McGraw-Hill.

Thurow, L. C. (1975). *Generating inequality: Mechanisms of distribution in the U.S. economy.* New York: Basic Books.

Trevino, L. K. (1986). Ethical decision making in organizations: A person-situation interactionist model. *Academy of Management Review* 11:601–617.

Vroom, V. H. (1964). *Work and motivation.* New York: Wiley.

Wagner, C., and Wheeler, L. (1969). Model, need, and cost effects in helping behavior. *Journal of Personality and Social Psychology* 12:111–116.

Wallach, E. J. (1983, Feb.). Individuals and organizations: The cultural match. *Training and Development Journal* 37 (2):29–36.

Wartick, S. L., and Rude, R. E. (1986). Issues management: Corporate fad or corporate function? *California Management Review* 29 (Fall):124–140.

Wartzman, R., and Barrett, T. (1989, Sept. 27). Government could stifle False Claims Act. *Wall Street Journal*: B1.

Weber, M. (1947). *The theory of social and economic organization.* New York: Free Press.

Weinstein, D. (1979). *Bureaucratic opposition.* New York: Pergamon Press.

Westin, A. F. (ed.). (1981). *Whistle-blowing: Loyalty and dissent in the corporation.* New York: McGraw-Hill.

White, R. W., Parmerlee, M. A., Near, J. P., and Jensen, T. C. (1979, Nov.). Sex discrimination in employment: Impacts of one legal remedy. Discussion paper #146, Indiana University, Bloomington.

Witkin, H. A., and Goodenough, D. R. (1977). Field dependence and interpersonal behavior. *Psychological Bulletin* 845:661–689.

——— (1981). Cognitive styles: Essence and origins—Field dependence and field independence. *Psychological Issues.* Monograph No. 51. International Universities Press.

Witkin, H. A., Goodenough, D. R., and Oltman, P. K. (1979). Psychological differentiation: Current status. *Journal of Personality and Social Psychology* 37:1127–1145.

Wolf, S. (1985). Manifest and latent influence of majorities and minorities. *Journal of Personality and Social Psychology* 48:899–908.

Wolf, S., & Latané, B. (1983). Majority and minority influence on restaurant preferences. *Journal of Personality and Social Psychology* 45:282–292.

Wouk, H. (1951). *The Caine mutiny.* Garden City, NY: Doubleday.

Wright, P. J. (1979). *On a clear day you can see GM.* New York: Avon.

Zalkind, S. S. (1987, Aug.). *Is whistleblowing climate related to job satisfaction and other variables?* Paper presented at the annual meeting of the American Psychological Association, New York.

Zalkind, S. S., and Eisenman, E. J. (1988, July). *Dimensions of whistleblowing climate: Individual and organizational correlations.* Paper presented at the eleventh annual meeting of the International Society of Political Psychology, Meadowlands, NJ.

Zuckerman, M. (1975). Belief in a just world and altruistic behavior. *Journal of Personality and Social Psychology* 31 (5):972–976.

Index